International Law, International Relations, and Global Governance

International relations and international law have developed in parallel but distinctly throughout the twentieth century. However, in recent years there has been recognition that their shared concerns in areas as diverse as the environment, transnational crime and terrorism, human rights and conflict resolution outweigh their disciplinary and methodological divergences.

This concise and accessible volume focuses on collaborative work within the disciplines of international law and international relations, and highlights the need to develop this collaboration further, describing the value for individuals, states, IGOs, and other non-state actors in being able to draw on the cross-pollination of international relations and international legal scholarship.

This book:

- examines how different elements of governance are interacting and shifting from one actor to another;
- analyses the cumulative effect of these shifts, and evaluates how they both enhance and challenge the world's governing capacity; and
- considers how the characteristics of an architecture for globalized governance are emerging.

Helping readers to examine and understand how accumulated actions over time have given rise to system-wide changes, this work is essential reading for all students of international law, international relations and global governance.

Charlotte Ku is Professor of Law, Assistant Dean for Graduate and International Legal Studies at the University of Illinois College of Law, and Co-Director of the Center on Law and Globalization.

Routledge Global Institutions Series

Edited by Thomas G. Weiss
The CUNY Graduate Center, New York, USA
and Rorden Wilkinson
University of Manchester, UK

About the series

The Global Institutions Series is designed to provide readers with comprehensive, accessible, and informative guides to the history, structure, and activities of key international organizations as well as books that deal with topics of key importance in contemporary global governance. Every volume stands on its own as a thorough and insightful treatment of a particular topic, but the series as a whole contributes to a coherent and complementary portrait of the phenomenon of global institutions at the dawn of the millennium.

Books are written by recognized experts, conform to a similar structure, and cover a range of themes and debates common to the series. These areas of shared concern include the general purpose and rationale for organizations, developments over time, membership, structure, decision-making procedures, and key functions. Moreover, current debates are placed in historical perspective alongside informed analysis and critique. Each book also contains an annotated bibliography and guide to electronic information as well as any annexes appropriate to the subject matter at hand.

The volumes currently published are:

61 International Law, International Relations, and Global Governance (2012)
by Charlotte Ku (University of Illinois)

60 Global Health Governance (2012)
by Sophie Harman (City University, London)

59 The Council of Europe (2012)
by Martyn Bond (University of London)

Books currently under contract include:

The Regional Development Banks
Lending with a regional flavor
by Jonathan R. Strand (University of Nevada)

Millennium Development Goals (MDGs)
For a people-centered development agenda?
by Sakiko Fukada-Parr (The New School)

Peacebuilding
From concept to commission
by Robert Jenkins (The CUNY Graduate Center)

UNICEF
by Richard Jolly (University of Sussex)

The Bank for International Settlements
The politics of global financial supervision in the age of high finance
by Kevin Ozgercin (SUNY College at Old Westbury)

International Migration
by Khalid Koser (Geneva Centre for Security Policy)

Human Development
by Richard Ponzio

Religious Institutions and Global Politics
by Katherine Marshall (Georgetown University)

The Group of Twenty (G20)
by Andrew F. Cooper (Centre for International Governance Innovation, Ontario) and Ramesh Thakur (Balsillie School of International Affairs, Ontario)

Feminist Strategies in International Governance
edited by Gülay Caglar (Humboldt University of Berlin), Elisabeth Prügl (Graduate Institute of International and Development Studies, Geneva), Susanne Zwingel (SUNY Potsdam)

Private Foundations and Development Partnerships
by Michael Moran (Swinburne University of Technology)

The International Politics of Human Rights
edited by Monica Serrano (Colegio de Mexico) and Thomas G. Weiss (The CUNY Graduate Center)

For further information regarding the series, please contact:
Craig Fowlie, Publisher, Politics & International Studies
Taylor & Francis
2 Park Square, Milton Park, Abingdon
Oxford OX14 4RN, UK
+44 (0)207 842 2057 Tel
+44 (0)207 842 2302 Fax
Craig.Fowlie@tandf.co.uk
www.routledge.com

International Law, International Relations, and Global Governance

Charlotte Ku

Routledge
Taylor & Francis Group

LONDON AND NEW YORK

First published 2012
by Routledge
2 Park Square, Milton Park, Abingdon, Oxon, OX14 4RN

Simultaneously published in the USA and Canada
by Routledge
711 Third Avenue, New York, NY 10017

Routledge is an imprint of the Taylor & Francis Group, an informa business

British Library Cataloguing in Publication Data
A catalogue record for this book is available from the British Library

Library of Congress Cataloging in Publication Data
Ku, Charlotte, 1950–
    International law, international relations, and global governance /
Charlotte Ku.
        p. cm. – (Global institutions)
        Summary: "This book focuses on collaborative work within the
disciplines of international law and international relations, to note sample
efforts to collaborate, and to assess the cultivation of an interdisciplinary
outlook"– Provided by publisher.
        Includes bibliographical references and index.
        1. International law. 2. International relations. I. Title.
    KZ1268.K8 2011
    341–dc23
    2011021495

ISBN: 978-0-415-77872-5 (hbk)
ISBN: 978-0-415-77873-2 (pbk)
ISBN: 978-0-203-15618-6 (ebk)

Typeset in Times New Roman
by Taylor & Francis Books

Contents

Illustrations

Foreword

James Crawford

Whewell Professor of International Law, Lauterpacht Centre for International Law, University of Cambridge

To those who practice it, international law is a set of practical functions, underpinned by a certain history and a less certain array of theories that have developed in the nearly four centuries since the Thirty Years' War ended with the 1648 Treaty of Westphalia. But while nation-states remain central to today's international system, over the past 100 years, international law has been applied through interaction by and between governments, organizations and individuals operating in one way or another beyond the realm of the single State. Charlotte Ku asks us to consider the evolving role of "operative" and "normative" international law in a system in which the state "is no longer the central locus of authority and control and has lost the competitive advantage over other forms of governance [that it had] from the seventeenth to the twentieth centuries." The ambitious aim of this work on international law, international relations, and global governance is to suggest that new methodologies are necessary to understand the multifaceted phenomena of international life today.

In exploring and synthesizing the contrasting concerns and various scholarly approaches in the fields of international law and international relations, Professor Ku demonstrates that the issues on the agenda of the two fields today reflect a growing recognition that their shared interest in global governance outweighs their historical disciplinary divergences. She describes and analyzes developments in the international system as it continues to move from "Westphalian" to "post-Westphalian" modes, a process that began with the creation of functional international organizations at the dawn of the twentieth century, but picked up speed with the founding of the League of Nations. While states remain the major players at the international level, other actors now interact—and sometimes work together—with states to wield global power and establish global order.

Professor Ku addresses both the means by which international law generates framework principles for these interactions and the partial shift from a state-based system to one which creates multiple-level responsibilities, implicating sub-state elements, and the public and private spheres. She thereby identifies those elements of governance—"power, authority, and legitimacy"—by which the acts and capacities of states and other entities operating on the international plane may be assessed. Traditional state power is constrained as never before by the need for legitimacy, and new articulations of the underpinnings of the international order are required. In this, international law has a central role to play. In attempting to "understand these interactions in a systematic, well-conceived, and theorized way," international lawyers can propose guiding principles, providing "common purpose and direction."

In this book, Professor Ku offers us a context in which to understand system-wide developments that influence the choices and condition the behavior of states and other actors. She suggests a means for both disciplines to bridge the historical tendency of international law and international relations theory to make sometimes mutually exclusionary claims in explicating recent trends toward global governance. Her work builds on the interdisciplinary work of earlier scholars and is a lucid overview of those historical and theoretical elements that influence the contours of human activity beyond the limits of the state.

Foreword by the series editors

The current volume is the sixty-first title in a dynamic series on global institutions. These books provide readers with definitive guides to the most visible aspects of what many of us know as "global governance." Remarkable as it may seem, there exist relatively few books that offer in-depth treatments of prominent global bodies, processes, and associated issues, much less an entire series of concise and complementary volumes. Those that do exist are either out of date, inaccessible to the non-specialist reader, or seek to develop a specialized understanding of particular aspects of an institution or process rather than offer an overall account of its functioning and situate it within the increasingly dense global institutional network. Similarly, existing books have often been written in highly technical language or have been crafted "in-house" and are notoriously self-serving and narrow.

The advent of electronic media has undoubtedly helped research and teaching by making data and primary documents of international organizations more widely available, but it has complicated matters as well. The growing reliance on the Internet and other electronic methods of finding information about key international organizations and processes has served, ironically, to limit the educational and analytical materials to which most readers have ready access—namely, books. Public relations documents, raw data, and loosely refereed web sites do not make for intelligent analysis. Official publications compete with a vast amount of electronically available information, much of which is suspect because of its ideological or self-promoting slant. Paradoxically, a growing range of purportedly independent web sites offering analyses of the activities of particular organizations has emerged, but one inadvertent consequence has been to frustrate access to basic, authoritative, readable, critical, and well-researched texts. The market for such has actually been reduced by the ready availability of varying quality electronic materials.

For those of us who teach, research, and operate in the area, such restricted access to information and analyses has been frustrating. We were delighted when Routledge saw the value of a series that bucks this trend and provides key reference points to the most significant global institutions and issues. They are betting that serious students and professionals will want serious analyses. We have assembled a first-rate team of authors to address that market. Our intention is to provide one-stop shopping for all readers—students (both undergraduate and postgraduate), negotiators, diplomats, practitioners from nongovernmental and intergovernmental organizations, and interested parties alike—seeking insights into the most prominent institutional aspects of global governance.

International Law, International Relations, and Global Governance

From the very outset of commissioning books for this series we knew that we would like to have a user-friendly introduction for non-lawyers to the field of public international law. Those studying and analyzing international politics tend to shy away from this essential building block for future global governance. Everything from the sources of international law to the interpretation of its "hard" and "soft" forms are all-too-often dismissed by social scientists as "just pieces of paper."

We were delighted when Charlotte Ku, Professor of Law and Assistant Dean for Graduate and International Legal Studies at the University of Illinois Urbana-Champaign College of Law, agreed to take up our challenge of writing an overview for this series. Charlotte is also Co-Director of the Center on Law and Globalization, a partnership of the University of Illinois College of Law and the American Bar Foundation.

Most importantly for our readers, Charlotte is a trained political scientist who served at perhaps the most prominent association of international lawyers: from 1994–2006, she was Executive Director and Executive Vice President of the American Society of International Law (ASIL) in Washington, DC. Not a "lawyer's lawyer" but a "political scientist's lawyer," Charlotte's service has included serving as the Chair of the Board of Directors of the Academic Council on the United Nations System (ACUNS) from 1998 to 2000. She was a founding director of the ACUNS-ASIL Summer Workshops on International Organization Studies. With a specialization in issues of global governance and international law, she is the author of numerous works, including *The Dynamics of International Law* and *Democratic Accountability and the Use of Force in International Law*.[1] As always, we welcome comments and suggestions from our readers.

Thomas G. Weiss
The CUNY Graduate Center, New York, USA

Rorden Wilkinson
University of Manchester, UK
June 2011

Acknowledgments

I owe the deepest thanks to Professor Thomas Weiss, with whom I have had the pleasure of collaborating for nearly 20 years, since he became Executive Director of the Academic Council on the United Nations System. I am grateful to Tom and to Professor Rorden Wilkinson for the opportunity they gave me to reflect on developments in global governance and the scholarly efforts undertaken in international law and international relations to understand them. Writing this book has allowed me to revisit familiar, classic texts and to discover the work of a new generation of scholars, and I thank Tom and Rorden for the invitation that led me to this learning experience.

Second, I want to thank Professor Edwina S. Campbell, who carefully read, critiqued, and made innumerable helpful suggestions to improve the text—not once, but twice. Thanks also to my University of Illinois colleague and frequent collaborator, Professor Paul Diehl, who commented on an early text and suggested useful references.

I want to acknowledge those with whom I spoke about this project in 2009 and whose insights and suggestions helped to shape the book: Karen Alter, José Alvarez, Michael Doyle, John Gamble, Tom Ginsburg, Laurence Helfer, Alan James, Lorna Lloyd, MJ Peterson, and Thomas Ulen. Talks with MJ Peterson and Tom Ulen were particularly helpful in moving the text away from an extended literature review to one that interweaves events with academic efforts to understand them. I have especially enjoyed, for many years, discussing the state of the two disciplines with John Gamble, Alan James, and Lorna Lloyd over our annual dinner during meetings of the International Studies Association.

For their contribution to deepening and broadening my own understanding of international law and international relations, I am indebted to many friends and colleagues. The list cannot be exhaustive because my debts are too many, but I want to acknowledge with gratitude all those who have played a role in my intellectual development, and most especially Jutta Brunée, Thomas Buergenthal, Hilary Charlesworth, Christine Chinkin, Inis Claude, James Crawford, Christopher Greenwood, Rosalyn Higgins, Karen Knop, Elihu Lauterpacht, Vaughan Lowe, Donald McRae, Andrew Morriss, Shinya Murase, Nico Schrijver, Dinah Shelton, Anne-Marie Slaughter, Stephen Toope, Peter Trooboff, Ruth Wedgwood, Edith Brown Weiss, and Cynthia Williams. Among colleagues who are no longer with us, but whose influence on my work remains, are Jonathan Charney, Louis Henkin, Harold Jacobson, Christopher Joyner, Douglas Johnston, Ronald St. John Macdonald, and Oscar Schachter.

I am deeply grateful to Professor Bruce Smith, Dean of the University of Illinois College of Law, for his encouragement and support of my scholarly pursuits. At the University of Illinois College of Law, I owe thanks to the staff of the Jenner Law Library and in particular, its International and Foreign Law Librarian, Jane Williams; and to my colleagues in the Office of Graduate and International Legal Studies, Christine Renshaw and Ann Perry, for their collegiality, support, and patience as I completed this manuscript.

For their help in the final preparation of the manuscript, I want to thank my niece, Elizabeth Ku (Cornell '10), for the painstaking care, patience, and astute eye with which she brought the manuscript into stylistic consistency with the Routledge Series on Global Institutions, Angie Adams for transmitting drafts and marked-up texts, and Christine Renshaw for help with formatting.

My final and most important thanks go to my family and especially to my mother, Agnes Ku, for her forbearance and understanding as I worked on this project (and the many others that preceded it). Wherever these projects have led, she has always encouraged me to pursue my intellectual interests and professional goals, for which I will always be grateful.

I have benefited from the insights and perspectives of all those named above, many other practitioners and scholars, and all my students. Any errors in the text, however, are mine alone.

Charlotte Ku
Champaign, IL
October 2011

Abbreviations

AFL	American Federation of Labor
AU	African Union
CICC	Coalition for an International Criminal Court
CIO	Congress of Industrial Organizations
CITES	Convention on the International Trade of Endangered Species
COMESA	Common Market for Eastern and Southern Africa
COP	Conference of the Parties to the Kyoto Protocol on Climate Change
CSCE	Conference on Security and Cooperation in Europe
ECOSOC	United Nations Economic and Social Council
ECOWAS	Economic Community of West African States
EPA	Environmental Protection Agency
ESG	Enlightened Shareholder Governance
EU	European Union
G-20	Group of Twenty Finance Ministers and Central Bank Governors
GEF	Global Environmental Facility
ICAO	International Civil Aviation Organization
ICBL	International Coalition to Ban Landmines
ICC	International Criminal Court
ICCPR	International Convention on Civil and Political Rights
ICISS	International Commission on Intervention and State Sovereignty
ICJ	International Court of Justice
ICRC	International Committee of the Red Cross
ICSID	International Centre for the Settlement of International Disputes
ICTR	International Criminal Tribunal for Rwanda
ICTY	International Criminal Tribunal for the former Yugoslavia

IGO	Intergovernmental organization
IL	International law
ILA	International Law Association
ILC	International Law Commission
ILO	International Labour Organization
IMF	International Monetary Fund
IO	International organization
IR	International relations
ITLOS	International Tribunal for the Law of the Sea
IWC	International Whaling Commission
JOE 2010	Joint Operating Environment 2010
KFOR	Kosovo Force
MONUC	UN Organization Mission in the Democratic Republic of the Congo
NASA	National Aeronautic and Space Administration
NATO	North Atlantic Treaty Organization
NGO	Nongovernmental organization
OAS	Organization of American States
OMB	Office of Management and Budget
OSPAR	Oslo/Paris Convention (on the Protection of the Marine Environment of the North-East Atlantic)
PCIJ	Permanent Court of International Justice
PICT	Project on International Courts and Tribunals
PRI	Principles for Responsible Investment
SALT	Strategic Arms Limitation Talks
UN	United Nations
UNA	United Nations Association
UNCTAD	United Nations Conference on Trade and Development
UNIDO	United Nations Industrial Development Organization
UNMIK	United Nations Interim Mission in Kosovo
UNSC	United Nations Security Council
USTR	Office of the US Trade Representative
WHO	World Health Organization
WTO	World Trade Organization

Introduction

- International law, international relations, and global governance
- The effects of globalization on governance
- Towards a globalized governing environment
- The international relations and international law divide
- Summing up
- The organization of the book

Why write another book about international law and international relations when decades of interdisciplinary work have produced a rigorous and distinguished list of scholarship? Part of the answer is that this book is less a plea for interdisciplinary collaboration than one urging the development of a broader understanding of the needs of governance in a global environment. Because the state and international law remain important factors in a globalized world, so will study of these subjects. Integration and synthesis of academic approaches can provide a multifaceted understanding of governance in the present globalized environment.

International law, international relations, and global governance

International law, international relations, and global governance are three distinct activities that carry out the world's business. They are studied and work individually or in combination, but cannot be fully understood or perform effectively without reference to each other. This book will highlight certain milestones drawn from practice to demonstrate changes in the international system. It will focus most heavily on developments in the twentieth century, but it will reach further back into history where a longer view makes a change clearer to observe. The book will feature selected academic approaches to show how scholars have explained and understood these developments. The purpose of this book is not to provide a comprehensive review either of the study or the practice of international law and international relations in the twentieth century. It is, however, to examine and to understand how accumulated actions over time have given rise to system-wide changes. The book focuses on the law and politics of global governance with a view to identifying:

how elements of governance are interacting and shifting from one actor to another;

how the cumulative effect of these shifts enhances as well as challenges the world's governing capacity; and

how the characteristics of an architecture for globalized governance are emerging.

This focus will serve as the framework for examining the contributions that international law and international relations have made to each other since the 1990s. It will further serve as the basis for considering ongoing interdisciplinary work between these two fields as scholars seek to explain, understand, and shape global governance.

This book assumes that international law is an important phenomenon in international politics. This is not to say that international law is the driving force behind all international actions or that it provides the solution to all the world's problems. But international law can make and has made significant contributions to the conduct of international affairs. International law may function in conjunction with a political decision or within a domestic system and therefore may not be regarded as the primary driver of change, but its presence still conditions the overall political environment. This is a key point the book will address. International law's contributions to global governance are unquestionably different from those of international politics and international relations, but they are present nevertheless. The practice of international law has also grown and today touches virtually every facet of public and private life.

Disaffection with international law has existed not only among students of politics, but also among lawyers who see international law either as politics only or as a form of utopian idealism. International lawyers themselves bear some historic responsibility for this, stemming from the classical legal thought advanced by the United States in the early twentieth century. It was influential in the early twentieth century as an alternative to the balance of power realism that was seen to be at the root of conflict and trouble in the world. This view saw law and legal institutions as neutral and apolitical honest brokers that served to manage conflict and competition. Conflict existed because of a "failure to provide proper institutional mechanisms" to resolve it.[1] This view further assumed that law embodied the values of a unified community. And finally, classical legal thought assumed that law evolved through formal and informal mechanisms and processes, and assumed that the weakness of international institutions like the League of Nations "did not signify fundamental problems but, rather, temporary difficulties on the way to more robust institutions."[2] Although there may be truth to this proposition, classicists underestimated the destruction that could take place en route.

The classicist school of thought was particularly strong in the United States in the years when it was stepping into its role as a world leader. At a time when the United States had little foreign policy infra- structure and a small professional foreign service, few opportunities to study international relations, and no think tanks, the US foreign policy establishment was dominated by lawyers, many of whom were leaders in the Republican Party that was the country's majority party from 1896 to 1932.[3] Typical of their views was the first article published in the *American Journal of International Law*, by the first President of the American Society of International Law, US Secretary of State Elihu Root:

> [T]he true basis of the peace and order in which we live is not fear of the policeman; it is the self-restraint of the thousands of people who make up the community and their willingness to obey the law and regard the rights of others. The true basis of business is not the sheriff with a writ of execution; it is voluntary observance of the rules and obligations of business life which are universally recognized as essential to business success.[4]

The assumption going into this study is that no single theoretical explanation can yet provide an adequate framework to help us fully understand the tools and units of governance today.[5] Much pioneering work has been done by political scientists and international relations and international law scholars, often together, to gain insight into what has worked in governance and why. Each major school of thought has something to offer and explains part of the puzzle. It may be the case that, as governance has evolved to connect a variety of pieces that previously had little to do with each other, explanations may also have to be eclectic in order to understand fully what is happening today and why.

Why undertake this kind of study now? Part of the answer is time. We are distant enough from the founding of the major international institutions functioning today to understand their development, to see the changes they have made, and the effects of their presence in world affairs. The increased volume of cross-border, transnational, and international activity also lends itself more to systematic study by simply providing more to study. It is difficult to predict behavior on the basis of one or two examples. Explanatory power and predictability are increased when a larger sample pool is available. The Routledge Global Institutions Series has provided an examination of a wide range of international institutions, practices, and phenomena. This book is an effort to provide a framework for understanding how these elements figure into the contemporary governance environment.

International relations and international law have both been interested in the ability and the capacity of actors in the international system to govern. The failure of international law to fulfill its promise to establish a war-free world discredited it in the eyes of many. Yet, the realist reaction that nothing but power and self-interest would compel state compliance has not provided a complete explanation of state behavior. International relations and international law scholarship have moved towards understanding that power, interests, and norms all have a role to play in governance. From that starting point, the interplay of structures, actions, and norms can be examined to understand their development and function in international governance. The global dimension adds another level of complexity because it introduces many more actors doing many more things that either contribute to or require governance. Much like moving from a traditional two-dimensional chessboard to a game played on three levels, the pieces and the moves may be familiar, but the game changes, and the strategy needed to win differs. In fact, it becomes a new game. Something similar is happening in the world today.

The units and tools of governance remain familiar and are fulfilling traditional roles, but at the same time, they are functioning in different ways with different expectations as to their effectiveness, output, and responsibilities. Global governance is therefore rooted in the units and tools of the classical state system, including international institutions, but has generated or enhanced other units and tools that are now playing important ongoing governance roles. How can we assess the durability and success of these developments? What will the structure of governance look like in this globalized world?

But first, how is governance defined in this study? A search of the web will provide a host of definitions, but they boil down to understanding governance as a term that covers the processes, systems, and controls to run an entity. Governance includes the authorities, processes, and procedures that guide strategic and key operational decisions. Governance therefore includes governments, law, and other forms of arrangements that regulate and facilitate human endeavor.

This book will examine the question of governance by highlighting key units in the international system and tracing their development from the end of the Second World War through the present globalized era. It will identify how each element emerged to become a unit of governance today and the questions this poses for the international system in which both international relations and international law take place. The intention of the study is not to provide a theory about global governance. It is rather an effort to draw together research strands that have helped to explain important aspects of political development to provide a broader framework for analysis that might then lead to further theorizing about global governance. These research strands are:

that governance is a social phenomenon and that behavior, including the pursuit of identity and interests, is shaped and influenced by social structure;

that governance orders behavior, but that the institutions of governance, including law, exist at different levels and need to be examined together in order to understand the full range of functionality on any given issue;

that governance is dynamic, with forces prompting change both from the inside and outside of systems and institutions, and that the validity and effectiveness of these activities must be regularly reaffirmed.

The book's conclusion will draw on this framework to delineate what a theory of global governance might address and encompass.

The effects of globalization on governance

What are the characteristics of globalization that seem to have triggered a need for change? For one thing, technology and the dramatic lowering of costs for cross-border activity have changed the world. At the dawn of the millennium, more information was sent over a single cable in one second than was sent over the entire internet in a month in 1997, and the cost of transmitting a trillion bits of information from Boston to Los Angeles fell from $150,000 in 1970 to 12 cents only 30 years later.[6] We can further see the changes that have occurred with a short backward glance to 1945. United Nations Secretary-General Kofi Annan wrote:

When the United Nations was founded two thirds of the current Members did not exist as sovereign states, their people still living under colonial rule. The planet hosted a total population of fewer than 2.5 billion, compared to 6 billion today. Trade barriers were high, trade flows miniscule and capital controls firmly in place. Most big companies operated within a single country and produced for their home market. The cost of transoceanic telephone calls was prohibitive for the average person and limited even business use to exceptional circumstances. The annual output of steel was a prized symbol of national economic prowess. The world's first computer had just been constructed; it filled a large room, bristled with 18,000 electron tubes and half a million solder joints, and had to be physically rewired for each new task. Ecology was a subject confined to the study of biology, and references to cyberspace would not have been found even in science fiction.[7]

For all the convenience in the shrinkage of distance and time and the reduction of costs in cross-border communication and economic activity brought about by the digital revolution, the increased interconnectedness has also created new and sometimes unexpected consequences. Take, for example, the initial eruption of the Eyjafjallajökull volcano in Iceland on 14 April 2010. This single event caused the cancellation of more than 100,000 transatlantic flights, stranding 10 million passengers and commercial cargo for a week.[8] Similar or even larger volcanic eruptions on record did not have the same effect because they took place before the advent of airplanes and the present network of air routes.[9] From a regulatory and governance standpoint, the 2010 disruption revealed "the limited level of integration achieved by the European Union (EU) in the civil aviation sector."[10] This meant that EU member states had to reach consensus on a coordinated response which took time—five days, during which European civil aviation was at a standstill. Regular flight schedules were not resumed for eight days after the initial eruption. In an increasingly close-knit world, we can expect more such widespread effects from single events.

More intense cross-border public and private sector interactions, denser networks of government accountability and civil society, and speedy and inexpensive information flows would have been enough to change how states relate to each other. The situation became more complex because these conditions have created basic shifts in political and economic relations. These shifts are all part of what we have come to know as globalization. David Held and Anthony McGrew wrote in 2002 that: "Globalization refers to a historical process which transforms the spatial organization of social relations and transactions, generating transcontinental or inter-regional networks of interaction and the exercise of power."[11]

On the eve of the new millennium in 2000, United Nations Secretary-General Kofi Annan described these shifts in *We the Peoples: The Role of the United Nations in the 21st Century*:

> ... while the post-war multilateral system made it possible for the new globalization to emerge and flourish, globalization, in turn, has progressively rendered its designs antiquated. Simply put, our post-war institutions were built for an inter-national world, but we now live in a *global* world.[12]

Another feature of today's globalization is what Robert Keohane and Joseph Nye describe as "thickness." An example of "thin globalization" is the trading route between Europe and Asia we have come to know as the Silk Road: " ... the route was plied by a small group of hardy traders, and the goods that were traded back and forth had a direct impact primarily on a small—and relatively elite—stratum of consumers along the road."[13] By contrast, "'thick' relations of globalization involve many relationships that are intensive as well as extensive: long-distance flows that are large and continuous, affecting the lives of many people."[14] Held and others distinguish the current wave of globalization from earlier waves of global forces in its "sheer magnitude, complexity, and speed." In terms of thickness, this means "that different relationships of interdependence intersect more deeply at more different points."[15]

This global political environment has created problems for existing channels and forms of governance because it challenges existing systems of national accountability.[16] James Rosenau characterizes these conditions as "turbulence" and describes them as follows:

> It is characteristic of a turbulent environment that, compared with other types, the actors in it are more numerous and interdependent, with the result that it becomes less stable and predictable, thereby altering the conditions to which the actors have to adapt and heightening the probability that increasing numbers of them will fail to adapt, developments which can in turn lead to changes in the environment's structures and processes.[17]

The number, dissimilarity, and interdependence of actors is high, making it difficult for any one entity or set of entities to exercise and to maintain control.[18] The state is no longer the central locus of authority and control and has lost the competitive advantage over other forms of governance that it held from the seventeenth to the twentieth centuries. We can see the reality of Rosenau's observation as we observe even superpowers "at the mercy of events and trends that they would like to redirect, terminate, or otherwise influence but cannot."[19] In more tangible terms, what this means is that governments have slowly faced an erosion of their authority with an increased emphasis on performance as a basis for legitimacy and compliance. Individual citizens are more vocal about what they like and do not like about governments, and the 24-hour news cycle plus the information disseminated through the internet provides plenty of air time to voice demands.[20] One manifestation of this is the difficulty states have in sustaining the use of force. As Rosenau observed, " … when they do resort to military action, states can no longer presume the domestic support necessary to carry out their goals in combat."[21] Access to the web and the erosion of state authority came together in the leak of documents related to the Afghanistan War and the conduct of US foreign policy on WikiLeaks in 2010 and the publication of reports based on classified material in the *New York Times*, the *Guardian* and *Der Spiegel*.[22]

Growing distrust of state authority means that "[a]s the external challenges to an organization become more intense, so do their internal consequences, in that they foster needs to revise strategies, streamline decisional processes, and ameliorate bureaucratic tensions; thus, the organization becomes part of the very interconnectedness in its environment with which it seeks to cope."[23] Again, we see this happening as states seek legitimacy through closer ties to international processes and standards. These systems of accountability are formal and informal and can include networks of private citizens committed to a common agenda. In retrospect, the Helsinki movement in the 1970s and 1980s was but an early example of this. Even in cases where state behavior may not be specifically regulated, countries may still choose to coordinate their behavior with international standards.[24]

We have already noted the effect technology had on creating today's globalized world. From a political perspective, Rosenau points to the 1960s and decolonization as a turning point that caused people to realize that the power balance and existing state system were far from immutable and were subject to change through political action.[25] Prior to the 1960s, the widespread and destructive forces unleashed in the two world wars and the Great Depression had occurred essentially within the frame of the classic state system. After the 1960s, not only was change seen as possible, but it was also taking place under conditions that made it harder and harder for states to control. See, for example, the "people power" phenomenon that occurred around the world in the late 1980s.

When considered in the context of exploding technologies, the contrast between the pre- and post-1950 eras can be drawn even more sharply. Under conditions in which it took hours or days to send messages, pictures, and money abroad and weeks or months to move people, soldiers, and goods from one part of the world to another, the governments of national and local systems were able to absorb and channel the complexity and dynamism introduced by the industrial era, thus enabling the parameter values of the global system to contain the subsystemic fluctuations within acceptable limits. Similarly, the mechanisms of international governance associated with the state system, while rudimentary and often temporary, were sufficient to manage change and complexity. But when the time required to transmit ideas and pictures was reduced to minutes and then to seconds, and the transportation of persons, goods, and explosives to days and hours (even to minutes in the case of explosives), interdependence became increasingly unmanageable, national governments increasingly ineffective, national boundaries increasingly permeable, and the durability of the global parameters of the past increasingly questionable. ... We happen to find ourselves in an era in which a great many past parameters are becoming variables.[26]

Towards a globalized governing environment

If we are in the midst of a historic shift in governance, and assuming that there are competing models for what governance in the globalized world would look like, what are the elements of this new governance and what functions does it need to fulfill? For example, at the dawn of the Westphalian system that has been the prevailing model of state interaction since the seventeenth century, competing models with the state were multiethnic empires, city leagues, and city states. These, in turn, replaced the earlier governing models of the Middle Ages that were empire, feudal lordships, and a theocratic church.[27] The territorial state prevailed in this competition in Europe because it "proved to be more adept at preventing free riding, standardizing weights and coinage, and establishing uniform adjudication."[28] It was also a more effective means to coordinate actions because it had a central "locus of authority" which the looser governing models did not. In the twentieth century, we saw pressures exerted on this locus of authority and responses undertaken that have changed and diffused this authority. Yet, the state remains an important actor in carrying out important functions in today's system of global governance.

As noted about globalization above, it is also the case that governance is thickening in the global era. State authority and functions are diffusing or disaggregating, as Anne-Marie Slaughter calls it, and new actors and processes have emerged to fill the gaps. At this point in time, we are therefore less likely to see an elimination or replacement of the state as a governing unit, but rather the emergence of a more complicated governing system that has multiple forms and units of governance operating simultaneously and whose elements may leverage and complement each other. These forms and units may also clash and come into conflict. To explore this idea, we will move to an examination of some of the key elements that constitute this governing system: states, institutions, individuals, and process interactions. Such a multilevel system will work only if it has adequate capacity to govern effectively, if all elements at all levels can connect to cooperate, and, perhaps most importantly, if the function and purpose of these elements is widely recognized and understood.[29] The role of states and governments has changed from being one of problem-solver to one of interdependence manager.[30]

If the proper conceptual adjustments can be made, international law can serve a facilitation role in moving the international system towards a juridical order with a respect for law by providing all of these elements with common purpose and direction to enhance coordination and to contribute to a generally stable governing structure. But accomplishing this may require of international law scholars a fundamentally changed view of world order. In a global governance system, states remain major actors, but state authority and capacity are supplemented—and challenged—by other strategic partners at the international, national, and subnational levels.

As Keohane observed: "Since there is no global government, global governance involves strategic interactions among entities that are not arranged in formal hierarchies. Since there is no global constitution, the entities that wield power and make rules are often not authorized to do so by general agreement."[31] Table I.1, developed by Keohane and Nye, identifies key elements and actors now active as part of global governance.[32]

As we begin to conceive and to operationalize a new globalized governing environment, it is important and useful to understand that governance is neither a static nor a finite phenomenon. And, the state—the principal governing unit within the international system—itself is changing. Saskia Sassen notes that " ... critical components of authority deployed in the making of the territorial state are shifting

toward becoming strong capabilities for detaching that authority from its exclusive territory and into multiple bordering states."[33]
It may also be useful to recall that the capabilities of the future are generated by the capabilities and capacity of present institutions and experiences. And, as Hendrik Spruyt observed, systemic change occurs in two stages: first will be observable new political coalitions followed by the second stage of different types of institutions competing for preeminence.[34] This book will proceed by addressing the specific capabilities and capacities of the major governing elements—where they have come from and where they are heading. It will identify where international law and international relations have undertaken specific theoretical explanations of these developments and will conclude with a chapter suggesting why a new form of inquiry may be required to understand fully the changes now underway.

This task is challenging because of the spatial and temporal dispersion "of units and actors that means that different influences may be acting simultaneously on different parts of the organization,[35] each imparting its own particular momentum to the developmental process."[36] Theorizing will help explain the observations of change as long as it does not lead to a compartmentalizing of perspectives that decreases rather than increases understanding.

Before proceeding, it may therefore be useful to consider some of the characteristics of the changes we will be examining:

Changes may be both cumulative and conjunctive where "characteristics acquired in earlier stages are retained in later stages" and "the stages are related such that they derive from a common underlying process."[37]

Change occurs in ways where a considerable time lag may exist between the formation of new institutions and practices and evidence of the growth or decline of existing institutions and practices.[38] Stephen

Table I.1 Key actors in global governance

	Private	*Governmental*	*Third sector*
Supranational	TNCs (transnational corporations)	IGOs (intergovernmental organizations	NGOs (non-governmental organizations)
National	Firms	Central	Non-profits
Subnational	Local	Local	Local

Source: Robert Keohane and Joseph Nye, "Introduction" in *Governance in a Globalizing world*, ed. Nye and Donohue (2000), 13.

Jay Gould's findings from evolutionary biology and his theory of punctuated equilibrium showed that "species emergence at the micro-level is sudden, but the diffusion of species that ultimately alters the characteristics of populations occurs through many individual events spread over quite long periods of time (on the order of millions of years)."[39] Institutions can learn and change "through the purposeful social construction among individuals within the entity."[40] Change can take place within a single unit or type of units or among multiple units or types, but then may have system-wide implications.[41] Change can occur as a cumulation of small changes that subsequently produce a larger or more fundamental change.[42] Rosenau uses the example of a regiment marching across a bridge as an example of this:

> ... numerous micro actions culminate in macro outcomes that lie outside the system's normal functioning. An oft-cited illustration of this process is that of a regiment marching in step across a bridge: the rhythm of the marching causes a swaying of the bridge (i.e., a new structural condition) that cannot be attributed either to the bridge or to the action of any single soldier but that nonetheless requires an adaptive adjustment on the part of each soldier.[43]

Change can provide a complete break with the past.[44]

The international relations and international law divide

The disillusion that caused a rejection of international law as a useful tool in shaping or studying governance that occurred after the Second World War has already been mentioned. There were good reasons for this skepticism about international law's role and promise, but the questions about governance posed by the end of the Cold War spurred the need for explanation and understanding of state behavior. The rejection of international law as a factor in international relations, however, was never complete. In the United States, scholars like Quincy Wright and Inis Claude were present in cross-disciplinary academic discussions of political science, international relations, and international law. Hans Morgenthau published in the *American Journal of International Law*. And the divide may never have been as stark in Europe, where international politics and law remained more closely taught and studied, although often in more theoretical than applied terms. A notable exception was in the British academy, where through the early 1970s, the London School of Economics, for example, taught a course on The Sociology of International Law. It included not only concepts of international law, but perhaps more importantly, the practice of international law, including the people and institutions that made and implemented it.[45]

What began to bridge the international law–international relations divide was the growing desire on the part of the international law community to understand more broadly the assertions it had made about the influence of international law on state behavior. Louis Henkin's famous declaration that "almost all nations observe almost all principles of international law and almost all their obligations almost all of the time" became the starting point for more than one investigation.[46] Both for law and for political science, the question was why states would behave in certain ways if it were not clearly in their self-interest to do so. There was a lingering feeling that self-interest alone did not provide a full explanation, but the skill to study state behavior systematically and rigorously was one that legal scholars had not yet developed.

This changed dramatically as scholars of international organizations and cooperation began to look into developments emerging through the 1970s, and legal scholars began to see the potential of social science research techniques to test the validity of what they had been taught as legal doctrine. Put simply, lawyers, like social scientists, began to ask "how and why" and were no longer satisfied with an answer that pointed only to legal dogma. What institutions work and why? What law works and why? How does all of this happen?[47]

International relations and political science scholars like John Gamble (treaties, law of the sea, and the International Court of Justice), Christopher Joyner (the commons, including the law of the sea, the United Nations and international institutions, and general international law), Anthony Arend (rule formation, jurisprudence, and the history of international law), Robert Beck (the use of force and globalization), and Lawrence LeBlanc (human rights and genocide) maintained teaching and research in international law, but did not bridge the research gap because their scholarship was largely in the dispositive style of mainstream law journal publishing without relying on conclusions drawn from the empirical analyses and observation of mainstream political science and international relations in the United States. With the exception of Gamble, who was an early pioneer in the use of quantitative methods to explain international law practice,[48] the others mentioned above relied on the traditional tools of descriptive legal analysis to produce their studies. Nevertheless, their presence in departments of political science and government kept the teaching of the subject available to non-law students at both the undergraduate and graduate levels.[49] An early bridge between international relations and international law was that of human rights scholarship and the work of David Forsythe, Jack Donnelly, and R.J. Vincent.[50] This work turned the lens back onto norms and their institutional underpinnings. The study of international institutions provided a bridge that has given us a group of important political scientists like M.J. Peterson, Kathryn Sikkink, Karen Alter, Paul Diehl and Gary Goertz, Karen Mingst and Margaret Karns, and Beth Simmons, who apply strong social science research techniques to understand the development of normative behavior and institutions.[51] The bases for the work of these leading scholars in international relations scholarship today were laid by important international cooperation scholars like Leon Gordenker, Keohane, and Nye.

On the law side, interdisciplinarity has been gaining momentum as the law and economics, law and society, law and philosophy, and legal history movements have matured. In this respect, international law is perhaps a late comer to embracing cross-disciplinary strategies for research, but their presence in the legal academy has no doubt helped develop interest among international lawyers in doing so.[52] It is also becoming evident that for practicing international lawyers, skill sets outside of law are increasingly required in order for them to practice law effectively. Lawyers recognize that for law to function well, they need to go beyond knowing the rules to understanding how they work and why they are effective or not.[53] Skill sets that require quantitative and business evaluation ability are central to successful law practice.[54]

A more institutionalized step to foster dialogue and collaboration between international relations and international law scholars was undertaken by the Academic Council on the United Nations System and the American Society of International Law from the early 1990s. Spurred by the Ford Foundation to undertake this collaboration, the two organizations have cooperated on a series of annual summer workshops that bring together international law and international relations scholars to raise awareness of the scholarship and outlook of the two perspectives. Since its inception in 1991, approximately 400 scholars and practitioners have participated in the annual workshop, and a number of the pieces cited in this study were developed in connection with the workshop program. This scholarship maintains separate but overlapping interests and employs multiple research techniques to understand how institutions, including law, work.

These efforts have not only produced valuable work that explains the function and effect of legal practice and dogma, but also have provided many international lawyers with the research skills to test their doctrinal hypotheses. These investigations, however, have lacked the ability to provide multiple explanations of a phenomenon and to assess behavior over time. Both of these dimensions are important to understanding global governance. Such multiple explanations require closer collaboration of international law and international relations scholars because the objective is to understand actions at a system-wide rather than an incident or topic-specific level.

Law can provide broad propositions with regard to governance, but needs social science to test and to understand law's specific effects. We realize more and more that the functionality of a governing unit may differ dramatically in different contexts. It is therefore important to create a mode of inquiry that can explain the behavior of actors at a fine grained level, but still maintain the ability to enhance understanding of the broader system within which these actions take place. It is important that this occurs so that new forms of governance can be readily identified and correlated within the governing order. The challenge is to devise a research methodology and strategy that can provide ready assessment of a law's effectiveness, a procedure's sustainability, and an institution's durability.

This task is made more difficult because governance may now emerge from a variety of public and private actors that include sub-national units of government, corporations, and other non-state actors. The research task is further complicated by having to understand the dynamic properties, interactions, and interconnections among elements because these properties and interactions taken together generate the capacities that shape governance. A mode of inquiry that can capture both the rigor of social science research and the broader doctrinal view of law is now needed to explain the shape and function of the emerging governing system. To facilitate the development of such an inquiry, this book will survey the developments in governance practice and scholarship with a particular emphasis on how each development has contributed to the capacity and structure of governance today.

Summing up

The backdrop of this book is that:

• Social science research has increasingly demonstrated that international institutions, including international law, matter in the conduct of international relations.

- Technology and the interaction of states, international institutions, non-state actors, and individuals throughout the twentieth century have created a globalized world.
- Governing in the globalized environment requires changed outlooks and capacities. Though evolving from presently existing institutions and processes of governance, our understanding of these changes is only piecemeal. Finding a way to theorize and to understand system-wide developments is the new and additional task for continued collaboration between international law and international relations scholars.

The organization of the book

The book begins in Chapter 1 with an overview of the academic disciplines of international law and international relations, the differences between the social science and the legal mode of inquiry, the motivations and contributions of collaborations between the two fields, and understanding pluralism. It continues in Chapter 2 to review the evolution of the state and state system to one of international community and international concerns. The chapter will examine the role states, international organizations (IOs), and non-governmental organizations played in this development. In Chapter 3 the book turns to the interactions of new issues and new actors with established institutions and their results. Chapter 4 covers the study and practice of international relations in a post-Westphalian context. Chapter 5 turns the focus to international law and its operation and development in the global environment. The book concludes in Chapter 6 with an outline for developing an integrated and synthesized understanding of global activity.

1 Points of departure

- **Mind the gap between scholars of international law and international relations**
- **Moving beyond realism and positivism**
- **The current state of the disciplines**
- **Summing up**

International law and international relations are distinct fields of study. Law and social science are distinct modes of inquiry. They are enterprises with different objectives and purposes. While this book acknowledges the importance of the collaboration that exists between international law and international relations scholars, it is important to understand that this collaboration does not replace the study of either subject as a distinct discipline. Indeed, the fruitfulness of interdisciplinary work would be mitigated if those working collaboratively were mere pale imitations of each other's fields. Maintaining disciplinary identity and continuing to push separately the frontiers of international law and international relations are key to understanding the value of each mode of inquiry and the contribution it can make to understanding the broader questions of global governance. As this chapter will show, interdisciplinary collaboration is less an effort to adopt another's methods than it is an ability to understand the additional insights provided by another form of inquiry and thereby enrich one's own work. Such collaboration can facilitate the development of new insights and accelerate the creation of new knowledge. This can, in turn, contribute to a broader systematic understanding of particular aspects of today's governing environment. The danger, however, is in becoming so focused on developing a mode of inquiry that conclusions become narrower and narrower, making system-wide evaluation and understanding harder.

Mind the gap between scholars of international law and international relations[1]

Accounts and descriptions of the present governing environment suggest the complex and even contradictory forces at play in today's globalized world.[2] These forces are redefining time and space. Yet our political and legal institutions remain rooted in a territorial and state-centric framework that appears inadequate to carry out core governing functions. At the same time, no clear alternative has emerged to replace the governance and authority structure of the state and its creations, including international organizations. There is little doubt, however, that these institutions, including law, function today in a more complicated governing environment where the state is not the only source of authority, but one of many authorities connected to each other and working simultaneously at different levels, including the private sector, civil society, and local communities.

It was not an accident that a great flowering of interdisciplinary work took place in the 1970s, as realization grew that the world was becoming a more complex governing environment. The Cold War masked the breadth and depth of these developments, but with its end in 1989, there was no doubt that much had changed since its start 40 years earlier. As we look back on the end of the Cold War itself, we can now recognize the importance of a social movement that successfully challenged the Soviet Union and its allies in eastern Europe, despite the state's command of vastly greater coercive power. These movements were made up of the human rights activists who dared to press for the right to travel and other individual liberties after the conclusion of the 1975 Helsinki Final Act of the Conference on Security and Cooperation in Europe (the CSCE Helsinki Final Act). In a series of follow-up conferences that grew out of the Helsinki Final Act, these individuals formed into coherent transnational social movements and became an effective international political force through networking and capacity-building.[3]

This extraordinary turn of events was acknowledged by long-time Soviet Ambassador to the United States, Anatoly Dobrynin, who reflected in his memoirs that such developments were "totally beyond the imagination of the Soviet leadership" that negotiated the Final Act.[4] Henry Kissinger, who served as US Secretary of State from 1973 to 1977, was equally surprised. He wrote in his memoirs:

> We did not foresee all the consequences of our policies, and I for one was initially skeptical about the possibilities of Basket III

[Co-operation in Humanitarian and Other Fields].[5] We did not expect the Soviet empire to collapse so quickly; we were content to loosen its bonds wherever possible and to push the right of peaceful change while awaiting the conditions that would enable the democracies to pursue it. ... We can rest on what was achieved without taking credit away from great men like Havel, Walesa, and their contemporaries who transformed a diplomatic enterprise into a triumph of the human spirit.[6]

The actions of states providing the basis for citizen activism and redefining the relationship between a government and its citizens is one of the most important contributing factors to globalization and a new governance environment. Helsinki was not the only catalyst for this. The move on the international level to end apartheid in South Africa and the human rights movements that stood up to the dictatorships in Latin America were all successors to Helsinki. People were using human rights standards to redefine their relationships to their governments. Activism in one country had ramifications in another, as was the case of the coupling of the US civil rights movement with the anti-apartheid campaign.[7]

The 1989 collapse of the Warsaw Pact eastern European dictatorships was preceded by moves away from military dictatorships in Latin America—Ecuador in 1979, Peru in 1980, Bolivia in 1982, Argentina in 1983, Uruguay in 1985, and Paraguay in 1989. Although many of these restorations to civilian and democratic rule in Latin America have been fragile, we can still see a trend towards democracy. Democracy and civilian rule have not, however, always led to a flowering of liberal democracy. See, for example, the elections of Alberto Fujimori in Peru in 1990 and of Hugo Chavez in Venezuela in 1998, who proceeded to weaken the democratic institutions in their countries following their elections. Fujimori was ousted after 10 years of rule and in 2011 was in jail serving prison terms for human rights violations and abuses of power. Chavez was re-elected after stifling democracy in what had been one of the strongest democracies in Latin America—Venezuela, with a tradition of civilian government going back to 1959.

Despite these setbacks, it is noteworthy that the transitions to civilian non-authoritarian governments have taken place against a backdrop of a strong regional human rights system. Becoming an active member of the Inter-American human rights system was often a first step taken by countries transitioning from dictatorships. The action served as a signal to both internal and external observers that a profound change had taken place. Internally, the signal was to a country's people that individual dignity and human rights would be respected where both had been previously ignored or abused. Externally, it was a signal to the world that the new government was prepared to carry out its international obligations and to meet international standards in the conduct of its affairs.[8]

Moving beyond realism and positivism

The desire to move beyond realism and to understand cooperation in the 1970s, in the case of international relations scholars, and from positivism to international institutions, in the case of scholars of international law, also provided impetus to look broadly at and to deepen understanding of international behavior. While states certainly acted in their own interest in the last decades of the twentieth century, pursuing that interest meant shaping the international decision-making framework or process. The privileged voting structure of the United Nations Security Council and the weighted management structure of international financial institutions like the International Monetary Fund and the World Bank are examples.[9] Those trained in the skills of empirical observation and quantitative analysis used such examples to test the influence of norms on international behavior and the normative propositions advanced and described by international legal scholars.

The interest of scholars in treaties and international agreements grew in the 1960s and 1970s as their number increased. Political scientists observed this as a possible indication that treaties were an important form of conducting international relations. The advent of treaty collections and the later development of online collections and searchable databases have heightened interest and facilitated research among empiricists by providing larger samples from which to extrapolate information and to test hypotheses. Such efforts include Peter Rohn's World Treaty Index project and the output of the University of Nottingham Treaty Centre under the direction of Michael Bowman and D.J. Harris.[10]

According to one comprehensive study of multilateral treaties, in the 250 years from 1648 to 1899, 524 multilateral treaties were concluded. Compare this to the 763 concluded in the following 25 years from 1900 to 1925.[11] This development led to the recognition by scholars through the last decades of the twentieth century that international relations "was not only built on power relations but also on explicitly negotiated agreements."[12] For international lawyers, the increased number of treaties and treaty topics fueled a desire to understand the social and political factors that gave effect to treaty obligations and other international norms. International relations could therefore try to explain what international law recognized and created.

In international relations, the experience of the Second World War and its aftermath saw the ascendance of realism as the dominant theoretical school, and of behavioralism as the dominant method of research. International law was reduced to a footnote, and regarded by international relations scholars as epiphenomenal, if at all. In a semi-autobiographical account of this development, Harold Jacobson described his early views of international law as a budding scholar of international relations:

> The 1950s and early 1960s were heady days for those studying international relations through the lens of political science. Many of us, like many who came before and after us, were deeply committed to our studies being relevant to achieving peace, prosperity, and human dignity. Having absorbed both E.H. Carr's *The Twenty Years' Crisis* and Hans Morgenthau's *Politics among Nations,* we knew we had to be realistic. At Yale and Michigan and many other places, we were also deeply committed to developing science. Quincy Wright's *A Study of War* provided a template for amassing data and systematically deriving generalizations and testing theories. We were convinced that we could be relevant, realistic, and rigorous. Political scientists attempting to develop generalizations about political behavior tended to deemphasize institutions, and international law did not figure prominently in our search for generalizations about international behavior.[13]

The disenchantment with international law's normative agenda, reflected in Carr and Morgenthau, stemmed from the perceived inability of international law and international institutions to prevent the Second World War or to stop its brutal realities. For the realists, normative pronouncements had no effect when confronted by a determined aggressor, and Carr and Morgenthau both rejected international law and legal institutions as effective bases for world order. To the extent that international law played any role, it was a mere reflection of power interests and distribution.[14] As Jacobson noted, disenchantment with international law coincided with the effort to move international relations away from the descriptive and prescriptive style of its early days to one more grounded in scientific rigor, with conclusions drawn from observation and empirical evidence.

Unlike their international relations (IR) colleagues, the basic objective of international legal scholars is not to explain the behavior of states, but rather to assess the status of legal norms. This is not to say that international lawyers are not interested in the behavior of states or power interests; they are, because both are crucial to the formation and development of legal norms. The primary objective of international law scholarship, however, is to determine which rules or standards have acquired the status of law. This classic emphasis on the status of law reflects a failure of legal inquiry to understand fully the influence norms, even if not full-fledged law, may have on behavior. Crossing the threshold of law, however, does trigger processes and frameworks that would not be available if the practice were other than law. And, as we will see, the existence of the structures and norms related to international law may shape the identity and interests of states and other international actors so that international law's effect may be felt even if it is not fully implemented and recognized as law by all.

Early twentieth-century work in international relations drew on political philosophy, outlining normative claims about how things "ought" to be, or diplomatic history, involving detailed descriptions and analysis of specific events. Theories, when they existed, were rarely subjected to rigorous empirical testing. This changed in the 1960s, when positivism came to dominate the field. The positivist approach to hypothesis testing and knowledge processing in the social sciences was modeled on approaches used by the natural sciences. The goal was to establish empirical facts, uncover causal relationships, and identify valid generalizations—or patterns—about human action.

A shared interest between legal and international relations scholars in understanding the behavior of international actors, however, does not mean that their reasons for undertaking research are the same. It is important to understand the difference. In the natural sciences, the most common research method is repeated experiments. In fields such as international relations, such experimentation is not possible, since history and events cannot be rerun to test specific conditions or factors. The IR alternative is to rely on statistical methods to collect findings, but this approach requires a large enough sample for analysis. Where a large sample is not available, qualitative methods are used, but still share the basic research strategy—hypotheses are derived from theories and then tested against specific observations and available empirical data.

How this works can be seen in the components of a typical social science research project. The research proposal involves not only stating and justifying the goals of the project, but also outlining a detailed plan for how those goals will be achieved. Justification for the significance of the project then needs to be established. First is the significance of the topic: for example, to understand the outbreak of interstate war. Second is the situation of the proposed research within the body of existing literature in order to avoid duplication of research already completed, and to illustrate how the study will further contribute to knowledge.

The research topic is usually stated as a question calling for an explanation. It is important to note that the question should relate to empirical facts rather than normative claims. At the same time, it cannot be limited simply to matters of fact and should also involve patterns and relationships. Identifying the research question is one of the most critical tasks confronting a researcher in the social sciences. Without a clear question, it is unlikely that the research will produce useful results.

A theoretical perspective is the second essential component of a social science research project. Theories help to identify what we expect to find in the empirical evidence when it is available and analyzed. The possibility of deriving hypotheses from the theoretical position that can be tested against empirical evidence is essential. Major theoretical outlooks in international relations are broadly classified as liberal internationalism, realism, Marxism, and structuralism. Although great attention is commonly given to the theoretical framework, the definitions of key concepts are a major problematic aspect of social science research. Most terms lack precise shared meanings, and will seldom correspond directly with the data accessible to the researcher. This makes both theorizing and communicating findings difficult. Therefore, making clear at the outset the boundaries of the concepts or phenomena being studied is important.

The final step in a research project involves the collection and analysis of data. Although the term "data" tends to bring to mind statistical material, evidence can take a variety of forms, including written archival materials, oral interviews, and other forms of observation. Analysis involves the testing of the original hypothesis against the data collected. If the evidence supports the initial expectations, the hypothesis is strengthened and is sometimes narrowed to test further its validity. If the evidence fails to support the expectations, then the hypothesis would appear to be inaccurate.

In contrast to international relations, the predominant mode of international legal analysis is descriptive and expositive. International legal scholars typically seek to uncover what rules of international law (IL) exist, with a view to suggesting where rules may need modification in order to be effective. Although there are a variety of approaches to this method, the primary purpose of these inquiries is to determine the present state of the law, and to examine such rules within a given political environment. This method of divining the law by searching for it in treaties and other documents dates back hundreds of years.

Another important approach is primarily prescriptive, undertaking critique and analysis as a basis for advocating what the law *should be* in light of perceived inadequacies or failures, rather than describing what it is. In neither approach is there an ability to explain or predict the actual development of international law or the dynamics behind its evolution.

Notable exceptions of legal scholars who tried to explain behavior based on observation and who sought to understand observance of norms regardless of their formal legal status, are Jonathan Charney, Stephen Toope and Jutta Brunée, Jack Goldsmith and Eric Posner, Kal Raustiala, Andrew Guzman, Laurence Helfer, and Joel Trachtman.[15]

Controversies among scholars of international law frequently reflect differences over the most fundamental question of jurisprudence: what does it mean to label something "law"? The three broadest approaches to this question are naturalism, legal positivism, and critical studies.

Naturalism teaches that, to be recognized as law, a body of norms must be based on a set of universal, immutable principles of justice accessible to human reason. Legal positivism seeks to reduce law to a matter of fact and insists on a strict separation between "law as it is" and "law as it ought to be." For positivists, law is an observable phenomenon. Critical studies challenge the premise that law is objective and find that it is conditioned by various political and social outlooks that may create inherent biases in the law against certain populations or issues.

In reality, these approaches are often blended. One reason is that empirical findings can have legal significance only within a pre-established conceptual framework. Certain basic precepts, such as the juridical equality of states and the duty to fulfill treaty obligations (*pacta sunt servanda*), are necessarily deduced from first principles rather than inferred from practice. Another reason is that the very notion of a legal system presupposes certain broadly shared ends of order, efficiency or justice that compel the making and operation of the law. While it is certainly possible to conceive of law that is unjust, and an entire legal system that is unjust, law rarely reflects random or arbitrary conduct and therefore is important to governance as a means of providing order and structure.

In determining whether a standard rises to the level of a legal norm, virtually all international law scholars make reference to an accepted set of "sources" of law—principally custom, treaty, and "general principles of law recognized by civilized nations."[16] Controversies nonetheless persist over the methods used to ascertain whether a given norm "exists" in international law, especially where state practice frequently contradicts apparent treaty commitment and ostensibly solemn pronouncements, as in the important areas of peace and security, human rights, and economic rights. These determinations are, in fact, tests of international law's authority, legitimacy, and power.

The methods by which international law scholars "find" international law then depend on the particular source of law at issue. With respect to custom, the goal is to find a consistent pattern of state practice, accompanied by a manifest sense of legal obligation (*opinio juris*). In other words, the customary law is that which states treat as binding on themselves. An articulation of standards does not suffice to establish law without conduct conforming to those standards, nor does conduct alone establish the existence of a legal norm in the absence of at least a tacit renunciation of the right to behave otherwise.

When confronted with a controversy, international jurists search the historical record for instances of state conduct in situations similar to the one at issue, as well as for pronouncements by state officials explaining, justifying, endorsing, denouncing, or acquiescing in relevant conduct. In collected accounts of practices and pronouncements, jurists seek to find patterns that indicate the existence of a legal norm. Instances that seem to contradict that indication may be either dismissed as isolated outliers or found to have resulted from special circumstances.

Although custom is theoretically the product of the consent of each state, consent may be imputed to states that, on notice of the custom's emergence in the community of states, fail to "persistently object," and to states that begin to participate in the relevant international activity subsequent to the hardening of the practice into custom. There are no clear specifications as to the amount or weight of evidence required to demonstrate the existence of customary law. Since states are presumed to be free to behave as they choose, the burden of persuasion ordinarily falls on the proponent of a legal restriction on conduct.

Where the legal issue involves a treaty rather than custom, a different set of methods comes into play. These methods are themselves dictated by the customary law of treaties, which governs such questions as what constitutes a binding treaty, how a treaty should be interpreted, and when treaty obligations may be suspended or terminated. This customary law of treaties was codified and further developed in the 1969 Vienna Convention on the Law of Treaties. Articles 31 and 32 of the convention establish an "objective approach" to treaty interpretation that emphasizes the "ordinary meaning" of the treaty language, permitting recourse to the records of negotiations (the *travaux preparatoires*) only in cases where the language is ambiguous, obscure, or conducive to a "manifestly absurd or unreasonable" result.

In reality, however, "ordinary meaning" is frequently elusive and the emergence of new circumstances may render uncertain the application of once clear terms. Efforts to specify meanings originally intended or subsequently adopted by the parties often produce controversy. To fill gaps in treaty language, jurists are obliged to employ methods similar to those used to derive customary law.

In addition to custom and treaty, international law encompasses "general principles common to the major legal systems of the world." To derive these, international jurists employ yet another method, canvassing the domestic law of states that represent a cross-section of legal traditions for evidence that certain principles are broadly shared. There is disagreement as to whether "general" principles include substantive legal norms—such as particular human rights—or whether the category is limited to more abstract norms—for example, one should not be permitted to benefit from one's own wrongdoing; rules of textual interpretation—a specific provision takes precedence over a general provision; and procedural principles—a party should not be allowed to relitigate issues that were previously the subject of a final judgment against it.

Since the late 1960s, international law has seen the emergence of a new category of norms not predicated on the consent—even "tacit" or implied—of individual states. These "peremptory" norms (*jus cogens*) may not be derogated from, and treaty provisions that contravene such norms are deemed invalid. No list of such norms has been authoritatively agreed upon, although the illegality of genocide, slavery, and torture are most frequently mentioned. Proponents are divided on how peremptory norms are to be derived; *jus cogens* may be predicated on *opinio juris* of an extraordinary character, on "general principles," or directly on natural law.

International relations and international law are distinct disciplines because their fundamental objectives differ. In international relations, the objective is to understand behavior. In international law, the objective is to direct behavior. Yet, there is a relationship, since those who wish to direct behavior benefit from understanding the behavior they seek to direct, that is, it is useful to know what works and why. And, those who seek to understand behavior need pools of behavior to examine. Keohane saw these as two different "optics." The IR optic is instrumentalist—directed to the pursuit of particular objectives, while the international law optic is normative.

According to this "normative optic," norms have causal impact. The impact of interests and power is by no means denied, but such explanations are not sufficient. Norms and rules exert a profound impact on how people think about state roles and obligations, and therefore on state behavior.[17]

Recognizing this fundamental difference of purpose should aid in understanding the various strategies pursued and the work produced in the two fields. Collaboration between the two disciplines is fruitful, but not because one imitates the methods of the other. Collaboration is most valuable when it strengthens the work of the two disciplines by increasing their ability to explain and to understand complicated matters like the requirements for effective governance in a globalized environment. Interdisciplinary work can also help to overcome the biases that may develop from a particular theoretical perspective or intellectual outlook. A challenge in studying social phenomena is that the research question and methodology will drive selection of the examples and therefore produce a result that may exaggerate the importance of a particular factor. At the same time, research has to be focused adequately to allow for the testing of hypotheses. An outsider's perspective can therefore be helpful in noticing factors that an expert may be constrained from seeing because of intellectual conditioning. Social scientists seek a generalizable proposition that lawyers resist. In fact, a generalized understanding of the functions, objectives, and tasks of behavior can be very helpful in predicting the outcomes of specific laws or standards. On the other hand, generalized understandings would have little validity without actual behavior to study. An inquiry into global governance provides an opportunity for both the social scientist and the legal scholar to take a broader view of developments in their fields. This broad view should include an understanding of how explanations of behavior may be limited in themselves, but stronger when used in connection with analyses from other theories or perspectives. A sampling of such perspectives follows.

The current state of the disciplines

The rejection of international law by postwar international relations scholars was mystifying to international law scholars and not even adequately recognized for a long time because of international law's role as a parent of modern international relations. IR scholars like Morgenthau, for example, were trained as lawyers, but moved away from their parent discipline.[18] The study of international relations can trace its roots to political philosophy and diplomatic history in ancient Greece and China as well as medieval Europe, as seen in the works of Thucydides, Sun Tzu, Mencius, Machiavelli, Bodin, and Kant. But the founding of what started as a primarily Anglo-American field of study is often traced to the creation of the Woodrow Wilson Chair of International Relations at Aberystwyth in 1919. Like its international law forebearer, international relations had a reformist bias and avowedly sought ways to prevent war. Early international relations scholarship, like its international law counterpart, was prescriptive, advocating "legal modalities for achieving peace."[19] The failure in the 1930s of these modalities to achieve that peace led to a desire to revise the discipline's approaches.

Harold Jacobson pointed to three books that "defined the new approach to the systematic study of international relations."[20] These were Carr's *The Twenty Years' Crisis, 1919–1939*, Wright's *A Study of War*, and Morgenthau's *Politics among Nations*.[21] All three pushed for the development of a less value-laden and more empirically rooted form of inquiry. One of their chief criticisms of inter-war international law projects was that they had been detached from "on the ground" reality. The objective of scientific inquiry as the basis for understanding international relations was therefore "to develop empirically-based generalizations about human behavior" to inform policy choices.[22] Making this distinction, however, did not mean the complete rejection of a reformist agenda, since seeking one possible outcome over another would still influence the choice of research question and appreciation of its significance to contribute to an agenda of peace, prosperity, and human dignity.

As a mode for undertaking inquiry, IR scholars emphasized quantitative analysis to provide the basis for generalization. Despite the slow progress towards identifying generalizations, this approach to international relations has nevertheless made important contributions:

> The search for generalizations about human behavior must be the core of the enterprise. Careful attention to the definition and the use of terms is essential to rigorous thinking. Accurate measurement is essential. Experience using the basic tool of statistical analysis in the social sciences, multiple regression, should make us deeply suspicious of deterministic and single factor explanations. Most developments are brought about by multiple causes that contribute in differing proportions. Developing middle range generalizations is a reasonable and realistic goal for international relations scholarship.[23]

Beth Simmons, who has also been a leader in using social science methods to understand international law, notes that:

> The challenge is to design research that is able to address the question as to whether legal considerations have any independent impact on states' decisions. ... The theoretical frontier is to determine why the law matters to behavior, if indeed it does. ... The most convincing explanations will be those that give a good reason to believe that the existence of legal institutions changes the interests governments have in particular kinds of behavior. We need to

think of what mechanisms could be at play in changing the context of choice: do legal commitments change expectations about behavior such that violating obligations increases costs? What kinds of costs are involved: domestic political punishment, market punishment, or punishment from other states or international institutions? Under what conditions can we expect these various mechanisms to come into play?[24]

Her study, *Mobilizing for Human Rights: International Law in Domestic Politics*, provides a good example of how social science inquiry can help to deepen understanding about the performance of international law. As such, it contributes both to international law and to international relations and helps those working separately in the two disciplines to gain from the knowledge and perspective of the other.

This interdisciplinary approach, however, has not developed in a vacuum. Simmons has been a leader in this effort to engage social science to explain the role international law might play in international behavior, and she acknowledges the "interesting new ways" that have been employed "to think about international law's effects on government actions and policies" over the last decade or more.[25] As Helen Milner so effectively argues, understanding international relations is incomplete without understanding the domestic situation—its interests, institutions, and distribution of information.[26] Simmons writes:

> Rational theorists have emphasized the role that law can play in crafting institutions that provide information to domestic audiences in ways that help them hold their governments accountable. Liberal theorists have argued that international legal commitments supplement domestic legal structures, and they view international human rights agreements as attempts to solidify democratic gains at home. Constructivist theorists have come to view " ... international law and international organizations [as] ... the primary vehicle for stating community norms and for collective legitimation," and some prominent legal scholars have explicitly incorporated such concepts as discourse, socialization, and persuasion into an account of transnational legal processes through which international law eventually puts down roots in domestic institutions and practices.[27]

Clustered under the heading of liberalism, we find the scholarship of Anne-Marie Slaughter, who has also been a leader in fostering inter-disciplinary study between international relations and international law, but takes a deep look inside the state for the capacities to govern in a globalized environment. By connecting more deeply with domestic political and legal orders, international law reaches those who are essential to its effective functioning—government officials at all levels networked with counterparts around the world—as well as those who require its protection—individuals and human rights.[28] Importantly, Slaughter finds that international law can provide structure and support if a state is unable to provide that for itself. Although this is not a permanent solution, the application of international law could provide a means for the international community to help fill a gap created by the collapse of a government or some other form of political transition.[29]

The English School encompassed scholarship that saw the international system as a society of states. By doing so, it opened the door to investigating how structure or rhetoric might shape state behavior and provided a middle path between realism and utopianism. It accepted that ideas can shape politics and behavior. Within the English School, scholarship divided into those who saw states as more pluralistic in their acceptance and practice of norms like the laws of war and humanitarian law and those who saw the world as more solidarist—that is, that states were more uniform in their acceptance and practice of these standards. Scholars following this tradition assumed that international relations are "governed by rules, and therefore, substantively, the interactions of states exhibit a degree of order that could not, under anarchy, normally be expected."[30] Following from that, they would then study "how satisfactorily any kind of institutional structure functions within a particular realm," and would undertake historical comparisons of systems. The name of this body of work derives from a group of scholars associated with the London School of Economics and the British Committee on the Theory of International Politics. Prominent names associated with this approach are C.A.W. Manning, Martin Wight, Hedley Bull, Alan James, Adam Watson, John Vincent, James Mayall, and Andrew Hurrell. With the end of the Cold War in 1989, interest was rekindled in the ideas of international society and world order—issues that had preoccupied writers of the English School decades before.

Constructivism is another social science approach that has found relevance among international lawyers. Its iterative and non-hierarchic characteristics seem to capture much of how law and international law work. Brunnée and Toope write:

> No law, even law in seemingly hierarchical state systems, is merely the imposition of authority (read as "power") from above. That is because, when understood as a purposive activity, law is inevitably

a construction dependent upon the mutual generative activity and acceptance of the governing and the governed.[31]

This approach theorizes that the framework and processes that facilitate activity among actors within a system can condition expectations and shape those within a system. In the language of constructivism, "law is constructed through rhetorical activity producing increasingly influential mutual expectations or shared understandings of actors."[32] Another characteristic of this approach is a recognition that for law to be effective and accepted, it should exhibit "a substantial degree of congruence between enacted laws and background informal social practices and conventions governing horizontal relations among citizens ... "[33] And, finally, in a vein reminiscent of the operating and normative systems approach Paul Diehl and I have taken to understanding international law, Brunée and Toope observe that " ... process is part of the ends that law serves because inclusive processes reinforce the commitments of participants in the system to the substantive outcomes achieved by implicating participants in their generation."[34] In this view, law has both a specific normative as well as a system-wide operating function. Law-abiding behavior will reinforce and further encourage lawabiding behavior, but only if the system credibly appears to facilitate the effective pursuit of interests and execution of responsibilities.

For IL scholars, the challenge is to understand "the difficulties arising from the diversification and expansion of international law."[35] The International Law Commission's Fragmentation Report posed the fundamental question: what role can international law play in the present environment of legal pluralism where there is international law and domestic law, but there is also transnational law, soft law, and private standards? These bodies of law and standards exist because they meet particular needs and are regarded as effective in meeting those needs. Many of these practices have grown out of *ad hoc* arrangements that subsequently gained wide acceptance so that their place in the legal hierarchy and relationship to other bodies of law may not be clear.

One aspect of globalization is the emergence of technically specialized cooperation networks with a global scope: trade, environment, human rights, diplomacy, communications, medicine, crime prevention, energy production, security, indigenous cooperation, and so on—spheres of life and expert cooperation that transcend national boundaries and are difficult to regulate through traditional international law. National law seems insufficient owing to the transnational nature of the networks, while international law only inadequately takes account of their specialized objectives and needs.[36]

Soft law is a term used to cover a variety of mechanisms that do not involve formal legal obligations or processes, but nevertheless represent a shared understanding or consensus about procedure or behavior among states. The term "soft law" has generated scholarly controversy because of the potential for confusion created by the notion that informal obligations could have the force of law. As will be seen in Chapter 5, although the theoretical and jurisprudential underpinnings of this concept may not be fully formed, a body of practice is growing and a view that soft law as part of the international legal scene "is here to stay."[37]

The potential for fragmentation exists not just because of different laws, but because the same dispute might give rise to multiple and possibly contradictory decisions. An example is the case involving the environmental effects of the "MOX Plant"—a nuclear facility at Sellafield, United Kingdom, that has been raised in three different institutional settings: an Arbitral Tribunal set up under Annex VII of the United Nations Convention on the Law of the Sea, the compulsory dispute settlement procedure under the Convention on the Protection of the Marine Environment of the North-East Atlantic (OSPAR Convention), and the European Court of Justice under the European Community and Euratom Treaties.[38] But is such competition or legal pluralism necessarily a bad thing? It can be if it unduly taxes the limited resources of the international legal system. It can, however, be positive if it provides a more comprehensive understanding of the outcomes from different sources of law and different institutional settings. It could also be regarded as positive if it provides more opportunity for access to international dispute settlement. These are, however, propositions that have yet to be tested and could benefit from a social science study once adequate examples are available.

Fragmentation further can occur through "conflicting interpretations of international law" as occurred in the *Tadic* case in 1999. The Appeals Chamber of the International Criminal Tribunal for the Former Yugoslavia (ICTY) disagreed with the finding of the International Court of Justice in the 1986 *Nicaragua* case, that the United States could not be held accountable for actions in a territory not under its "effective control." The ICTY decided that "effective control" was too high a threshold for holding an outside power accountable for domestic unrest and that it was sufficient to hold the power accountable if it exercised "overall control" over the forces causing the unrest.[39] This shows the practical difficulty of developing law incrementally—that the prevailing standard may be unclear and inconsistent when it is in formation. Ongoing adjudication can help to clarify it, but in the meantime, questions about the standard will remain. Of course, the situation is similar in a domestic legal system.

Although seeking a simpler and more consistent jurisprudence and one option for dispute settlement might seem desirable, it is no longer possible in today's more complicated and inter-related world of affairs. The fragmentation was driven by the need to be responsive to new initiatives and needs and to generate additional capacity to carry out necessary tasks. These include the vast new body of law associated with the work of international organizations and generated by these institutions.[40] The challenge is to maintain the strength and effectiveness of these diverse elements by keeping them within a structure or framework of international law that continues to function as the general language or operating system for activities between states.[41]

The fragmentation of the international political world has attained legal significance especially as it has been accompanied by the emergence of specialized and (relatively) autonomous rules or rule complexes, legal institutions, and spheres of legal practice. What once appeared to be governed by "general international law" has become the field of operation for such specialist systems as "trade law," "human rights law," "environmental law," "law of the sea," "European law," and even such exotic and highly specialized knowledges as "investment law" or "international refugee law," etc.—each possessing its own principles and institutions. The problem, as lawyers have seen it, is that such specialized law-making and institution-building tends to take place with relative ignorance of legislative and institutional activities in the adjoining fields and of the general principles and practices of international law. The result is conflicts between rules or rule systems, deviating institutional practices and, possibly, the loss of an overall perspective on the law.[42]

If an overall framework can be maintained, such pluralism may not only increase the general capabilities of the legal system to meet changing needs, but by doing so, may also create new capabilities to respond to further changing needs. The level of intrusion into their activities that states have permitted since the middle of the twentieth century provides a good example of this. For historic reasons related to the Cold War in the 1970s and 1980s, decolonization in the 1960s, and political transformation in Latin America in the 1970s, states became willing to allow outside monitoring, either from international institutions or from other states, and even non-governmental organizations, as assurance that international obligations would be met. President Ronald Reagan succinctly expressed this in the context of concluding arms control agreements with the Soviet Union when he said, "trust, but verify." International inspections, monitoring, and reporting are now taken for granted and accepted to a degree that would have been considered impossible only a few decades ago. Consider, for example, the vilification of North Korea stemming from its refusal, even at the cost of forfeiting much needed international assistance, to allow any international inspection or monitoring of its arms development program or even of the condition of its population.[43]

The cumulative effect of international inspections and reporting requirements has created an international system where all countries large or small, powerful or less powerful, understand that their actions may be subject to scrutiny, often within the framework of an international institution. States subjected themselves to these standards as a way to get target states to agree to the same standards. But agreements that might have started as symbolic gestures have taken on substantive significance as webs of interstate accountability have become denser and denser in the areas of arms control, human rights, and, for members of the European Union, EU directives. Such a cumulation was possible and discernible because it took place within a general international law framework that could capture the behavior for observation and analysis. Whether one believes that international law has any effect or not, that states and other actors were acting within a framework is a starting point to understand motivation and purpose. This was noted by the UN International Law Commission as follows:

> Fragmentation moves international law in the direction of legal pluralism but does this, as the present report has sought to emphasize, by constantly using the resources of general international law, especially the rules of the V[ienna] C[onvention on the] L[aw of] T[reaties], customary law and "general principles of law recognized by civilized nations."[44]

For international law, these general provisions help to situate pluralist developments within the field.

Understanding and studying law, including international law, has also become more complex under the influence of the critical legal studies movement that has challenged the assumption that law is value-free. Scholars following this school of thought demonstrate how gender, race, and historic conditions such as colonialism are reflected in the law and serve to reinforce existing social practices unless consciously revised. They see law as a tool that can be used to check the excessive or unjust use of power. A related approach that engages international law is legal pluralism, defined by Sally Engle Merry as follows:

Recent work defines "legal system" broadly to include the system of courts and judges supported by the state as well as non-legal forms of normative ordering. Some of these are part of institutions such as factories, corporations, and universities and include written codes, tribunals, and security forces, sometimes replicating the structure and symbolic form of state law. Other normative orders are informal systems in which the processes of establishing rules, securing compliance to these rules, and punishing rulebreakers seem natural and taken for granted, as occurs within families, work groups, and collectives. Thus, virtually every society is legally plural.[45]

Embracing legal pluralism is an important way for international law to understand its interactions with other systems of law and "to move away from its fixation on state sovereignty."[46] It can provide a more nuanced approach and capture a fuller range of international law's influence. As Brunée and Toope note: "We should stop looking for structural distinctions that identify law, and examine instead the processes that constitute a normative continuum bridging from predictable patterns of practice to legally required behavior."[47] By looking at the effects rather than the form, this pluralist outlook allows for including non-governmental organizations, corporations, epistemic communities and others who are now "actively engaged in the creation of shared understandings and the promotion of learning amongst states."[48] It provides for the conceptual expansion that includes actors who have not been part of the formal international law-making system in the past. By drawing on multiple sources and overlapping layers of authority, this form of analysis may more closely reflect how law functions and facilitate understanding of its operation in a global environment.

Summing up

Disillusioned by the failure of international law and the League of Nations to prevent the Second World War, international relations scholars dismissed international law as epiphenomenal. International relations instead embraced realism and the development of a less value-laden and more empirically rooted form of inquiry. Yet, the break was never complete, as interest continued in the development of international society and world order. The study of international institutions provided an important bridge between the normative pursuits of international legal scholarship and the empiricism of social science. Finding that "institutions matter" through empirical observation provided an important insight into how the interests and behavior of states could be shaped by exogenous factors. As the understanding of state conduct and behavior became more complicated, so did the understanding of international law. With the advent of critical legal studies, international law moved away from its claim to be value-free with an increased attention to the origins and functions of norms. The international legal environment is also one that now includes a number of courts and tribunals, each issuing separate and sometimes contradictory opinions about the same case. International law further faces growing specialization, leading to concerns about its possible fragmentation.

These observations lead to two conclusions: 1) the world as seen through either international relations or international law is more complicated and nuanced than their academic pre-dispositions might suggest; and 2) international law plays a role in shaping the interests and politics of the international system that in turn shape the ongoing development of international law. International law and international politics have an interactive and iterative relationship that further functions at the international, national, and now sub-national levels. The next four chapters will take a look at these cumulative interactions over time.

2 International concerns and the international community of states

- The state and the development of an international community
- International organizations as international actors
- The development of international human rights as a matter of international concern
- Summing up

A characteristic of the globalized governing environment is that those who govern are now subject to greater demands for transparency and scrutiny than ever before. States today tolerate intrusion into their affairs in ways that would have been unthinkable only a few decades ago. This level and form of international activity did not develop by accident, and was initially created and promoted by states themselves to pursue particular objectives. What states promoting such practices failed to realize, however, was that once introduced, they would not stay contained to one issue area, activity, or state. The outcome of the accumulated changes and adaptations made by actors in the international system to meet specific needs is the development of an international community and a vibrant civil society expressing international concern on its behalf. What remains under-studied is how these actions have changed the actors themselves and the system within which they act and govern.

Another area worthy of attention is how governing capacity is generated within the international system. This chapter will draw on the experience of developing today's human rights system to show how capacities are initiated, practiced, and perfected over time to become a permanent part of the governing environment. It further shows that the search for capacity to support a particular political or normative agenda can be far-ranging, and that even practices that may not have been regarded as altogether successful may, nevertheless, prove to be important in a future application. When a new mode or tool is introduced, it contributes to the governance toolkit by being available and adaptable for further use. From a theoretical perspective, understanding how a problem is solved is important, but further understanding regarding how governing capacity has been affected—increased, made more complicated, or likely both—is needed.

This chapter will examine the development of the practice of expressing international concern either by or on behalf of an international community. It will demonstrate how rhetorical or symbolic expressions can connect powerful political forces and bring about dramatic changes. It will do so by examining two major actors in the creation of both international concern and the international community—states and international organizations. It will further demonstrate the power of using their activities to create the worldwide connections and political infrastructure that can be mobilized to promote change. Human rights will be used as an example of how capacity is built over time and how that capacity can generate further opportunity for governance. Human rights is selected for study because of its relatively short history, but one that demonstrates how connecting an idea to governance capacities can facilitate political and normative development.

The state and the development of an international community

In his study, *The Sovereign State and Its Competitors*, Hendrik Spruyt identified a "distinct central locus of authority" as one of the key assets provided by the sovereign state over other models of political organization such as city states, feudal lordships, or multinational empires bound together by personal allegiance to a sovereign.[1] The looser forms of authority made sense at a time when physical control of vast territories was difficult. However, once economic, social, and political needs required more regularized forms of cooperation and coordination, the looser forms became less effective, particularly at waging war:

> Success in war ... may indicate the effectiveness and efficiency of types of organization. Although Venetian defeat at the hands of the French was not such that Venice disappeared as an institutional type, it did prove that some forms of organization were institutionally superior. Sovereign states were better, in the long run, in raising more revenue and larger numbers of troops. War did not work as an evolutionary process that selected among types of units, but it did indicate to political elites and social groups which type of organization was the more efficient, and they subsequently adopted the most competitive institutional form.[2]

The state was the form that most ably met the governance needs of the seventeenth century. It remains the central international actor today, although in a vastly changed governance environment. The state now meets its governance obligations by negotiating with international organizations, private actors, civil society, and its own citizens. This governance network did not appear overnight, but developed as a result of steps taken by states over the centuries to enhance their capacity to govern. Historically, the state's role was further advanced "by mutual empowerment," that is, "[s]overeign actors only recognized particular types of legitimate players in the international system"—other states.[3] We see this "mutual empowerment" at work after 1960 as the United Nations (UN) gained members with the independence of Europe's colonies. From its original 51 members in 1945, the United Nations expanded to 76 in 1955 and then to 99 in 1960. These newly independent countries led in the development and passage of UN General Assembly Resolution 1514 in 1960, declaring that: "Immediate steps shall be taken, in Trust and Non-Self-Governing Territories or all other territories which have not yet attained independence, to transfer all powers to the people of those territories, without any conditions or reservations, in accordance with their freely expressed will and desire, without any distinction as to race, creed or colour, in order to enable them to enjoy complete independence and freedom." This call for "immediate steps" is in contrast to the language of Chapter XI of the UN Charter: Declaration Regarding Non-Self-Governing Territories, that emphasized stewardship and responsibility in the governing of non-self-governing territories and assistance "in the progressive development of their free political institutions" (UN Charter Article 73(b)). UN membership in 2010 was 192, with the most recent member, Montenegro, joining in 2006.

The emphasis of the 1960 UN General Assembly resolution was on independence and freedom from external rule as attributes of sovereign statehood. International law acknowledges these attributes in the concept of the equality of states. It does, however, also provide for four generally accepted criteria for statehood, as reflected in Article 1 of the Montevideo Convention on Rights and Duties of States, 1933.

- A permanent population;
- A defined territory;
- A government; and
- The capacity to enter into relations with other states.[4]

While international law recognizes these general criteria, it is flexible on how each of them is met.[5] International law does not establish how many people constitute a population, how settled the boundaries of a territory have to be, or what form a government should take, nor does it define how much effective control is required over the territory claimed. In fact, control can be minimal and still prevail as long as it is greater than that of any other claimant.[6]

In international law, the law of state responsibility provides the legal basis on which states seek remedy for breaches of international obligations or duties by another state. The evolution in the concept of state responsibility since 1955, led by the UN's International Law Commission (ILC), provides a snapshot of the expanding scope of responsibility that states now have to each other. The law of state responsibility was the subject of an unsuccessful codification conference in 1930 under the auspices of the League of Nations. Twenty-five years later, the UN's ILC initially "focused on State responsibility for injuries to aliens and their property, that is to say on the substantive rules of the international law of diplomatic protection," but a significant number of the ILC's members found this too narrow an understanding of state responsibility and worked to broaden its scope of coverage.[7]

By 1961, the ILC agreed that, beyond diplomatic protection, states were now held responsible to each other in the areas of human rights, disarmament, environmental protection, and the law of the sea.[8] There was also an effort to expand the concept of state responsibility beyond the responsibility of one state to another to include the responsibility of a state to the international community. Article 19 of the 1976 Draft Articles of State Responsibility states:

> An internationally wrongful act which results from the breach by a State of an international obligation so essential for the protection of fundamental interests of the international community that its breach is recognized as a crime by that community as a whole constitutes an international crime.[9]

In hindsight, it is clear that, as the Westphalian state form was a response to domestic economic and political needs that required a distinct locus of authority, by the late twentieth century, states began to respond to complex cross-border issues that involved a range of emerging authorities and governing capacities. A state authority remains vital, but flexibility and agility are now also the hallmarks of statehood within a complex governance network of international organizations and private entities. Think, for example, of the international response required to the terrorist attacks on the United States on 11 September 2001. For one analysis of this new environment and its challenges to states and the traditional tools of states, including war, was the US Department of Defense's 2010 study, the Joint Operating Environment (JOE) 2010. One conclusion the JOE 2010 draws is that: "As they [nonstate actors] better integrate global media sophistication, lethal weaponry, and potentially greater cultural awareness and intelligence, they will pose a considerably greater threat than at present. Moreover, unburdened by bureaucratic processes, transnational groups are already showing themselves to be highly adaptive and agile."[10]

The need for flexibility as well as authoritative decision-making was created by the kinds of issues increasingly faced by governments. Multiple authorities even within one government have to be coordinated to pursue a policy. For example, Abram and Antonia Chayes noted that in the United States, the "interagency process" dealing with arms control issues (Strategic Arms Limitation Talks—SALT I and SALT II, 1972–79) involved: "the National Security Council staff, the Departments of State and Defense, the Arms Control and Disarmament Agency, and sometimes the Department of Energy or the National Aeronautic and Space Administration (NASA)."[11] Subjects like environmental protection are even more complicated. The final US position drafted in preparation of the Montreal Protocol to the Vienna Convention on the Protection of the Ozone Layer—adopted 1985 and entered into force 1988—was prepared by the Department of State "and was formally cleared by the Departments of Commerce and Energy, The Council on Environmental Quality, EPA [Environmental Protection Agency], NASA [National Aeronautic and Space Administration], NOAA [National Oceanic and Atmospheric Administration], OMB [Office of Management and Budget], USTR [Office of the US Trade Representative], and the Domestic Policy Council (representing all other interested agencies)."[12]

Within each agency, there are additional levels of clearance and coordination. In the US Department of State alone, an issue like the Montreal Protocol has to be cleared by multiple offices, including the regional bureaus, the office handling environmental issues, that handling international organizations, the Legal Adviser's office, the legislative liaison office to Congress and several others. And this is only at the level of the US federal government. Where compliance with international obligations requires changes in the laws of the constituent states of the United States or any country with a federal system, the "interagency minuet" in that country becomes that much more complicated.[13]

That state interaction with international law, international obligations, and international institutions can and does change the state itself should not be surprising if we recall Inis Claude's description of states seeking cooperation to meet their objectives. He wrote that "states must develop an awareness of the problems which arise out of their coexistence, and, on this basis, come to recognize the need for creation of institutional devices and systematic methods for regulating their relations with each other."[14] States therefore pursue cooperation when they are unable to meet certain objectives on their own and seek ways to bolster their capacity to do so.

Alexander Cooley and Spruyt further remind us that state sovereignty is not absolute, but is a condition that can wax or wane depending on political circumstances. Cooley and Spruyt apply a theory of "incomplete contracting" to these situations to demonstrate how relations can move from partial sovereignty to full sovereignty over time.[15] Incomplete contracts are those that "leave terms to be specified because of procedural and strategic uncertainty."[16]

Territories gaining independence have struck special arrangements with their former colonial masters for trading privileges or other preferential arrangements in the interest of maintaining stability and for economic gain. New states and other states whose sovereignty may be conditional in some respects can also improve their circumstances in rounds of re-negotiation to eliminate any special privileges. Forms of conditional sovereignty are not limited to newly independent territories, but also include areas where transitional governments sanctioned by the UN are in place or where special political circumstances make such conditions desirable. A prime example of a UN-sanctioned transitional government was that of Kosovo in 1999. UN Security Council Resolution 1244 placed the territory under the authority of the UN Interim Mission in Kosovo (UNMIK) and established the Kosovo Force (KFOR) to back its authority. Another form of an incomplete contract was the agreement between the United Kingdom and China covering the terms of the return of Hong Kong to Chinese sovereignty in 1997. Although it was made clear in the agreement that China would become the sovereign authority in Hong Kong, the territory was allowed to maintain certain attributes of its British past, including the use of the common law and the English language for an initial period of 50 years with no clear indication about what would happen in 2047—50 years after Hong Kong's return to Chinese sovereignty.[17]

What we have seen is the state governance framework responding to the adaptations and adjustments made by states to fulfill their new responsibilities to people in their jurisdiction, stewardship of their territory, and multilateral coordination and cooperation. As such, domestic political systems are being affected when international obligations shift the internal balance of power. This can be troubling if the internal shift results from actions taken by international organizations whose decision-making processes are regarded as opaque and unresponsive to public scrutiny and pressure. The failure of institutions to allow for participation in their decision-making processes or means to review decisions made has created suspicion and hostility against actions taken at the international level. In democracies, this leads to questioning of the lack of democratic accountability in the operations and decision-making of international institutions.[18]

Similar concerns arise with regard to treaties that create obligations or set up institutions that "establish regimes that, typically, allocate implementing powers to committees of diplomats or representatives of governments, to administrators, bureaucrats, and, occasionally, to international judges or arbitrators."[19] The US Supreme Court case of *Missouri v. Holland* provides a good example of where meeting an international obligation, even without the involvement of any international institutions, changed the power structure within the United States in the area of the management of migratory birds. Under the Constitution, international obligations can be used to preempt the jurisdiction of states within the United States if the Congress and the President choose to do so in compliance with an international agreement. The US Supreme Court ruled in 1920 that the protection of migratory birds was a national interest that could only be protected by national action, and that the 1916 treaty between the United States and the United Kingdom (for Canada) to protect migratory birds, ratified in 1918, did not violate the Tenth Amendment.[20] The federal government thus assumed responsibility at the expense of the local powers and placed greater distance between the people and the basis for the law—in this case, a treaty.

The tolerance of national governments and their citizens for such deference to international obligations varies. In the cases of countries transitioning from authoritarian governments, international obligations may be regarded more positively as a means to move into an era that is more respectful of private rights and interests. See, for example, the inclusion of international human rights standards in the Constitution of South Africa. Jed Rubenfeld sees the difference as one of constitutional outlook. He describes two forms—an international constitutionalism and an American or national constitutionalism. The international outlook is prevalent in Europe: "From this viewpoint, it's not particularly important for a constitution to be the product of a national participatory political process. What matters [to those holding the international outlook] is that the constitution recognizes human rights, protects minorities, establishes the rule of law, and sets up stable, democratic political institutions, preferably of a parliamentary variety, in which the chief executive is not directly elected by the people [but indirectly through political party consensus or vote]."[21] In contrast, the American or national approach "holds that a nation's constitution ought to be made through that nation's democratic process, because the business of the constitution is to express the polity's most basic legal and political commitments."[22]

While a state may resist being constrained by a complex web of formal and informal connections and networks, it also seeks to use those connections and networks as enablers of its own national action. Despite the reluctance of the US government to conform to international practices just because they are internationally accepted, we can see that the United States recognizes that it must embed itself into international networks in order to pursue its security, economic, and political interests. This was certainly the case when the United States asked the UN Security Council (UNSC) to pass UNSC resolution 1373 as part of its response to the attacks of 11 September 2001. Acting under Chapter VII of the UN Charter, the Security Council obligated all states to do a series of things to prevent and to suppress the financing of terrorist acts.[23]

The state remains a powerful and vital political institution as the focus of political interests both local and global. It may not be the only broker of power and interests, but it remains a universally accepted actor that has already proven its own capacity to adapt to the changing needs of domestic governance since the seventeenth century. Given the current need for forms of governance to address global interests and concerns, the state will remain an essential player, even if it is not always the only or most powerful player.

Whether the state's continued importance in governance is permanent or transitional is not yet known. What we do know is that the state has the most developed and recognized infrastructure for governance. This includes the capacity to organize its people and to coordinate other units of governance like municipalities, counties, tribes, and provinces. The state therefore maintains its importance as a nexus between the international and the sub-national levels of governance. It is not the only possible nexus, but it remains an important one in a variety of ways. It provides widely recognized and authoritative pathways for international obligations to reach local governments and people. See, for example, the 1980 Hague Convention on Child Abduction that provides that a court order in one country to release a child will go directly to the judge in the country where the child is located without going through diplomatic or other channels. The state provides relevant personnel to address regulatory issues through networks of regulators. The state remains the most efficient means to mobilize national and sub-national resources for international action. One example of this is the contribution of national military forces to the United Nations for peacekeeping and peace-building operations.[24]

If the early history of the development of the state was that it was the most competitive institutional type to raise revenue and troops, then the current history of the state is one in which it seeks means to enable national action. This enabling comes from domestic forces like elections and debate, but it also now increasingly comes from international forces like those found in international institutions or international law. Legitimacy is part of enabling, but the principal interest here is one of how relevant elements to meet state objectives connect and operate. As we will see in the rest of this chapter, the domestic and the international are coming together in ways that make international issues and concerns a growing factor in domestic politics.

All of this relates to the idea of an international community. There is no single common understanding of what the international community is or who comprises it. Its meaning will therefore be shaped by the context in which it is used. For example, for international lawyers, the international community may mean all those who have a right and a reason to be involved in some normative development. For the UN, it may mean a substantial portion of the UN membership. For civil society, it may mean a collection of like-minded individuals and organizations. What all of these meanings hold in common, however, is the sense that an expression by an international community is something that should be noted. The reasons any view should be noted—and by whom—will also differ depending on the nature of the community. In the case of the UN, an expression on behalf of the international community might warrant attention because it will signal to a state that its behavior may have a negative effect on its relations with a large number of UN member states. What is changing is the emergence of some recognized voices for the international community. Many of these voices are associated with international organizations.

International organizations as international actors

One of the reasons for the durability of the state has been its adaptability. This has included the creation of institutions to enhance its capacity to provide for the well-being of its citizens and for strong economic development. The establishment of international organizations changed the landscape of international relations Inis Claude's *Swords into Plowshares* provided a concise history of international organizations organized around "streams of development."[25]

The first phase can be traced to the nineteenth-century Concert system, starting with the Congress of Vienna in 1815 that introduced a "system of multilateral, high level, political conferences," to ensure an acceptable balance of power among the major world powers of the time—the United Kingdom, the Austrian Empire, the Russian Empire, Prussia, and France.[26] The last of these meetings took place in Algeciras in 1906 in an effort to resolve the conflict between France and Germany over the French desire to establish a protectorate over Morocco. A contemporary version of this would be the G-20 (Group of Twenty Finance Ministers and Central Bank Governors), which includes the finance ministers of 19 countries plus the EU and representatives from the International Monetary Fund and the World Bank. Since the financial crisis of 1997–99, a G-20 ministerial is held each fall. Summits of the G-20 were held to address the financial crises in 2008, 2009, and 2010.[27]

Claude called the second stage the Hague system, starting with the Hague Conference of 1899 to limit armaments. Differing from the first stream, in which only select states took part, the Hague conference system aspired to universal participation. Its participants also agreed to meet on a regular basis—once every seven to eight years. The motive for expanding participation was a practical one: effective control of the spread and use of excessively destructive armaments required participation by as many countries as possible. A second conference was held in The Hague in 1907, but the third scheduled for 1915 was pre-empted by the First World War and never took place.

The legacies of both the Congress and Hague systems can be seen in the structure of contemporary international organizations where there is often a smaller council of important powers or stakeholders, together with an assembly of all members that meets on a regularly scheduled basis. International organizations today typically have a plenary body in which all members are represented on an equal basis, that is, each member state casts one vote. This is a legacy of the Westphalian system and an important reflection of the formal equality that international law attributes to each state. Organizations like the UN have therefore become important diplomatic venues for countries that do not have the capacity to have direct contact with countries around the world through bilateral embassies.

That each state casts one vote in the General Assembly leads to alliance-building among the members to advance their agendas. Such successful alliance-building occurred in the UN General Assembly through the 1960s and 1970s when members newly independent from their colonial masters pressed for a rapid end to colonialism everywhere.[28] The enlarged General Assembly also successfully pressed for the end of such neo-colonial practices as apartheid in southern Africa. In 1962, UN General Assembly resolution 1761 called on member states to boycott South Africa and on the Security Council to impose sanctions and to establish a Special Committee to monitor the racial situation in South Africa until the practice of apartheid was ended.[29]

Although UN General Assembly resolutions do not have the force of international law, as a reflection of world opinion, they become part of the governance and norm-creation process. In democracies, this may mean leverage for pressure groups to lobby their own governments and other powerful entities like corporations to take actions to bring objectionable practices to an end. Reflecting the public sentiment expressed through the anti-apartheid stance of the UN, the Reverend Leon Sullivan, a member of the Board of Directors of General Motors, developed a code of conduct, commonly referred to as the Sullivan Principles, for corporations doing business in South Africa in the 1970s. In the Preamble to these Principles, Reverend Sullivan wrote:

> The objectives of the Global Sullivan Principles are to support economic, social and political justice by companies where they do business; to support human rights and to encourage equal opportunity at all levels of employment, including racial and gender diversity on decision making committees and boards; to train and advance disadvantaged workers for technical, supervisory and management opportunities; and to assist with greater tolerance and understanding among peoples; thereby helping to improve the quality of life for communities, workers and children with dignity and equality.[30]

UN General Assembly resolutions can, therefore, provide a focus and a call to action for both public and private actors even if the resolutions do not compel action as a matter of legal obligation.

A major innovation of the UN was the move towards majority voting, rather than unanimity, as was the practice in the League of Nations. The unanimity requirement was a crippling one for the League, rendering its members unable to respond to situations as they occurred. To overcome this, the UN Charter provided for a General Assembly and a Security Council that could both make decisions on the basis of a majority. In the case of the Security Council, the majority carried an important condition. UN Charter Article 27 provided that on non-procedural matters, the majority had to be two-thirds of the members, including "the concurring votes" of the five designated permanent members of the Security Council—China, France, the USSR/Russia, the United Kingdom, and the United States.[31]

"The third major stream of development in the organization of international life arose from the creation of public international unions— agencies concerned with problems in various essentially nonpolitical fields."[32] This stream included the creation of the "functional unions" by states to gather expertise and information and to facilitate cross-border activity. Generally created by treaty, the Universal Postal Union, the International Telecommunications Union, the International Civil Aviation Organization, and the Food and Agriculture Organization are examples of such international or intergovernmental organizations (IGOs) created to set standards and to regulate a particular area of cross-border activity. These institutions typically have a permanent secretariat made up of specialists charged with monitoring their mandated activity. Although the twenty-first century has seen an increase in hybrid organizations working in the regulatory area, institutions of hybrid governance also have forebears dating back to the League of Nations.

Established in 1919 to protect workers' rights and to promote good working conditions and employment opportunities, the International Labour Organization (ILO) functions in a tripartite structure with representation from governments, workers, and employers provided for in its constitution. The three groups have equal voice in all ILO deliberations, although governments have a larger number of delegates and therefore a larger total number of votes. Each delegate casts one vote whether representing an employers' or workers' group. In the early twentieth century, this governing structure was quite novel, and it created an important precedent for the participation of private stakeholders in the work of an organization created by states.[33]

The ILO's method of requiring member states to submit ILO conventions to domestic political branches and to enact appropriate legislation is also a precursor to what many conventions require states to do today, that is, enact implementing legislation. Laurence Helfer notes that the ILO worked to ensure state compliance with its obligations in two ways. One was through interpretation that was used to reassure states that they would not be taking on any obligation beyond what they could meet.[34] The second was to collect and to publish these interpretations and non-binding recommendations. The reasoning for this practice was to make known to the entire membership the questions and answers individual countries were asking. The practice foreshadows the human rights General Comments system used by the Human Rights Committee.

Following the Second World War, member states convened a constitutional convention to consider the ILO's role in the new system of international institutions. It was concluded that the ILO should expand its treaty-monitoring authority and require "states to disclose whether they had implemented the organization's nonbinding recommendations."[35] Since this monitoring was over domestic lawmaking activity, this new authority effectively "gave an international organization agenda-setting power over *domestic* lawmaking processes by requiring governments to submit all treaties to the legislature and to take a position on whether the treaties should be ratified."[36] And, as we will see later, this power to put into effect non-binding recommendations blurs the distinction between the ILO's binding and non-binding obligations and further shows how the authority of an international organization can expand without it necessarily receiving specific member state authorization to do so.

This contrasts with the more classic structure of the International Civil Aviation Organization (ICAO), where non-governmental organizations are invited to participate, but do not take part in the formal governance of the organization, as in the case of the ILO. Established in 1944 by the Convention on International Civil Aviation (the Chicago Convention), ICAO works to ensure the safe and orderly functioning of civil aviation. To do this, ICAO works in cooperation with several UN agencies such as the World Meteorological Organization, the International Telecommunications Union, the World Health Organization, and the International Maritime Organization. It also works closely with several non-governmental organizations: the International Air Transport Association, the Airports Council International, the International Federation of Air Line Pilots' Associations, and the International Council of Aircraft Owners and Pilots Association.[37]

The International Committee of the Red Cross (ICRC) and the Hague Conference on Private International Law are yet another form of public and private cooperation.[38] These two organizations facilitate the development of and compliance by states with specific bodies of law. In the case of the ICRC, this is humanitarian law and the laws of war. The Hague Conference works in three general areas: international protection of child, family and property relations; international legal cooperation and litigation; and international commercial and financial regulation.[39]

The latest entrants on the international and global regulatory scene are from the private sector. Examples of self-regulatory schemes are the World Diamond Council's warranty system for conflict diamonds created in 2004; the Sustainable Forestry Initiative started by the forest industry in 1994 to protect forests; and the Responsible Care initiative developed by the chemical industry following the release of poisonous gas from a Union Carbide plant manufacturing pesticides that killed nearly 4,000 people in Bhopal, India in 1984. The Sullivan Principles, initially directed in 1977 at promoting racial equality in South Africa, were expanded by corporations to apply globally in 1999; the Rugmark labeling project warranting against the use of child labor in the manufacture of rugs started in 1994; and in 1997, Amnesty International created Human Rights Guidelines for companies.

Trade associations have also moved into this regulatory area through labeling schemes to assure buyers that products are not made using child labor (Rugmark and athletic wear labeling); that farmers and producers receive a fair price (food and other Fairtrade products including cosmetics and clothing); that resources are protected and renewable (Forest Stewardship Council labeling); and that their origins are known (International Federation of Organic Agriculture Movements). Most of these labeling programs date from the 1990s, with the earliest one developed for organic food labeling in 1972. The private International Organization for Standardization has had widespread regulatory influence through its adoption of such important standards as the 14001 environmental management standard, the size of credit cards, and the distinctive ring tones that are used in automated telephone systems.[40]

The Concert system, the Hague system, and the functional international organizations represent the three streams of intergovernmental consultation and cooperation that provided the foundation for the development of the general multipurpose international organization with a permanent headquarters, secretariat, and regularly scheduled meetings. The UN and its predecessor, the League of Nations, are the principal examples of this kind of institution. The UN embodies all three streams of development, with a Security Council of important powers dedicated to issues of peace and security, a General Assembly that meets regularly and is universal in its membership, and a system of specialized agencies, many of which originated in the need to address the specific regulatory issues brought about by twentieth-century technology and higher levels of cross-border economic activity. In the nearly one hundred years since the founding of the League of Nations, we now recognize that its direct heir, the UN, sits in the center of a network of organizations—public, private, and hybrid. The UN further serves as the model for international organizations, both regional and international, and provides specialized administrative services, like those dealing with employment disputes, to agencies within the UN family.[41] Like states, the international organization form has not stood still. It has adapted to create new capacities and has evolved from its classic form while retaining many of its original forms and functions. As the work of international organizations identifies new issues and generates the need for new mandates, these issues have led to the creation of emanations—new organizations within existing ones. Most international organizations are no longer created by states. In fact, those that governments establish by treaty have been in the minority since some time before the First World War. Currently, most IGOs are created by other IGOs. The Food and Agriculture Organization, for example, spawned the European Commission on Agriculture as well as about 20 other agencies; the European Commission on Agriculture then created its own spin-off IGOs. In 1992, emanations comprised more than 70 percent of the IGO population; of these, almost 25 percent were third-, fourth-, or fifth-generation IGOs; that is, they were themselves created by emanations or even emanations of emanations. States become members of such organizations by passive assent simply by virtue of their membership in the parent organizations.[42] Creating new organizations within existing organizations in this way has effectively ended the state's monopoly on creating international organizations.

In operation, some group of member states will still need to support an emanation, since the additional funding required for the new organization will likely be through voluntary contributions. But small groups of states can and have pushed decisions with institution-wide effects including the creation of emanations. The consequence of moving the locus of decision-making away from states is to widen the accountability gap as citizens in member countries are unable to use elections as a means to challenge decisions made at the international level. On the other hand, an emanation may represent a portion of a country's domestic agenda, for example, in the area of environmental protection and the formation of an organization like the Global Environment Facility to provide assistance to improve environmental safeguards.[43] Either way, the accountability gap can be overcome if citizens broadly accept the decision-making authority of an international institution, as occurs in the EU, for example.[44]

Creating an organization through the regular voting procedures of existing international organizations is less costly and much easier to achieve than negotiating a treaty to create a new organization. First, since emanations emerge from decisions that IGOs take via their normal decision-making channels rather than through the classic procedures of international treaty making, the most powerful states wield less influence over the evolution of IGOs than they would were all

IGOs created by traditional means. Because their assent can be crucial to a treaty's creation, powerful states have greater influence in the treaty-making process than they do within international institutions, where they are subject to procedural rules that limit their influence. Second, although decisions made within IGOs involve governmental representatives, they also grant a voice to international administrative staff and non-governmental organizations, thus giving new and different actors a role. Through a web of emanations a country can represent its interests broadly and become eligible for an array of institutional resources, but individually it has little control over the package of subsidiary agencies to which it belongs and what those agencies do. The United States, for example, argued against the creation of the UN Industrial Development Organization (UNIDO). When that organization was launched anyway, the United States had to decide how best to manage it. Secretariats and representative staffs, often those of the most powerful states, now create new IGOs; home governments then decide whether to refuse membership.[45]

Although states continue to be the principal law-making authorities because of their long-established role, they are increasingly working through frameworks created by international institutions. This has in turn created international political space for participation by a range of non-state actors. The established role of settings like the UN General Assembly means that debates that are sustained in such organs may themselves ultimately become a part of the law-making process.[46] When issues require world-wide attention, a convenient starting place to raise them is in a body like the General Assembly, UN specialized agencies, or UN-sponsored conferences. As Jonathan Charney concluded, "[t]he augmented role of multilateral forums in devising, launching, refining and promoting general international law has provided the international community with a more formal lawmaking process that is used often."[47] This law-making process is used not only by states, but also by private entities, individuals, non-governmental organizations, and other international organizations.

By creating and working with international organizations, states in the twentieth century increased their capacity to deal with new cross-border issues. They did so in part by using the institutional and procedural frameworks of international organizations to raise issues of concern with an international organization's membership that often represented either a majority of states or key states on an issue. So while the state increased its governing capacity by working with international organizations, it also increased the number of actors that could initiate action and set the international agenda, thereby decreasing its relative influence on international relations. Change did not take place only in one direction, but had a recursive effect that generated new demands, issues, and challenges to tax enhanced state capacity. The development of international human rights as a matter of international concern provides an example of how creating awareness in an issue area has led to additional responsibilities and obligations on the part of states.

The development of international human rights as a matter of international concern

Although selected individuals—monarchs, diplomats, religious personnel—have had privileges and special status in international law throughout history, these privileges were granted by states to other states or recognized sovereign entities like the Roman Catholic Church and not to the individuals themselves. Individuals benefited from such status, but that status was derived from state interest and ability to serve as a guarantor to ensure that the rights were respected. This changed fundamentally in the course of the twentieth century as individuals gained rights in their own name. States, international organizations, and non-governmental organizations contributed to the development of the present system in which states have incorporated international human rights in their constitutions. However, human rights have not left the system that created them untouched. By changing the monopoly of states in the granting of rights and privileges, human rights have developed new responsibilities and capacities in global governance.

From idea to norm to institution to practice, international human rights have moved steadily to become one of the foundations of today's global order. Although traceable directly to the post-Second World War order, we can see glimmers of these ideas as the world struggled to create a new order after the First World War. In January 1918, President Woodrow Wilson had set out American war aims. Point V of his Fourteen Points Speech introduced the idea that in colonial territories the "interests of the populations concerned must have equal weight with the equitable claims of the government." The efforts of the League of Nations, the predecessor organization to today's UN, to implement these ideas from 1919 to 1945, provided an important bridge from a world of generally unfettered state actors to one in which states were obligated to respect the rights of people, particularly their own citizens and those entrusted to their care.

The concept of responsibility to the people governed by a state started with the League's practice of mandates whereby the mandatory power was expected to govern its mandate "to ensure the humane transition of non-western peoples from tradition to the 'strenuous conditions of the modern world'."[48] The system applied only to specific territories, but created an important mechanism of reporting and oversight in the treatment of designated populations. The mandate system was instituted to deal with the colonies and dependencies of the defeated powers of the First World War—Austria-Hungary, Germany, and the Ottoman Empire. That there would be external oversight by the league was a dramatic departure from historic practice where a victor state took the territories of the vanquished and ruled those territories and the people in them as the victor saw fit, with little if any reference to any other standards or entities. The post-First World War system assigned temporary authority over a territory to one of the victor powers, but under the supervision of an international organization—the League of Nations. The mandate agreements made clear "(1) that the mandated territories are not under the sovereignty of the mandatories, and (2) that the inhabitants of these territories are not nationals of the mandatories."[49] The mandatory power was obligated to produce annual reports to be reviewed by the League's Permanent Mandates Committee with an eye to the development of the people under its *temporary* care.

This followed the general League practice of fact-finding, introduced as a required step in cases of disputes both between members and between members and non-member states, as provided in Articles 15 and 17 of the League Covenant. Although these investigations were not effective in averting war, they did introduce the special role of investigation and fact-finding by international organizations. This has proven to be a particularly important tool in enforcing human rights obligations both at the international and regional levels. Individuals living in the mandated territories were permitted to submit written petitions directly to the League's Permanent Mandates Committee and to provide information on their condition. In allowing this, the mandate system created "an international administration that helped transform a principle into a program."[50] Rajagopal acknowledges the significance of this innovation in governance as follows: " ... the techniques that the P[ermanent] M[andates] C[ommission] developed for dealing with the petitions essentially remain unchanged in the institutional practices of subsequent international petition processes, from the UN human rights procedures to the ... World Bank Complaints Panel."[51]

The new outlook with regard to the rights of individuals, however, met its limits in the mixed application of the concept of "self-determination" that was a centerpiece of Wilson's post-First World War world. The 1919 Paris Peace Conference sent the clear message that individuals would be granted rights as long as these were consistent with state interests. To ensure compliance, the Allied Powers agreed to guarantee the rights through League bodies. The mandate system was part of this compromise. With these caveats, specific rights were recognized and granted, like language rights and the right to attend school in one's own language in parts of the former Austro-Hungarian Empire. Other claims, however, including the return to China of German-controlled interests in China, were not granted.[52] The granting of those German rights to Japan on the basis of a secret treaty touched off a firestorm of national resentment and anger in China that ultimately brought the Chinese Communist Party into power 30 years later.[53]

The successor states formed after the break-up of the multi-ethnic Austro-Hungarian Empire were obligated by the victorious Allied Powers to protect minorities who were on these territories as the result of the redrawing of the borders in the region. Ten of the peace treaties emerging from the 1919 Paris Peace Conference contained minorities provisions. These were the Allies' treaties with Poland, Czechoslovakia, the Kingdom of the Serbs, Croats, and Slovenes, Romania, Greece, Armenia, Austria, Bulgaria, Hungary, and Turkey. An example of such a provision is Article 12 of the Polish treaty:

> Poland agrees that the stipulations in the foregoing articles, so far as they affect persons belonging to racial, religious or linguistic minorities, constitute obligations of international concern and shall be placed under the guarantee of the League of Nations. They shall not be modified without the assent of the Council of the League of Nations. The United States, the British Empire, France, Italy and Japan hereby agree not to withhold their assent from any modification in these articles which is in due form assented to by a majority of the Council of the League.
>
> Poland agrees that any member of the Council of the League of Nations, shall have the right to bring to the attention of the Council any infraction, or danger of infraction, of any of these obligations, and that the Council may thereupon take such action and give such direction as it may deem proper and effective in the circumstances.[54]

The League served as guarantor of these rights and set up a committee mechanism to review petitions from minorities claiming violations of their rights. It is worth noting that the major powers of the time were explicitly obligated to support the actions of the League Council in this treaty provision. This can be seen as a precursor to the majority decision-making requirement of the UN Security Council, where nine of 15 votes have to be affirmative, with no negative votes from the Security Council's five permanent members as provided by UN Charter Article 27.

As with the mandates, the League's contribution came in the process it developed to deal with issues arising from these minorities' provisions. Instead of a commission made up of state representatives, as was the case with the Permanent Mandates Commission, minorities' issues were the responsibility of the Minorities Section of the League Secretariat—a permanent body of international civil servants who were not to receive instructions from governments, but were to work on behalf of the League. The concept of a permanent, professional, and independent staff is enshrined in Article 100 of the UN Charter, but this development in the League was a novelty when the organization was established and was the brainchild of the first Secretary-General of the League of Nations, Sir Eric Drummond.

The minority treaties provided for a petition mechanism and League member states constituted a Minorities Committee to receive and to review these petitions. Petitions were for information and were not authorizations for action either by the League or its member states.[55] Nevertheless, providing that individuals within these territories could address a body outside of the governing authority was an important innovation.

On receiving the petitions, the Minorities Committee performed two functions. The first was to determine whether a petition contained information that would require Council attention. The second was to confirm the information contained. The purpose of these tasks was to provide "the Council a safer basis of action than they already have in the form of the petition and the comments of the government concerned."[56] These responsibilities evolved through League Council authorization.[57]

Unlike the UN Charter that devoted five articles to the Secretariat, Article 6 of the League of Nations Covenant only provided for a Secretary-General "and such secretaries and staff as may be required." The Secretary-General was to appoint the staff "with the approval of the Council." With little guidance, Drummond set out to create a secretariat modeled on the British permanent civil service of professional and independent staff. This, too, is a lasting legacy of the League of Nations. Two important features that Drummond initiated remain part of the international scene. First, UN Charter Article 100 provides explicitly for an independent secretariat as follows:

1   In the performance of their duties the Secretary-General and the staff shall not seek or receive instructions from any government or

from any other authority external to the Organization. They shall refrain from any action which might reflect on their position as international officials responsible only to the Organization.

2 Each member of the UN undertakes to respect the exclusively international character of the responsibilities of the Secretary-General and the staff and not to seek to influence them in the discharge of their responsibilities.

Second, the UN Secretary-General is given a special role by UN Charter Article 99: "The Secretary-General may bring to the attention of the Security Council any matter which in his opinion may threaten the maintenance of international peace and security."[58]

While Drummond was allowed to address the Council and the Assembly, the Covenant did not give the League's Secretary-General the right to initiate discussion of an issue. In contrast, the UN Secretary-General acting under Article 99 of the Charter can appeal directly to the Security Council to act on a matter that might threaten peace and security even if no state raises it. This right was first used by UN Secretary-General Dag Hammarskjold in 1960, with regard to the crisis in the Congo created by the departure of the Belgian colonial government. The right was last used by UN Secretary-General Kurt Waldheim in 1979 on the eve of the Iraqi invasion of Iran. Article 99 empowered the UN Secretary-General to exercise a prerogative that was otherwise reserved for states only—to call to the attention of the UN Security Council threats to international peace and security.

Legal questions arising out of minority claims were referred by the League Council to the Permanent Court of International Justice (PCIJ). The PCIJ produced a well-recognized jurisprudence that included *Advisory Opinions on Minority Schools in Albania*;[59] on *Questions Relating to Settlers of German Origin in Poland*;[60] and on the *Consistency of Certain Danzig Legislative Decrees with the Constitution of the Free City*.[61] These cases established the practice of oversight by an international organization of the treaty obligations of states. They further developed the advisory jurisdiction of international judicial institutions.

The aftermath of the First World War thus saw states accept concepts of responsibility to specified populations entrusted to their care by the Allied Powers that won the war. The Powers delegated oversight of these obligations to the newly established League of Nations that was to act not only in their name, but also in that of all the League's member states. It may be worth noting that the phrase "international concern" in the Minorities Treaties indicated a responsibility not just to the victor powers, but to the international community generally. International concern has also become a phrase much associated with the UN when it tries to spur action on the part of UN member states. The basis for this concept of responsibility was provided by treaties—a classic form of state-to-state transactions. But the use of a permanent international organization to provide the procedural infrastructure for the supervision of these obligations was something novel. It is one of the important legacies of the League of Nations that we have seen replicated and expanded upon in the UN.

The violence and brutality of the Second World War and the clear international leadership role of the United States after that war prompted further re-examination of the relationship of governments to those placed under their care—this time, not just specially designated populations, but all people. On 6 January 1941, US President Franklin D. Roosevelt described four freedoms on which the postwar world would be based:

- Freedom of speech and expression;
- Freedom of every person to worship God in his own way;
- Freedom from want; and
- Freedom from fear.[62]

Guaranteeing these aspirations became even more urgent when Nazi atrocities against the Jews came to light in the last months of the Second World War. Including these freedoms in the UN Charter was the achievement of a small group of non-governmental representatives from the United States.[63]

Knowing the opposition to joining the League of Nations that Woodrow Wilson had encountered in the United States, Roosevelt and the post-Second World War planners decided to engage the American public early. Representatives of private non-governmental associations were therefore included as consultants to the US delegations working on finalizing plans for the UN. Those represented included the National Association of Manufacturers, the Chamber of Commerce, the American Federation of Labor (AFL), the Congress of Industrial Organizations (CIO), the American Farm Bureau Federation, the Federal Council of Churches, the American Jewish Committee, and the American Association of the UN—the precursor to the present-day UN Association (UNA).[64] Joseph Proskauer and Jacob Blaustein of the American Jewish Committee, James Shotwell of the Commission to Study the Organization of Peace,[65] and Clark Eichelberger of the American Association for the UN, led efforts to include an international bill of rights in the UN Charter. Chile, Cuba, and Panama joined this effort, but were strongly opposed by the United Kingdom and the Soviet Union. Nevertheless, such language was included, and a foundation laid for the subsequent development of human rights within the UN system. William Korey wrote:

> So it happened that the single most important treaty of the twentieth century, the United Nations Charter, which led to the creation of mankind's most elaborate international institution ever, was obliged to incorporate not a passing and extremely limited note about human rights but rather seven major references to human rights, several of enormous consequences.[66]

These included language in the UN Charter's preamble, and Charter Articles 1, 13, 55, 56, 62, and 68. UN Charter Article 55 states:

> With a view to the creation of conditions of stability and well-being which are necessary for peaceful and friendly relations among nations based on respect for the principle of equal rights and self-determination of peoples, the United Nations shall promote:
>
> (a) higher standards of living, full employment, and conditions of economic and social progress and development;
> (b) solutions of international economic, social, health, and related problems; and international cultural and educational cooperation; and
> (c) universal respect for, and observance of, human rights and fundamental freedoms for all without distinction as to race, sex, language, or religion.

However, efforts to include a bill of individual rights in the Charter failed. Proponents of this did not give up, and they found a powerful and effective advocate for their cause in Eleanor Roosevelt, whose work brought about the adoption of a Universal Declaration of Human Rights in 1948.

UN Charter Article 56 obligated state members of the UN "to take joint and separate action in co-operation with the Organization for the achievement of the purposes set forth in Article 55," quoted above. UN specialized agencies were further directed to develop and work towards the purposes of Article 55. UN Charter Article 2(7), on the other hand, assured member states of non-interference in their domestic affairs. Nevertheless, Thomas Buergenthal saw the UN Charter as an important step in the development of human rights law, as "states were deemed to have assumed *some* international obligations relating to human rights."[67] He further noted that Article 56 of the UN Charter provided the UN "with the requisite legal authority to embark on what became a massive lawmaking effort to define and codify these rights."[68]

With the addition of more and more newly independent states to UN membership in the 1960s—37 new states joined between 1960 and 1970 alone, these former colonies exerted pressure on the UN to act in cases of mass violations of human rights, such as the practice of apartheid in South Africa. On the basis that states practicing apartheid were not "promoting human rights," as required by Article 55, the UN Economic and Social Council (ECOSOC) passed resolutions calling for an end to the practice by the Republic of South Africa and by Southern Rhodesia. The focus on apartheid grew to include other gross violations of human rights, whether they dealt with apartheid or not, as matters addressed by the UN Economic and Social Council and its Sub-Commission on Prevention of Discrimination and the Protection of Minorities.[69] These are now recognized as "Charter-based mechanisms for dealing with large-scale human rights violations" and include special rapporteurs and other missions, as well as the Office of the High Commissioner for Human Rights.[70]

The Universal Declaration of Human Rights adopted in 1948 served as the cornerstone of international human rights law later set out in such treaties as the International Covenant on Civil and Political Rights (ICCPR) and the International Covenant on Economic and Social Rights adopted by the UN General Assembly in 1966, the Convention Against Torture (1984), the Convention on the Prohibition and Prevention of Genocide (1948), the Convention to Eliminate All Forms of Racial Discrimination (1966), the Convention to Eliminate All Forms of Discrimination Against Women (1979), and the Convention on the Rights of the Child (1989). Following the model of the Minorities Treaties of the League period, each of these treaties established "a treaty body"—a committee of independent experts to monitor and to provide international oversight of state compliance with their obligations. Over time, the interpretive work done by these bodies through comments and reports has taken on a normative character. Noteworthy in this regard because of its broad scope is the practice of General Comments on thematic issues that has grown out of the Human Rights Committee's review of International Convention on Civil and Political Rights reports submitted by countries.[71] As Buergenthal observed: "While one can debate the question of the nature of this law and whether or not it is law at all, the fact remains that the normative findings of the treaty bodies have legal significance, as evidenced by references to them in international and domestic judicial decisions."[72] But notable in the original UN Charter structure was the clear separation between the organs charged with security (the UN Security Council) and those charged with the stability and well-being of individuals (the Economic and Social Council, the Trusteeship Council, and the specialized agencies). Under the provisions of UN Charter Article 10, the General Assembly "may discuss any questions or any matters within the scope of the present Charter ...," except for issues dealt with by the Security Council. The General Assembly was to refrain from acting on matters before the Security Council unless the Security Council requested General Assembly action, or if the procedures of the Uniting for Peace Resolution were activated once the Security Council became deadlocked because of the threat of a veto by one of its Permanent Members.[73] So, although the importance of the well-being of individuals was recognized in the UN structure, human welfare was still regarded as an issue separate from—and subordinate to—issues of state security.

This changed as Holocaust survivors and human rights advocates like Rafael Lemkin worked to complete the Convention on the Prevention and Prohibition of Genocide in 1948. This was followed by the International Covenant on Civil and Political Rights in 1966. For the United States, interest in human rights beyond the rhetorical was initially focused on the Soviet Union and its satellites. The 1974 Jackson-Vanik Amendment, for example, restricted trade with the Soviet Union and other controlled economies by prohibiting most-favored nation trading status if countries denied emigration by persecuted populations like Jews, religious minorities, and political dissidents. Through the 1970s, the United States began to incorporate human rights into its foreign policy as countries in Latin America moved from military dictatorships to new forms of civilian government, and through the Helsinki Process begun in 1975 that would help end the Soviet empire.

The immediate aftermath of the Cold War, however, provided a reminder that the mere existence of law was not good enough if states were unwilling to hold other states to those obligations. The will to do so was tested in the 1990s as the international system faced episode after episode of governments brutalizing their own people. Cambodia, Rwanda, and then the break-up of Yugoslavia brought things to a head as the international community sat on the sidelines, seemingly unable to respond in any way. As the International Commission on Intervention and State Sovereignty (ICISS) put it in 2001: "For some, the international community is not intervening enough; for others it is intervening much too often. For some, the only real issue is in ensuring that coercive interventions are effective; for others, questions about legality, process and the possible misuse of precedent loom much larger."[74]

Intervention has generated an impassioned debate, with the discussion focusing on the distinction between legitimacy and legality. The question was whether legitimacy alone could overcome the strictures of existing law where it seemed inadequate to respond to new situations. Although the need for an exception may be thought compelling, as in the cases of mass brutality against one's own population, there has been an understandable reluctance in the scholarly and policy communities to accept any intervention on a self-judging basis. The fear, of course, is that powerful states would use any pretext to pursue their own interests in the name of some community interest. The flip side of this issue is where there are international calls to action, for example, in response to the killings in Rwanda in 1994, but a failure by states to act on the basis of such calls. Another example is the extended period of time (two years) it took for the UN Security Council to refer the situation in Darfur to the International Criminal Court for investigation. These are examples of where changes in international attitudes and values may have occurred, but where the mechanisms of the international system—including the right to intervene, are not yet fully developed to realize those values.[75]

In the decades since the end of the Cold War, the world of states has struggled to react when governments turn against their own people. As the world has faced these crises, it has taken steps to move beyond rhetorical expressions of outrage to recognition that gross violations of human rights are threats to international peace and security. Yet, it continues to struggle with ways to undertake collective action. In this context, the international community encompasses the world of states, public and private institutions (international organizations, foundations, civil society organizations), and individual experts focused on security. In the words of the ICISS:

> For some, the new interventions herald a new world in which human rights trumps state sovereignty; for others, it ushers in a world in which big powers ride roughshod over the smaller ones, manipulating the rhetoric of humanitarianism and human rights. The controversy has laid bare basic divisions within the international community. In the interest of all those victims who suffer and die when leadership and institutions fail, it is crucial that these divisions be resolved.[76]

Responding to a plea by the UN Secretary-General to "put people at the center of everything we do," the Japanese government initiated the Commission on Human Security. Led by the former UN High Commissioner for Refugees, Sadako Ogata, and Nobel Laureate Amartya Sen, the Commission's report in 2003 described this changed environment:

> The international community urgently needs a paradigm of security. Why? Because the security debate has changed dramatically since the inception of state security advocated in the 17th century. According to that traditional idea, the state would monopolize the right and means to protect its citizens. State power and state security would be established and expanded to sustain order and peace. But in the 21st century, both the challenges to security and its protectors have become more complex. The state remains the fundamental purveyor of security. Yet it often fails to fulfill its security obligations—and at times has become a source of threat to its own people. That is why attention must now shift from the security of the state to the security of the people—to human security ...[77]

In an attempt to refashion the debate, the Canadian-sponsored ICISS developed the concept of the *responsibility to protect*—the idea that sovereignty carries with it the responsibility to protect a state's population. When there is a failure to do so or, even worse, when a state is the perpetrator of violence against its own people, the international community must act. This responsibility includes those occasions when the UN Security Council becomes deadlocked by virtue of the veto of one of the Council's permanent members (see UN Charter Article 27 for voting procedures). The ICISS urged use of the Uniting for Peace Resolution and regional organizations to provide a mandate in that case and admonished the Security Council that "states may not rule out actions to meet the urgency and gravity of the situation" and that the credibility of the Security Council would suffer if it failed to respond.[78] The ICISS and its report also noted the importance of preventing mass violence. But the key shift was that the ICISS acknowledged that the well-being of a brutalized population *may* require overcoming the structural legal barriers in the present international security system in order to take action. The Commission's report is careful to urge that these actions be rare and taken on the basis of *some* international mandate—even if on a regional rather than a universal basis.

In December 2004, the United Nations released the report of its High-Level Panel on Threats, Challenges and Change, *A More Secure*

World: Our Shared Responsibility.[79] This was done at the request of the UN Secretary-General after the bitter divisions created prior to the US invasion of Iraq in 2003. The report recommended that the UN security system address security in a comprehensive way and not focus only on the use of military force. The report noted conditions including poverty and disease that breed unrest and lead to conflict and urged a comprehensive strategy to tackle conflict at its source.[80] This focus on the human condition as a key to state security is the latest development that increasingly places the well-being and interests of individuals at the center of contemporary international relations and international law.

Although international institutions have outgrown their initial role as acting only at the specific direction of states, the ability of international institutions to gather resources and to mobilize collective responses remains tenuous. In areas like public health and the alerts declared in cases of serious health threats like possible flu pandemics, we see that collective responses can be effective, but still very much rely on national and local authorities to carry out. What we see now is a partnership whereby an alarm may be sounded or an issue for general attention may be raised in an international institution. The institution then remains in action as a coordinating mechanism for national or local action. We therefore see the need for strengthened international capacities to spot issues and to coordinate responses at the same time that we see the need for strong national and local capacities to carry out needed action. If local capacities are not available, the international, including the capacities of states external to the region, may have to fill in until they are developed.[81] With the expected continued increase in global interactions and connections, this reality puts a premium on the capacities of states to take needed actions within their jurisdictions and to provide the resources to respond to international calls to action and international concerns.

Summing up

As we focus on the inadequacies or challenges of the existing units and structures of governance, it is easy to forget that the present globalized governing environment is the product of actions taken by these units and structures. The two principal units and structures are the state and, a product of their creation, the international organization. History tells us that the eventual dominance of the state form of governance was the result of a competitive exercise. The state triumphed because it best served the organizing needs of the time—it provided the financial and political resources to field the armies needed to protect and to advance a state's interests. Once established, states and their leaders undertook steps to mutually empower other entities that most closely resembled them, thereby squeezing out alternative units of governance over time. A similar form of mutual empowerment took place in the 1960s with the increasing intensity of calls for an end to colonies that came from the concerted efforts of newly independent states. These states worked assiduously through the UN General Assembly to maintain focus on the issue, to pressure states into acting, and ultimately to vilify and to shun states that failed to conform. The dramatic end to this chapter of world history may have been the actions taken by the UN in South Africa to advance both the causes of human rights and decolonization that ultimately ended South African control over South West Africa (originally a League mandate), and led to the independence of Namibia in 1988, the ending of apartheid in South Africa, and the election of Nelson Mandela as President of South Africa in 1994.

That a forum like the UN was available to new states to set and to pursue this agenda of decolonization shows how the existence of a structure facilitated the promotion of a new agenda. The novelty and irony here is that those successfully using the structure—in this case an international organization—were not the creators of the organization, but new states using the organization against the interests of some of its creators. IOs were initially established to help states meet their objectives, but we have seen that IOs develop independent capacities of their own—including secretariats. This has led to new organizations, emanations, and processes to address further needs and objectives. Each such step potentially introduces a new dynamic or actor to the international system that can create new capacity, but may also add to the complexity of international relations.

The creation of the mandates system under the League of Nations and the development of human rights as a normative and political reality demonstrate the iterative steps taken by states and international organizations to build an international community, to establish an area of international concern, and to create an international responsibility. Although these terms originally may be rhetorical devices, their exploration, including investigation of how specific needs might be met within existing frameworks, helps to create new pathways and identify new capacities and responsibilities. The human rights story shows how quickly a new agenda can be developed and put into operation if appropriate connections between international frameworks and domestic politics are made. The incorporation of international human rights in provisions of national constitutions, for example, has facilitated the entry of post-authoritarian transition governments into the ranks of respectable states, thereby enabling them to function effectively as international actors. Present efforts to operationalize a *responsibility to protect* show how states, public international organizations, and private entities have tried to raise international concern and to work within existing international frameworks like the UN system to meet new needs. Once adopted, such new concepts and practices become part of a specific area of law and international relations. Their acceptance, however, also affirms the utility of the modes or pathways used to achieve this recognition. Working in the UN General Assembly to advance an agenda, for example, would be one such pathway. In the case of the *responsibility to protect*, these modes include association with the UN Secretary-General, public input individually or through non-governmental organizations, and engagement with experts and those affected by the concept through town meetings, and adoption and codification by UN organs and states themselves. Each such initiative and accretion there-fore adds to the content of international law and politics. Perhaps as importantly, each such effort adds to the overall governing capacity of the international system by highlighting accepted and useful pathways for pursuing such initiatives and putting them into operation.

3 The expanded international political and juridical arenas

- Expanding the international political arena
- The expanded international juridical space
- The consequences of these expanded arenas
- Summing up

Flashed across the front pages of newspapers and magazines across the world, the picture of a man dressed in a white shirt and black trousers facing down a column of tanks on one of Beijing's main avenues during the Chinese government's crackdown of the pro-democracy movement in June 1989 is one of the iconic images of that dramatic period. The photo has greater significance as a manifestation of the convergence of several worldwide "patterns of conduct" that emerged from the twentieth century with important implications for the international system of the twenty-first century.[1]

One such pattern is the growing prominence of individuals and private entities like corporations as actors and subjects at the international level. Human rights and transnational economic activity were the bases for this development. In the economic realm, Ronald Brand noted that:

> The twentieth century has seen new recognition of the direct application of international law to relationships between individuals and states. The law of economic relations is one area in which international law (traditionally considered only applicable between and among "sovereign" states) has grown to encompass rules that provide rights for individuals in their relationships with states.[2]

The second important development that had its origins in human rights, arms control, and environmental protection was the acceptance by states of outside inspections to monitor and verify whether a state was complying with its international obligations. In the mid-1990s, Louis Henkin observed:

> State autonomy remains a powerful value, but the distinction between state and human values continues to converge. The right of a state "to be let alone" subsumes the rights of its inhabitants to be let alone, to maintain their traditions and culture, as well as their ways of life.[3]

The result is that in contemporary international relations, individuals have gained access to a political and legal arena long occupied by states alone. We know that states voluntarily undertook obligations that contributed to this transformation. It is useful to identify the conditions that created a fertile environment for this development as a step towards looking into the future of global governance. These initially included the desire to avoid recurrence of the genocide of the Holocaust. Later, both the wave of decolonization in the 1960s and the promotion of individual liberty—the Helsinki movement—in the 1970s and 1980s to counter Cold War totalitarianism required states to examine and to redefine their relationships with the people they governed. As a result of these developments, the international political and juridical arenas have expanded and now provide more opportunity for non-state actors to play roles in governance that were once reserved almost exclusively to states and state-created institutions.

This chapter will examine these developments first in the political realm and then in the juridical arena. It will conclude with a discussion of the implications for global governance of these new expanded arenas.

Expanding the international political arena

If we take international obligations as a benchmark for expanding interests in the business of the international system, then treaties would be a place to begin. Remarkably, only 10 percent of all 6,000 multilateral treaties are characterized as addressing matters of human welfare, but these few treaties have had a profound influence in the 60 or so years of their existence.[4] The International Covenant on Civil and Political Rights, the European Convention on Human Rights, and the Convention against Torture and Other Cruel, Inhuman or Degrading Treatment or Punishment are all widely accepted conventions that obligate state parties to some form of reporting and outside review of their treatment of individuals under their jurisdiction.[5] These treaties have been influential, not only through their specific provisions, but also through the structural and political changes they fostered in specific countries and in the international system more generally.[6] Thomas Buergenthal notes that:

> The proliferation of human rights treaties and the emergence of international and regional human rights tribunals with jurisdiction to interpret and apply these treaties have prompted an increasing number of states to accord human rights treaties a special status in their national constitutions. That status facilitates the domestic implementation of the decisions of those tribunals. It also contributes to a legal and political climate in the countries concerned that enables their judiciaries and legislatures to take international and regional human rights obligations into account without having to face some of the constitutional obstacles that have traditionally impeded effective domestic compliance with international judicial and quasi-judicial decisions.[7]

The expansion and maintenance of international trade first brought individual, national, and international interests together in a systematic way. After the mercantilist aspirations of the great European state trading companies like the Dutch and British East India Companies in the seventeenth and eighteenth centuries gave way to free enterprise in the nineteenth century, states began to promote the interests of their private entrepreneurs in international competition. The collapse of global trade in the 1930s as a result of high national tariff barriers and ruinous exchange rates caused planners during the Second World War to focus on creating the institutions and conditions that would provide for a stable postwar monetary and trading environment.

In July 1944, 44 countries met in Bretton Woods, New Hampshire, to finalize agreements for the establishment of several post-Second World War international financial institutions. These institutions were created to stabilize an international economic and trading system that had been traumatized by the Great Depression and the Second World War. The International Monetary Fund (IMF) was set up to address the problem of unregulated exchange rates. The IMF was charged with monitoring exchange rates and establishing reserves to lend to countries whose currency had lost value due to trade deficits or other damaging economic conditions.[8] The International Bank for Reconstruction and Development was created to help Europe recover from the Second World War. It is now one of five institutions that belong to the World Bank Group and focuses on loans to "middle-income and creditworthy poorer countries to promote sustainable, equitable and job-creating growth, reduce poverty and address issues of regional and global importance."[9] An International Trade Organization was also planned, but failed to secure the needed agreement to get underway and was replaced by the General Agreement on Tariffs and Trade that developed into the World Trade Organization in 1995.[10]

These institutions bore the hallmark of the United States, which was determined to transfer its Depression-era domestic institution-building experience to the international scene. This meant a heavy reliance on regulatory institutions and a "liberal conception of the rule of law" that saw "citizens rather than states as subjects" and "the imposition of affirmative rather than negative duties."[11] To achieve the objectives of free trade, financial stability, and economic development ultimately led to the present practice, whereby private actors can assert their legal rights directly at the international level without a state pursuing a claim on their behalf. Investment flows and trade would be impeded without such access to dispute settlement. By creating mechanisms for direct access to dispute settlement, such as the International Centre for the Settlement of Investment Disputes (ICSID) in 1966, states assured investors that they could seek effective redress if investments were lost.[12] As of 2010, the ICSID had facilitated the settlement of 194 investment disputes stemming from bilateral investment treaties. As Brand describes the role of the private merchant in international law:

> The twentieth century witnessed the return of the merchant to a significant role in determining the rules applicable to commercial conduct. National codes have been accompanied by rules established directly by merchant groups, and ultimately by the movement to treaties through which the rules once again become truly international in nature and context. In the process, "international law" rules are developed specifically for the purpose of measuring the conduct of private parties. ... Thus, private parties participate in the creation and become the subjects of international legal rules.[13]

A series of changes in world financial practices further facilitated the increase of foreign direct investment. This included the lifting of restrictions throughout the European Union that had previously made the movement of funds across borders in Europe extremely difficult. The end in the early 1970s of the system of fixed exchange rates, that was put into place after the Second World War, and the move towards floating exchange rates further opened the flood gates for investment flows. In 1960, foreign direct investment was valued at $60 billion; by 1980, it was over $500 billion.[14] Today, the United Nations Conference on Trade and Development's (UNCTAD) World Investment Report expects foreign direct investment to reach $1.2 trillion with growth towards $1.6 to $2 trillion in 2012.[15] The combination of removing structural barriers to the flow of investment funds together with the reassurance of access to dispute settlement for investors facilitated the growth in cross-border investments. From a governance standpoint, the ICSID dispute resolution system provided a structure for private actors to engage a state in the international realm as a near equal by allowing an individual to pursue a claim against a state through the ICSID. This has been a revolutionary contribution to contemporary governance, but is not yet general practice. For example, the World Trade Organization restricts use of its dispute settlement system to states only.

But where does this leave the state in today's international system? In his study of structural change, Hendrik Spruyt examined the "long historical process" that led to the system of sovereign states. His study concluded with some scenarios for contemporary change. One such scenario is described as self-help, where "there will be relatively little change in the nature of formal political institutions but considerable change in how social actors order international transactions among themselves."[16] As Spruyt reminds us, the important question when examining systems change is to understand the function and status of the system's units that create "patterns of conduct."

The development of international human rights created an international political environment characterized by a more participatory and populist approach to international affairs. This expanded international political space made possible not only passive protection, but also the active participation of private associations and individuals at the international level. Anne-Marie Slaughter and Walter Mattli provide an example of this development in the European Court of Justice:

Until 1963 the enforcement of the Rome treaty [the 1957 treaty that established the European Economic Community], like that of any other international treaty, depended entirely on action by the national legislatures of the member states of the community. By 1965, a citizen of a community country could ask a national court to invalidate any provision of domestic law found to conflict with certain directly applicable provisions of the treaty. By 1975, a citizen of an EC country could seek the invalidation of national law found to conflict with self-executing provisions of community secondary legislation, the "directives" to national governments passed by the EC Council of Ministers. And by 1990, community citizens could ask their national courts to interpret national legislation consistently with community legislation in the face of undue delay in passing directives on the part of national legislatures.[17]

After the Second World War, international institutions expanded the political space by serving as the vehicle for the appearance of more than 100 new states through decolonization, but they also were the medium for establishing the rights of private individuals and associations in international public discourse and increasingly in the law-making arena. United Nations (UN) Secretary-General Kofi Annan recognized this change in his reflection on the UN's role in the twenty-first century, *We the Peoples*, when he wrote that: "We must also adapt international institutions, through which states govern together, to the realities of the new era. We must form coalitions for change, often with partners well beyond the precincts of officialdom."[18] As M.J. Peterson had already concluded: "[T]he state does not monopolize the public sphere."[19]

Beyond access to the legal and political space, individuals have grouped to form social networks in the pursuit of specific objectives within that space. The anti-slavery, temperance, and women's rights movements are early examples of such networks. Apart from a specific substantive agenda, these networks also pressed for and achieved more participatory governance in both public and private organizations. This has led to an increasingly active role for individuals in shaping the future direction of governments, public policy, and private entities such as corporations. The effective harnessing of this force will be an important aspect of global governance.

As with the human rights story, the seeds of the current wave of social networks were sown in the nineteenth and early twentieth centuries. Margaret Keck and Kathryn Sikkink note as precursors to current advocacy networks, the Anglo-American anti-slavery movement between 1833 and 1865, the primarily Anglo-American suffrage movement to give women the right to vote—ending in the United States in 1920, the move to eradicate foot binding in China (1874–1911), and the effort to end female circumcision among the Kikuyu in Kenya in 1920–31.[20] The success of these movements depended on the ability of the movement to tap domestic political forces and create political alliances that produced the desired change. Lessons learned and experience gained by each movement strengthened and empowered the next. For example, the second-class status of women in the anti-slavery movement helped create the women's suffrage movement, which used organizing and messaging lessons learned from the anti-slavery movement. This learning process is more powerful today, when a movement's record can be traced, broadcast, and followed by anyone with access to the Internet.

The strength of social movements is that they may be highly organized, but do not require buildings and large secretariats that can become costly. As such, social movements are organized around some sense of shared identity or cause. The flexibility that comes from a lack of institutionalization, however, creates longer-term challenges for keeping a movement together. One of the characteristics of this fluid structure is that a movement can relate and connect to political and social forces beyond its own immediate location or area of interest. This can have either positive or negative consequences, depending on the situation. For example, local movements might be empowered by outside forces, thereby gaining legitimacy and credibility in an otherwise hostile environment. Or, a democracy movement might be regarded as subversive, as was the case in the totalitarian states of the Communist bloc during the Cold War and in Iran in 2009. The "outside" need not be at the international level, but can be at a federal or central government level. This, for example, was the case reported by Balakrishnan Rajagopal in his study of the Working Women's Forum in India that bypassed local opposition by gaining status with the Indian federal government.[21] In the United States, we can see the same phenomenon with regard to the civil rights movement and Prohibition to ban the sale and to restrict the use of alcohol. The "outside" can also be provided by private philanthropy. The Ford Foundation's support of the Mexican Academy of Human Rights, established in 1984, which helped it become a center for Mexican human rights activism, is an example here.[22]

Social movements can respond to opportunities provided by outside forces and thereby advance their cause. For example, a powerful alliance was struck between those foreign missionaries leading the campaign to end the mutilating practice of foot binding women in China and the Chinese working to modernize the country following the end of the imperial dynasty in 1911. This alliance won the cause local acceptance and became associated with forward-thinking and Chinese republican nationalistic aspirations.[23] Keck and Sikkink call this a "boomerang" effect, "which curves around local state indifference and repression to put foreign pressure on local policy elites."[24] Keck and Sikkink emphasize the importance of and need to engage with domestic politics and political structures in order to fully understand global politics today.[25] Beyond involving civil society in international activities, this has created a new form of global politics:

> ... liberalism, as currently formulated, lacks the tools to understand how individuals and groups, through their interactions,

might constitute new actors and transform understandings of interests and identities. We argue that individuals and groups may influence not only the preferences of their own states via representation, but also the preferences of individuals and groups elsewhere, and even of states elsewhere, through a combination of persuasion, socialization, and pressure ... Modern networks are not conveyor belts of liberal ideals but vehicles for communicative and political exchange, with the potential for *mutual transformation of participants*.[26]

There is now a two-way flow of pressures, with the international community setting up expectations for national and local standards of conduct, and the failure of the national or sub-national level to carry out its responsibilities generating pressure for further international action. As Rajagopal notes: "Social movements are often the chosen vehicles to register protest, but these can have enduring effects on the institutions they encounter."[27] Sidney Tarrow sees transnational activism as "the start of a new fusion of international and domestic politics" and a "scale shift" in terms of issue advocacy or advancement.[28]

There were 300 non-governmental organizations (NGOs) represented at the 1972 Stockholm Conference on the Environment, but 1,400 at the Rio de Janeiro Environmental Conference 20 years later. The NGO Greenpeace, for example, has repeatedly created conditions that provoke a response by international and national public authorities, notably when French intelligence services sank Greenpeace's vessel, *The Rainbow Warrior*, in 1985 as it was docked in the port of Auckland, New Zealand, on its way to disrupt French nuclear testing in the South Pacific.

The asymmetry does not always, however, favor the state. Indeed, the traditional power of a state in military forces and hardware may be a disadvantage in fighting non-traditional enemies who may not wear uniforms or otherwise look like traditional warriors. In fact, the more such fighters can blend into the general civilian population, the greater the disadvantage of the traditional military who may face criticism and even condemnation for killing civilians—even if some of those civilians may be harboring the combatants or are combatants. Since the wars to suppress independence movements in the 1950s and 1960s, the use of military power by states against civilians, even if they might be combatants, is also becoming harder and harder to justify.

Social movements have been important in reshaping major international institutions. Perhaps the most dramatic shifts can be seen in the work of the international financial institutions as they have adjusted to a more focused development agenda that takes into account the impacts of projects not only on people, but also on the environment. Rajagopal tells this story in *International Law from Below* with specific reference to the outcomes of the World Bank's Polonoroeste and Narmada projects in Brazil and India, respectively. In the case of the Polonoroeste road project, the Bank's record of failing to consider the effects of its projects on people led to the adoption of environmental review procedures for its projects. The Narmada dams project led to the creation of the Inspection Panel system in 1993 that remains in use today to assess individual complaints about the impact of World Bank-financed projects. The Inspection Panel practice has led to more open access by the public to World Bank documents and reports.[29]

Social movements and transnational networks have provided pathways for individual activism at a global level using several techniques, including information politics, symbolic politics, leverage politics, and accountability politics. Networks stress gathering and reporting reliable information, but also dramatize facts by using testimonies of specific individuals to evoke commitment and broader understanding. Activists use important symbolic events and conferences to publicize issues and build networks. In addition to trying to persuade through information and symbolic politics, networks also try to pressure targets to change policies by making an implied or explicit threat of sanctions or leverage if the gap between norms and practices remains too large.[30]

Social networks can also be extremely important in providing information or gauging local conditions in situations where outside forces could not possibly gain access. This is important in gathering information with regard to human rights practices or activities with environmental consequences.[31] The information provided is similar to that submitted to the League of Nations Mandates Commission by people in a mandated territory. (See discussion of the League Mandate system in Chapter 2.) Unless the monitor knows local conditions well, abuses and violations could be hidden from plain view.

Private efforts to advance a public policy agenda and new normative development such as the one that helped to bring an end to apartheid can also be seen in the shift within corporate practice from the traditional emphasis on the need to deliver the most robust profits to shareholders to attention to other interests, such as the welfare of the environment, employees, and local communities.[32] This change has been encouraged by the UN's Principles for Responsible Investment (PRI), finalized in 2006.[33] The six core Principles of Responsible Investment are:

Incorporate ESG (enlightened shareholder governance) issues into
investment analysis and decision-making;
Adopt an active ownership strategy and engage portfolio companies
around ESG issues;
Seek appropriate ESG disclosures from portfolio companies;
Promote acceptance and implementation of the PRI among service
providers and others within the investment industry;
Collaborate with other signatories to implement the PRI; and
Disclose to beneficiaries and the public how ESG issues are integrated
within investment practices, policies toward service providers, and
active ownership activities.[34]

The principles were developed through the joint effort of 20 institutional
investors working with government, inter-governmental organization,
and NGO representatives, academics, and civil society representatives
under the auspices of the United Nations Environmental Programme's
Finance Initiative and the UN Global Compact.[35] The PRI's objective
is to push awareness of social issues to the "financial intermediaries"
and portfolio companies that help to channel the investment funds of
individual investors.

What we see in these developments is that new actors can change the
governance environment and facilitate the entry of the private sector
and the individual into the public legal and political arena. Procedural
changes and adaptations to meet specific objectives have enduring effects
on the overall structure and function of governance.[36] With the passage
of time, the initial agents of change, that is, international organizations,
have themselves become the object of protest or complaint as they
become identified with the existing governing structure and particular
values. The World Bank and the International Monetary Fund have
been particular targets for NGO protests. A notice that appeared on
www.choike.org, "a portal dedicated to improving the visibility of the
work done by NGOs and social movements from the South," protested
the IMF/World Bank 2006 meeting in Singapore. In advance of the
meeting, a notice was posted on the choike.org site that "an international People's Forum vs. the IMF and the World Bank" would
be convening and inviting people from around the world to join the
protest.[37]

The movements behind these kinds of protests may not endure, but
the changes they help to initiate will. The World Bank has initiated
Inspection Panels to allow those affected by Bank projects to lodge
protests and concerns. Reflecting this development, John Rawls envisions
a more explicit role for civil society as part of the overall governing

environment: " ... it may turn out that there will be many different kinds of organizations subject to the judgment of the Law of Peoples and charged with regulating cooperation among them and meeting certain recognized duties."[38] Important developments in governance need not result in new institutions, but can take place through change in existing organizations. That change may be initiated either by forces within the existing governing structure or by forces external to it or both.

The practice of seconding staff from national to international institutions was thought to be a useful way to build support for the work of an international institution within national governments. Similarly, prominent NGO leaders like Bernard Kouchner can play important roles in policy development when they move from an NGO—as co-founder of Medecins Sans Frontières/Doctors Without Borders to government—Foreign Minister of France from 2007 to 2010. It would be useful to know how many NGO leaders move to/from government or positions of influence within the UN or other international organization networks. For example, a number of important human rights advocates have served either as Special Rapporteurs or Special Representatives of the UN Secretary-General in the human rights area. Notable examples are Juan Mendez, Theo van Boven, Manfred Nowak, Stephen Toope, Philip Alston, John Dugard, James Anaya, Nigel Rodley, and Radhika Coomaraswamy.[39]

In similar fashion, we see the influence of academics and public intellectuals in national and subsequently international policy formation. In the run-up to the adoption of UN Security Council Resolution 1973 (March 2011) to use all necessary measures to stop Muammar Qaddafi from killing civilians in rebel strongholds, it was reported that French intellectual Bernard-Henri Levy warned President Nicolas Sarkozy that "there will be a massacre in Benghazi, a blood bath, and the blood of the people of Benghazi will stain the flag of France."[40] Levy then arranged meetings between Sarkozy and rebel leaders that convinced the French president to press forward with the UN resolution and North Atlantic Treaty Organization (NATO) action. In the United States, it was reported that US Permanent Representative to the UN Susan Rice told National Security Council staff member Samantha Power: "I swore to myself that if I ever faced such a crisis again, I would come down on the side of dramatic action, going down in flames if that was required."[41] Rice was on the staff of the National Security Council in 1994 during the Rwandan genocide that failed to elicit any international response. Power, in charge of multilateral affairs and human rights at the National Security Council, is a former Harvard professor and 2003 Pulitzer Prize-winning author for her book, *A Problem from Hell: America and the Age of Genocide.* Today's international governing structure provides for dispute settlement. The emergence of arbitration as an established means of settling disputes is an example of practice creating a body of law by vesting individuals with certain judicial powers. This practice has over time facilitated and produced substantive changes in international law, specifically with respect to international commerce. As a result, arbitration institutions such as the International Chamber of Commerce in Paris, the London Court of International Arbitration, and the Stockholm Chamber of Commerce have risen to prominence. Although there no longer seems anything novel about a private party bringing action against a government in an international tribunal over investment disputes, Salacuse and Sullivan are correct to remind us that this is indeed a "revolutionary innovation" in international investment law.[42] There is, for example, no similar right in international trade law. Since 2000, there has been a proliferation of such arbitration cases and rulings resulting both from the increase in the use of bilateral investment treaties and the availability of dispute settlement mechanisms such as international commercial arbitration and ICSID. Treaties and mechanisms for dispute settlement are part of international law's operating system that has facilitated the flow of investment funds into developing countries.[43]

This institutionalization of arbitration proceedings has implications for the normative development of international investment and commercial law. The practices of these principal arbitration institutions influence the making of contracts, agreements, and treaties by signaling which provisions arbitrators have found consistent with existing international agreements and practice, thereby setting the parameters for the provisions of future agreements. As the London Court of International Arbitration notes,

> Ad hoc clauses are frequently either inadequate or overly complex. By incorporating institutional rules into their contract, the parties have the comfort of a comprehensive and proven set of terms and conditions upon which they can rely, regardless of the seat of the arbitration; minimizing the scope for uncertainty and the opportunity for delaying or wrecking the process.[44]

This might involve precluding certain provisions as well as suggesting to the parties that new elements will be received favorably by arbitration panels. The process involves an interactive cycle of contracts, awards and rulings, and new contracts, which is likely to accelerate in the future. The arbitration process is becoming fixed as part of the investment law landscape, "which in turn has increased the rate of publication of awards and accentuated public aspects of the arbitral process."[45] These, in turn, shape future contracts, arbitrations, and awards.

The expanded international juridical space

In Chapter 2, we saw the emergence of "emanations" within international organizations—structures and organizations created by existing organizations. We noted the idea of "mutual empowerment" whereby an important governance form seeks to crowd out competing forms by empowering those most like itself. The advent of emanations within international organizations is a form of self-generating mutual empowerment.[46] Another form of institutional expansion is in the development of regional organizations to complement the universal ones. A good example of this kind of expansion is in the emergence of a strong system of regional human rights law and judicial institutions.

These have not only added to international human rights monitoring and protection capacity, but are instrumental in relieving violations of an individual's human rights. As Buergenthal observed: "The UN system is better equipped to deal with large-scale violations of human rights, for which it commands the necessary political, military, and public relations resources."[47] For relief and protection of an individual's rights, the regional human rights systems seem more effective. The European Convention on Human Rights began the regional human rights movement that was followed by the Inter-American and African systems. These human rights systems build on the UN system of rights, but also codify "those rights to which the region attaches particular importance because of its political and legal traditions, its history and culture."[48]

The western European member states of the Council of Europe signed the European Convention on Human Rights and Fundamental Freedoms in 1950 and it came into force in 1953. They were concerned that the UN was acting too slowly to enact a binding international bill of rights. Forty-six European states are now party to this convention. It began with 12 basic civil and political rights and has now expanded to 15 through a series of protocols.[49] The European Convention established a Commission in 1954 to investigate charges of violation and to determine their admissibility to the European Court of Human Rights, created in 1959. Originally, only states and the Commission had standing before the European Court, but Protocol No. 11, which came into force in 1998, abolished the Commission and gave individuals the right to file cases directly with the Court.

Although the institutional framework of the European system is noteworthy, the record of compliance by states members of the European system is its most significant contribution to human rights. Buergenthal reports that: "Its judgments are routinely followed by the national courts of the states parties to the Convention, their legislatures, and their national governments. The Convention itself has acquired the status of domestic law in most of the states parties and can be invoked in their courts."[50] Over its 50-year history, the Court has delivered more than 12,000 judgments binding on member states, and they have undertaken changes in legislation and administrative practices in response to the Court's decisions. More than 119,000 cases were pending in 2010 before the Court.[51]

The Inter-American system has also emerged as an important human rights system since 1959 when the Inter-American Commission on Human Rights was established as an autonomous organ of the Organization of American States (OAS).[52] The Commission's mandate comes from Article 106 of the OAS Charter (1948) and Chapter VI of the American Convention on Human Rights (adopted 1969; entered into force 1978) that details the functions and procedures of the Commission. The Commission is made up of seven members elected by the OAS Assembly who serve in their personal capacity (American Convention on Human Rights Chapter VII). In 1966, the Commission was authorized to receive individual communications "charging large-scale violations of a selected number of basic rights set out in the American Declaration, including the right to life, equality before the law, freedom of religion, freedom from arbitrary arrest, and the right to due process of law."[53] The Commission promotes human rights by collecting and reviewing reports from OAS member countries and reviewing petitions from individuals and representatives of organizations claiming violations of human rights. It makes site visits and issues special reports (see American Convention on Human Rights Article 41).

The American Convention detailed the petition process and other work of the Inter-American Commission on Human Rights and established an Inter-American Court of Human Rights. The Court is made up of seven judges who are elected by the OAS Assembly to serve in a personal capacity for a term of six years (American Convention on Human Rights Chapter VIII). The Commission is empowered to hear complaints brought by individuals against their own governments, but individuals have no direct access to the regional human rights court. The system therefore resembles the pre-Protocol No. 11 European system. A case can be referred to the Inter-American Court by the Commission following its own examination of its merits. Only states accepting jurisdiction of the Inter-American Court can be brought before it. Individuals have no standing before the Court, although since 2001 individuals have been permitted to appear before the Court once their case is referred to it. More than 2,000 petitions were received by the Commission in 2009 (see Annual Report, Inter-American Commission on Human Rights, Chapter III). Of these, 12 cases were referred by the Commission to the Court.[54]

The African Charter on Human and Peoples' Rights was concluded by members of the Organization of African Unity—African Union since 2002—in Banjul, The Gambia, in 1981 and entered into force in 1986. Article 30 of the African Charter established the African Commission on Human and Peoples' Rights within the Organization of African Unity. The Commission has 11 members—each from a different African Union (AU) member country who are elected by the OAU (now AU) Assembly. They are not government representatives and they serve in a personal capacity.[55] The Charter did not, however, provide for a Court. An 11-member Court was subsequently created by the AU by means of a protocol in 2004 and came into existence in 2006. Individuals do not have the right to petition the Commission, but they can bring violations of human rights to the Commission's attention. States are obligated to file reports once every two years on actions taken to give effect to the African Charter. The Commission can make recommendations to governments to address their human rights records and may provide advisory opinions on matters of interpreting the African Charter. The relationship of this African Court of Human Rights to the African Court of Justice, established as an organ of the African Union in 1999, is yet to be determined.[56]

In the more than 60 years since the adoption of the Universal Declaration of Human Rights by the United Nations General Assembly, the development of both international law and international institutions has capitalized on a political environment that has increasingly found mass brutality intolerable. The "CNN effect" of a 24-hour news cycle contributed to this development by bringing stories of savagery, like that of the former Yugoslavia, into the homes of viewers around the world. This has, in turn, generated political pressure for action. It is not accidental that the media are often the first institution to be shut down when a government is on the verge of some brutal action. The German Basic Law (Grundgesetz) and many other democratic constitutions, including the US Constitution, explicitly safeguard the freedom of the press. In the *Freedom in the World* survey conducted by Freedom

House to determine "the state of global freedom as experienced by individuals," one of the areas surveyed is Freedom of Expression and Belief, including four questions touching on the independence of the media.[57]

The use of human rights as a foreign policy tool that started in the 1970s was supported by the dramatic normative and institutional developments of the 1950s and 1960s. The CSCE (Helsinki) framework, in turn, provided the focal points and the expectations that inspired the steady development of people power as an alternative to the traditional tools of state power in countries throughout the world. Beth Simmons captures this phenomenon in her study about the effects of international human rights treaties on state behavior:

> The importance of an opportunity to influence a country's rights future is supported by the finding that ratified treaties have their strongest effects in countries that are neither stable democracies nor stable autocracies. The findings show, for example, that governments' willingness to reduce interference in the free practice of religion was associated with ratification of the ICCPR, but this effect was especially strong in this large, heterogeneous set of countries. Even more striking, *only* in these partially democratic or transitioning countries did the ICCPR have any effect on provisions for a civil liberty as important as fair trials.[58]

International human rights seem to have a particularly strong opportunity to become part of the governing system and mores of a country when it is in transition from one form of government to another. This is borne out by the fact that 28 percent of the pending 119,000 petitions before the European Court of Human Rights are from Russia, 11 percent from Turkey, 8 percent from Ukraine, and 8 percent from Romania. As to judgments of violation between 1959 and 2009, nearly 19 percent were against Turkey with Italy at 17 percent and Russia at 7 percent.[59]

International human rights has also moved further to hold individuals to account for their conduct in mass murder and other crimes against humanity. The International Criminal Tribunals for the Former Yugoslavia and for Rwanda were created by UN Security Council Resolution 827 (1993) and UN Security Council Resolution 955 (1994), respectively, to prosecute individuals for actions taken in those conflicts and pave the way for establishing a permanent international criminal court. Drawing on the jurisprudence of the International Military Tribunal in Nuremberg that tried high officials of the Nazi war machine following the Second World War and the Tokyo trials, the ICTY has rendered 91 judgments and the ICTR 27 judgments for various war crimes up to 2010.[60] The ICTY's judgments have defined the offenses, modes of criminal liability, and the scope of superior responsibility. These tribunals have also made particular advances in the area of gender crimes, which were not addressed in the Nuremberg and Tokyo tribunals. In this respect, the Čelebić Case (Trial Judgement, ICTY, 16 November 1998 and Appeal Judgement 20 February 2001) and the Furundžija Case (Trial Judgement 10 December 1998 and Appeal Judgement 21 July 2000) pioneered the development of defining rape as torture and an international crime.[61]

Responding to broad support among UN members for a permanent tribunal to address such crimes, the International Criminal Court (ICC) was established in 2002 when the Rome ICC Statute, signed in 1998, entered into force. Although not part of the UN system, the ICC is located in The Hague, as are the International Court of Justice—successor to the League's Permanent Court of International Justice—and the ICTY, both of which are UN bodies. The ICC has proceeded carefully in prosecuting its first cases, but it has already taken the unprecedented step of indicting a sitting head of state and government of war crimes, Sudan President Omar al-Bashir. He has been found to be complicit in the genocidal murders that have taken place in the Darfur region of Sudan.[62]

The move towards judicial enforcement of international human rights shows the ongoing need for work at both the national and international levels. At the national level, the effort continues to meld international human rights into national standards through constitutional or legislative guarantees that will ensure judicial review of a government's treatment of its people. At the international level, the focus is on developing institutions and procedures that can prosecute and otherwise hold individuals to account for actions they have taken in violation of international human rights whether they are holding public office or not.

If the rejection of "superior orders" as a defense was thought to be the start of individual international responsibility in matters of mass violations of human rights, the ability to indict and to question the behavior of incumbent government officials is a major further increase in the ability of the international community to act in response to mass violations of human rights, when domestic systems are unable to do so. It may be worth noting that national or domestic systems of accountability still bear primary responsibility for prosecuting these crimes under the International Criminal Court.[63] The international criminal law system complements national systems and takes action when national systems fail to act. It further helps to set standards for proper prosecution and investigation of such crimes and serves as a general resource and repository of information on the prosecution of international crimes.[64]

As we look back at the development of international institutions in the twentieth century, the last decade of that century is distinguished by the number of international judicial bodies created at that time. Cesare Romano of the Project on International Courts and Tribunals (PICT) noted 12 judicial bodies that became active or were extensively modified in the decade after 1989 compared to the six or seven that existed prior to 1989.[65]

In addition to the numbers, another important characteristic of late twentieth-century international judicial institutions is the opening of proceedings to non-state actors, including international organizations, individuals, and national courts. International organizations have had standing before international judicial institutions to perform intermediary functions and to seek legal advice. Examples of the intermediary function are the old European Commission on Human Rights and the Inter-American Commission on Human Rights, where an international body is charged to investigate and to determine the justiciability of a complaint before the relevant court, in this case, the European Court of Human Rights and the Inter-American Court of Human Rights, respectively.

In the UN system, the International Court of Justice (ICJ) serves as the principal judicial organ of the UN. As such, UN organs and specialized agencies are authorized to seek legal opinions from the court. Such Advisory Opinions have included the 1949 Reparations for Injuries Advisory Opinion, where the ICJ articulated the concept of "functional immunity," to describe the status of UN officials on mission and subsequent responsibility for their safety and well-being.[66]

Given the level of institutional development at both the international and regional levels and the increasing scope of international organization (IO) responsibilities, it is not surprising that this has been the area of greatest non-state activity before international judicial bodies. In addition to the UN system and the ICJ,

> advisory opinions also can be requested of ITLOS [International Tribunal for the Law of the Sea] by the [UN] General Assembly or the Council of the International Seabed Authority; of the E[uropean] C[ourt] of J[ustice] by the Council and the Commission of the European Communities; of the European Court of Human Rights by the Committee of Ministers; of the Inter-American Court on Human Rights by several organs of the Organization of American States; of the Central American Court of Justice by the organs of the Central American Integration System; and of the COMESA

[Common Market for Eastern and Southern Africa] Court of Justice by the COMESA Authority and Council.[67]

Increased access by individuals to international judicial process and institutions has been described above particularly in connection with the European Court of Human Rights. With individuals now increasingly able to access international institutions and jurisdictions to press their own claims, whether for human rights violations or for property loss and damage, the practice of diplomatic protection, whereby a state presses the claim on behalf of its national, is eroding. At the same time, direct access to international judicial institutions has raised the level of a state's responsibility to its nationals and increased external review of a state's conduct.

This has led to the growth in national courts seeking interpretations from international judicial institutions of national law or other law under their jurisdiction. This can be significant since "[t]he interpretation of the legal regime's norms given by the regime's judicial body, by way of preliminary ruling, is typically binding upon the requesting national court."[68] National courts seek such preliminary rulings in order to avoid being overruled by an outside body. Romano explains:

> Preliminary rulings originate from the initiative of individuals who decide to claim the direct applicability of a regime's law or the incompatibility of national legislation with it before national courts. This is a further explanation for why direct inter-state litigation has become an exceptionally rare event, and why [courts] which grant non-state entities standing are constantly expanding in number and scope.[69]

By incorporating international obligations into their domestic legal systems, national courts bypass national parliaments that typically have had the responsibility for turning international obligations into enforceable domestic law. By connecting to national judicial institutions and thus becoming part of a country's jurisprudence, international obligations can reach more deeply into a country and touch all—individuals, corporations, other non-state actors—who have access to a country's domestic court system.

The increased number of international judicial institutions and the expansion of the jurisdiction of these institutions to include international organizations and individuals has created concern about overlapping jurisdictions and inconsistent rulings. An additional concern is that multiple institutions would encourage forum shopping and detract from the regular and systematic development of international law. As Zachary Douglas observed:

> Forum shoppers of the future will be less concerned with the remedial possibilities in proceedings before domestic courts of different states, but will instead seek advantage from the absence of hierarchy and coordination among the various types of international tribunals and from the often strained relationships between such tribunals and municipal courts.[70]

On overlapping jurisdictions, we have the example of maritime boundary cases that can go before the ICJ as well as the International Tribunal for the Law of the Sea. In the area of genocide, we see the 2007 case of Bosnia and Herzegovina v. Serbia and Montenegro where the ICJ took note of the ruling of the ICTY that genocide had occurred in Srebrenica, but that Serbia was not directly responsible.[71] Or, we can see the inconsistency in the relationship between international and national courts demonstrated by a pair of death penalty cases. In the case of *Thomas v. Baptiste,* the British Privy Council acting as the High Court of Trinidad and Tobago concluded in 2000 that the execution of a prisoner had to await the ruling of the Inter-American Court of Human Rights. This contrasts with the 1998 experience in the United States where the state of Virginia executed a Paraguayan national, Angel Breard, despite an order by the ICJ to delay the execution until the ICJ could determine whether the United States had violated its treaty obligations with Paraguay by failing to provide Mr. Breard with access to Paraguayan consular officials.

The general concern is whether the accumulation of judicial bodies and their potentially inconsistent jurisprudence over time might threaten the coherence of the international legal system.[72] Campbell McLachlan notes the venues where parallel proceedings and such conflicts might arise:

> ... [I]ssues of parallel proceedings may arise between all levels of international litigation: as between national courts; between national courts and arbitral tribunals; between international tribunals; and as between international tribunals and national courts.[73]

The potential for these overlaps and inconsistencies is not new and was noted by the Permanent Court of International Justice in 1925 in the case concerning *Certain German Interests in Polish Upper Silesia,*[74] with no useful resolution. But how much of a problem is this, since it could also be argued that it serves the rule of law to have multiple forums that parties can make use of. To answer this question, Jonathan Charney undertook a review of the jurisprudence of the ICJ, the European Court of Justice, the European Court of Human Rights, the Inter-American Court of Human Rights, the dispute settlement forums of the World Trade Organization and the General Agreement on Tariffs and Trade, the Iran-United States Claims Tribunal, ad hoc tribunals established to decide issues of international law, and several administrative tribunals. He reviewed their jurisprudence in several core international law areas: the law of treaties, sources of international law, state responsibility, compensation for injuries to aliens, exhaustion of local remedies, nationality, and international maritime boundaries. Charney concluded that

[I]n those core areas of international law, the different international tribunals of the late twentieth century do share relatively coherent views on these doctrines of international law. Although differences exist, these tribunals are clearly engaged in the same dialectic. The fundamentals of this general international law remain the same regardless of which tribunal decides the case.[75]

The problem may become more complicated if we include the work of national courts and dispute settlement mechanisms like arbitration where general public access to the proceedings may be limited. Although there may be cross-fertilization and a consideration of available jurisprudence on a specific topic like international maritime boundaries, each court and tribunal will function on its own. This makes inconsistency and differences inevitable. However, the number of institutions now in existence that were created by states for specific reasons—for example, limited membership or specific issue areas—means that there are multiple opportunities available for international law to be tested as to its applicability and relevance to a variety of situations. It may also mean that the work of the judicial bodies will fall into some patterns where more general or interstitial questions would go to the ICJ while other narrower ones might go to the regional, subject matter, or other judicial institutions. As such, the ICJ could take a leadership role in setting out the contours of a problem and the applicable law. If it is the first international judicial body to face a question, this initial articulation could have influence over the framing of the law and the decision-making of other courts and tribunals.

The international judicial system started with the League of Nations PCIJ in 1922 as the first permanent court of general jurisdiction. In a

Westphalian system of sovereign equals, this was quite a remarkable achievement and a move back towards the pre-Westphalian era when states would seek and accept the decision of a third party when they found themselves in dispute with another state or sovereign.[76] It is therefore even more remarkable that in less than a century, the idea of judicial settlement at the international level has expanded to include a number of permanent tribunals—the ICJ that succeeded the PCIJ, the International Tribunal for the Law of the Sea, dispute settlement bodies of the World Trade Organization, and most recently, the International Criminal Court. These are complemented by the permanent tribunals that exist at the regional level, including the European Court of Human Rights, the Inter-American Court of Human Rights, the European Court of Justice, the Benelux Economic Union Court, the Court of First Instance of the European Communities, the Economic Court of the Commonwealth of Independent States, the Common Court of Justice and Arbitration of the Organization for the Harmonization of Corporate Law in Africa, the Court of Justice of the Common Market for Eastern and Southern Africa, the Court of Justice of the African Union, the Court of Justice of the Economic Community of West African States (ECOWAS), the Court of Justice of the West African Economic and Monetary Union, the East African Court of Justice, the Court of Justice of the Andean Community, and the Central American Court of Justice.[77]

Add to this the national judicial institutions that also play a role in developing international jurisprudence and we see the emergence of a vibrant and dynamic judicial system. In an ideal world, rulings by the various courts would be evaluated by each other, replicated where applicable and in agreement, refuted or expanded where less relevant or not in agreement. Over time, one might expect that the best and most effective ideas will be adopted widely and become part of general international law.[78] Unless a hierarchy among judicial institutions is established, cross-fertilization and evaluation of legal concepts and principles that come out of international courts will need to be facilitated by the judges and personnel of these institutions themselves through some form of ongoing dialogue, communication, judicial comity, academic commentary, and review. Such dialogue and scholarship are supported by access to judgments, pleadings, and other materials related to cases that come before the various tribunals.

Though early in their institutional development, we see an increase in the number of permanent international judicial bodies, an emerging relationship of complementarity between national and international judicial institutions in the areas of human rights and international criminal law, and a heightened awareness among judges that they do not work in isolation from courts outside their borders at the national, regional, and international levels. None of this is moving towards a hierarchy of institutions unless explicitly provided for by treaty, as is the case in the European Union. There is, however, a need for integrated information resources and for greater knowledge and awareness of the practice of judicial institutions and bodies around the world.

Whatever scholars and jurists conclude about the pros and cons of this fragmented international judicial system, it is one development that is unlikely to change because of the advantages such fragmentation presents to those seeking justice and remedy through a legal proceeding. It may be that, over time, the effectiveness of various judicial bodies will help to drive traffic to one or another institution. Should the institution become overwhelmed, as is presently the case with the European Court of Human Rights, the institution might then seek to discharge its obligations in cooperation with others, including national courts and parliaments, and help to overcome conflicts through some form of coordination. This functional test, however, will take time to work out. In the meantime, as McLachlan suggests: "The emerging practice of direct judicial communication, if regulated in order to secure due process for the parties, may reduce the risk of conflict between courts, and greatly facilitate their interaction in solving problems of litispendence."[79]

The consequences of these expanded arenas

The preceding chapter demonstrated the importance of frameworks to provide initial space for political engagement and discussed the capacity of existing frameworks to adapt and to shape the future. This takes place when parts of an existing governance system create conditions that facilitate the move to a new governing system. When existing units and frameworks serve as the basis for broader systemic change, those elements that once may have seemed minor or symbolic can take on greater significance under changed circumstances. The capacities generated and created by existing units of governance in response to new conditions therefore hold the seeds of the system to come.

The challenge for decision-makers, analysts, and states is to be able to discern between an *ad hoc* accommodation and broader system-wide change. In the midst of such change, it may be difficult to imagine how the new system will work in the long run. For example, the mandates and minorities treaties of the League of Nations provided an important foundation for today's governance by giving international institutions monitoring and oversight functions. These functions are now widely accepted and take place in a variety of areas from arms control to human rights to the protection of wildlife and the environment. But, in the early days of international organizations, the ground-breaking significance of inviting international scrutiny into the actions of governments, including the opportunity for individuals to hold their own governments to account before an international body, was unclear. As we saw in the years following the 1975 Helsinki Final Act of the Conference on Security and Cooperation in Europe, the formality of having states report to the follow-up meetings provided in Basket III of the agreement created opportunities for local and external political forces to connect and to leverage each other's resources and capacities. The lowering of the cost and time of travel and communication transformed reporting and monitoring into political and governing tools that would have been unthinkable in the early twentieth century. Their work facilitated by technology and after nearly a century of experience with monitoring, public and private organizations continue to expand the level of influence they can exert on governments by using these techniques.

The conditions that generate change and create new capacities are new needs, accumulated practice, and available opportunity. The appearance of needs that require new structures or processes in order for governments to respond effectively can be an important engine for change. That something new is required suggests a lack of capacity in the existing system. The broader the agreement that change or adaptation is needed, the more likely new structures become. The change that takes place, however, does not end with a single application. Capacities created in one area can be adapted or enhanced for use in another area. For example, the tools of inspections, monitoring, and reporting are used across the board in arms control, human rights, and many other areas. Follow-up or review conferences are another example of increasing capacity in international governance. They provide regular opportunities not only for ongoing normative development but also for the fostering of political and advocacy networks in an issue area. The follow-up conferences convened to implement the 1975 Helsinki Final Act led to strong human rights movements throughout eastern Europe, and over a decade of UN-sponsored conferences on various subjects like human rights, women's rights, and the environment has created advocacy organizations worldwide.[80]

The widespread recognition of need alone, however, may not be adequate to prompt immediate change in the international system. Consider, for example, the crime of genocide and the establishment of the International Criminal Court in 2002 to address the failure—or incapacity—of states to "end impunity for the perpetrators of the most serious crimes of concern to the international community."[81] The Convention on Prevention and Punishment of the Crime of Genocide was signed in 1948 as a reaction to the Holocaust in the Second World War. The Convention entered into force in 1951, but was not given immediate effect, since there was no legal system other than national legal systems that could prosecute this crime and hold individuals to account for their actions.

This changed with the courts created by the UN Security Council in 1993 and 1994 to deal with crimes committed during the conflicts in the Former Yugoslavia and Rwanda. Their record of prosecution established the strong view that there should be no impunity for perpetrators of mass crime. The international community further realized that a permanent court might be desirable to address these situations rather than constituting a body on an *ad hoc* basis. The ICC's website notes that an important factor that made possible its creation was the consensus achieved in the international community on defining genocide, crimes against humanity, and war crimes.[82] But it still took four years from 1998 to 2002 before the Statute of the International Criminal Court came into force, and the United States has refused to become a party to the Statute.

Accumulated practice that over time can create habits and acceptance of activities that were previously considered revolutionary is another important condition in fostering change and generating new capacity. The increasing willingness of member states of the Council of Europe to comply with decisions of the European Court of Human Rights (see, for example, the 1961 *Lawless* Case and the 1958 *Case relating to Certain Aspects of the Laws on the Use of Languages in Education in Belgium*) and of European Union members to comply with decisions of the European Court of Justice, even when compliance requires change in national practice and law, is an example of how attitudes change as state practice accumulates over several decades.[83] But we know that establishing an institution alone is inadequate to foster such profound change. It also requires the will and support of the people and institutions—domestic, political and legal systems, it seeks to address. Where this is absent, establishing an institution will not, alone, suffice. See, for example, the failure of the Andean Court of Justice to exercise the same level of influence over countries in its region.[84]

Available opportunities can create new capacities. We see this in the interpretive work performed by international institutions that fill important gaps in normative development, much as constitutional courts do when they interpret their countries' constitutions. Two international examples are the General Comment practice of the United

Nations Human Rights Committee and the doctrine of the margin of appreciation used by the European Court of Human Rights. As provided by Article 40 of the ICCPR, the United Nations Human Rights Committee[85] studies the reports submitted by state parties and can issue general comments to promote further compliance and implementation of the Covenant.[86] Interpretations of provisions of the ICCPR are published by topic on the UN High Commissioner for Human Rights website at www2.ohchr.org. There have been 33 general comments, including General Comment 32 issued in 2007, that addresses the right to equality before courts and tribunals and the right to a fair trial, and General Comment 29, issued in 2001, that addresses ICCPR Article 4 and derogations during a state emergency. The accepted process of review by the Human Rights Committee has created a new capacity to interpret ICCPR provisions that, over time, is likely to shape the expectations created by those obligations.

In the case of the European Court of Human Rights, the practice known as the "margin of appreciation" grew out of a 1976 case, *Handyman v. U.K.*, indicating that application of the provisions of the European Convention on Human Rights might differ from case to case and country to country, depending on the right in question and the circumstances. The essential point was that the balancing of these rights would take place "under a European-level supervisory mechanism," that is, the Court, and that the Court would stay out of certain domestic spheres.[87] This further meant that the Court's oversight might differ from country to country, depending on historical, cultural, and social factors.[88]

By the late twentieth century, there was already a full range of capacities, devices, methods, accumulated experience, and resources that set the stage for a new phase of development. First, the League of Nations and then other regional and universal organizations since 1945 were important law-makers and creators of additional international organizations.[89] Before the century ended, opportunities to engage in global politics had increased for both state and non-state actors at international conferences, preparatory meetings, and follow-up conferences that were focal points for like-minded states, NGOs, and social movements to organize and to coalesce around specific issue areas.

The cycle of six preparatory conferences that began in 1996 and ended with the Rome intergovernmental conference that produced the Statute of the International Criminal Court in 1998 was a classic example of twentieth-century institution and capacity-building. A Preparatory Commission was then charged with drafting the Court Rules of Procedure and Evidence and other administrative matters, including privileges and immunities and financial regulations. The Court opened for business in 2003 after its Statute came into force in 2002, and a Review Conference of its Statute took place in Kampala, Uganda, in May–June 2010. Additional work will continue into 2015 and another Review Conference will take place in 2017. The Kampala Review Conference was attended by more than 4,000 representatives of states, intergovernmental organizations (IGOs), and NGOs.

In 1986, political scientists Harold Jacobson, William Reisinger, and Todd Mathers wrote that the "web of IGOs was dense and complex" and numbering over 1,000.[90] States belonged to organizations ranging from the multipurpose and general to the specific and regional. Denmark was found to be at the top of the list of countries with 164 full and associate memberships in various IGOs. In this study, the United States was listed as having 122 memberships, while Iceland had 105, India had 102, and Brazil had 100. The study concluded that:

> The evolving web of international governmental organizations has modified the global political system, as functionalism argued that it would, but it has not yet radically transformed this system, as functionalism hoped would happen. The radical transformation may yet come. In the meantime, however, international governmental organizations, in addition to modifying the political system, institutionalize aspects of traditional international politics.[91]

In 2010, the radical transformation is underway. Even if it is not yet complete, its contours are clear. The independent Westphalian state continues to exist, but in a world in which its existence depends on its participation in a global network that encompasses all states, international organizations, the private sector, media, NGOs, non-state actors, and individuals. Any one of these actors has the ability to have an existential impact, positive or negative.

For 300 years, this was not the case: only states could have such an impact on each other. But in the last half century, the actions of states themselves to enhance their capacity and the information and technological revolutions have globalized what was once a state monopoly of power. That globalization is both vertical and horizontal. States are affected by actions occurring thousands of miles from their borders, and can be affected by actions taken by a single individual. In such a world, the idea of autonomy is an illusion, a luxury to which some states still cling, but which most—even the United States—abandon in moments of crisis like the aftermath of September 11, 2001. States, however, have not yet completely abandoned the structures or processes of the Westphalian system, so that the traditional tools of interstate relations like diplomats and embassies now function alongside the newer phenomena of NGOs and private advocates.

Whether viewing these developments through the functionalist or the rational choice lens, the need to fulfill particular aspirations or accomplish specific tasks has often been the starting point for change.[92] Neither international law nor international relations is particularly good at capturing the cumulative effect of change, in terms of both new capacities and new demands. For example, the development of the post-Second World War system of international institutions can be partially attributed to greater international and domestic attention to social issues such as standards of living. It has also been attributed to a "distinctively liberal conception of a world under law" conceived by the United States as the international form of the New Deal.[93] As Slaughter wrote:

> The similarity in substance and scope between the domestic law of the liberal welfare state and the international law of cooperation in the postwar world has long been recognized. By taking a closer look at and examining the ways in which the American plans for the postwar order also reflected the specific institutional *forms* of the New Deal, projected onto the world by many of the domestic architects of the New Deal, I have suggested that the roots of contemporary multilateralism lie in one particular liberal state's vision of the world as a domestic polity, economy, or society writ large. It is thus no accident that the distinctive features of the international law of cooperation correspond to domestic law: "domestic" concerns like health and welfare, citizens rather than states as subjects, the imposition of affirmative rather than negative duties.[94]

The New Deal represented the US experience. It also offered a middle ground for a postwar world between those who believed in capitalism and the free market and socialists who believed in an interventionist, but not authoritarian state. The New Deal form of social liberalism allowed for an interventionist state in certain areas of individual well-being like social security, but also fostered capitalism and a free market. The focus in common was the individual. On the one hand, the individual was to be provided a safety net in the face of catastrophic economic collapse like that of the Great Depression. On the other, governments would support capitalism and work to make it flourish, support economic growth, and produce wealth. By the 1970s, the focus on the individual and the right of the individual to be heard combined with the information and communications revolutions to create domestic populations that were increasingly aware of and sophisticated about activities outside their countries' borders.

Individual stories have a ready outlet in the international media that need material to fill the 24-hour news cycle created by news channels like CNN in the 1980s and now by the Internet. CNN created the 24/7 non-stop news cycle. The information gathered to fill this news cycle comes not only from professional journalists, but also increasingly from anyone with a cell phone and a story to tell. An event is known around the world within minutes of its occurring and can serve as a rallying cry for activism, as was seen in the overthrow of Egyptian President Hosni Mubarak in February 2011.

The difference between the reporting of the 1989 student movement that led to the government crackdown in Tiananmen Square in Beijing, China, and the reporting of the Abu Ghraib prisoner abuses in 2004 is instructive. Student organizers took full advantage of the presence of a large corps of international media covering the visit of Mikhail Gorbachev to Beijing in May 1989 to press their demands for some level of free speech. As interest grew in the story of the student demonstrations, the foreign press stayed and kept watch. Following the crackdown, however, the foreign media were not welcome in China, and Tiananmen Square was sealed off. Although fax machines enabled some reporting after the government intervened, the world could not see what was happening. Fifteen years later in 2004, photos of the terrible conditions at the Abu Ghraib prison in Iraq were taken and released on the Internet by cell phone. Web reporting is now commonplace from virtually anywhere in the world, but technological advances are only part of the reason why this is possible. These changes exist because of steps taken by states and their agents, including IGOs, to empower individuals and to reap the economic benefits of connectivity. The state encouraged the public to demand accountability, and connectivity makes this demand visible worldwide.

Among scholars, this development is reflected in legal pluralism and critical legal studies that seek to understand international law's context. In their writings, critical legal scholars demonstrate the interactions and political factors that condition international law's creation and operation. Legal pluralism does not privilege the state as a law-maker or international actor, but sees it as one of several actors that have influence in decision-making. It sees international law as a "sphere of complex, overlapping legal authority,"[95] but one that has not yet fully theorized the relationships of the levels of law-making. Sally Engle Merry defines legal pluralism as "a situation in which two or more legal systems coexist in the same social field."[96] She expands on this:

A legal system is pluralistic in the juristic sense when the sovereign commands different bodies of law for different groups of the population varying by ethnicity, religion, nationality, or geography, and when the parallel legal regimes are all dependent on the state legal system.[97]

International law is pluralistic in its operation. It functions through domestic legal and political institutions and their legislation and judicial rulings. Understanding international law in this way permits "conceptualizing a more complex and interactive relationship between official and unofficial forms of ordering,"[98] and more closely describes the functioning reality of international law today. A key interest of legal pluralists is the ways in which law shapes the normative order through its effects on legal institutions both domestic and international.

For those in critical legal studies, law is "a system of signs that represents or distorts reality through the mechanisms of scale, projection, and symbolization."[99] Viewed this way, international law is neither objective nor value-free, but very much part of the political environment that supports any normative order. David Kennedy describes this situation:

A common disciplinary vocabulary … can extend and reinforce the profession's accumulated knowledge about what works and what doesn't, which may be all to the good. But, of course, a disciplinary vocabulary can also have limitations, characteristic blind spots and biases. A professional vocabulary can have unacknowledged bad effects when it legitimates, explains away, apologizes for or simply distracts professional attention from injustice.[100]

Kennedy further demonstrates that "money, access to institutional resources, relationships to underlying patterns of hegemony, and influence – is central to the chance that a given idea will become influential or dominant within the international law profession."[101] Given this reality, Kennedy cautions the user of international law to understand the influences—political, economic, cultural, and social, that affect law's formation.

That international law, like domestic law, is subject to these influences is not surprising, but the failure to understand that this is the case is problematic. A belief in its freedom from such influences will over time not only discredit, but also possibly degrade the capacity of international law to function. Two important examples of such blind spots are the failure to represent women in the making and operation of international law that feminist international law scholars like Christine Chinkin and Hilary Charlesworth address,[102] and the failure to understand the deep effects of colonialism on the development of post-colonial states in Africa, Latin America, and Asia (even China) as they struggle to have their views and interests fully represented in the international norm-making environment.[103] A common theme among critical legal scholars is the disenfranchisement or exclusion of certain actors from the power structure of a particular law-making era. Kennedy explains:

> Much of this work does not fit easily into traditional academic disciplines. Some of these writers are public international law scholars, others focus on particular issues, like the environment, nationalism, or trade. Some come from legal sociology, comparative law or legal philosophy. Some use the insights of other disciplines, including anthropology, economics, and feminism. Some have been interested in progressive or critical dimensions of contemporary legal philosophy or method. Some think of themselves as deeply progressive; others eschew political affiliation of all sorts. Whatever their intellectual roots, most of these scholars see themselves as challenging the dominant intellectual style or assumptions of their field.[104]

Summing up

The enhanced role of the individual in the international arena today has created a post-Westphalian situation where the international level can join directly with the local level or individual without a state intermediary.[105] This creates a form of cosmopolitan democracy where individuals have direct access to international activities and may even be able to assert rights and challenge their own government's actions either in court or through institutions like the World Bank Inspection Panels. For this more active role, individuals have also now acquired direct international responsibility and can be held accountable for mass violations of human rights as in the case of the indictment of Sudan's President Omar al-Bashir for the genocide in Darfur.

This new form of global politics is unstructured in comparison to traditional Westphalian international politics. It may function through networks and social movements rather than institutions. Important political movements like that to end the use of landmines may shrink or go out of existence even if their institutional legacies are significant.

The new global political environment is shaped by ongoing interactions rather than abrupt system-wide changes.[106] These interactions create denser and denser political connections between the local and the non-local, the individual and the institutional, and the national and transnational. The other characteristic of these interactions is that they are not necessarily hierarchical. Political and social movements that can create momentum can become important global actors. Factors that make for an effective advocacy network are "issue resonance, network density, and target vulnerability."[107]

The international political arena has changed not only in how politics are now practiced, but also in how issues are addressed. Although states maintain primary responsibility for any failure to meet international standards, the ability of states to pick and choose the standards with which to comply is diminishing. Simmons describes this in the area of human rights:

> ... from its apogee in the nineteenth century, the idea of exclusive internal sovereignty has been challenged by domestic democratic institutions, by international and transnational private actors, and even by sovereigns themselves. The result today is an increasingly dense and potentially more potent set of international rules, institutions, and expectations regarding the protection of individual rights than at any point in human history.[108]

The partnership required of the rules, institutions, and expectations at the international level with those at the national or sub-national levels, however, is not yet well developed, and aspiration and expectation presently exceed the ability to deliver. This will likely change as the international discourse enters the national discourse and the two over time increasingly blend together. The process, however, is likely to stress existing institutions further and produce unexpected, and even undesirable, outcomes, at least in the short term. The international system's ability to assess shortcomings and develop governance institutions and processes at all levels will be critical over the long term. International law is one of the governance institutions that can contribute to this task—an understanding that may be more important than its ability to sanction individual acts of non-compliance.

4 International relations in a global context

- The state as global actor
- Global scripts and collective legitimation: states and international organizations
- NGOs and global politics
- Summing up

What we see in the globalized governing environment are changes in how states and international organizations (IOs) carry out their functions. The domestic and the international are now engaged in a more extensive, intense, and complex relationship than ever before. States and IOs are becoming more closely tied and dependent on each other to discharge their functions. We see the need for international authorization or legitimation in many state activities, but we also know that implementation remains in state hands. As a result, implementation gaps exist, and the formal international legal structure may suggest more normative cohesion than actually exists.

Another factor that affects the effective implementation of international standards is their association with particular political and economic values that not all countries—especially those being asked to make profound adjustments—share. This causes resistance and skepticism about whether international engagement is worth the price that must be paid to comply. Both states and IOs increasingly find themselves bound by structures and values that may neither serve their interests today nor be effective at meeting objectives over the long run. States adjust as they seek ways to function more effectively, but these adjustments do not yet constitute a coherent governing system.

Effective regulation and governance require flexibility and adaptability on the part of individuals and institutions that govern today. *Ad hoc* arrangements and soft law practices seem to offer that flexibility and adaptability. But one disadvantage of *ad hoc* arrangements over time, is that they may only add to environmental complexity if they are not part of a governance framework generally recognized by governments, an international institution, or other accepted authority. At the same time, international law's less developed reliance on any single implementation framework may be an advantage by making it possible for international law to function in multiple institutional settings both domestic and international.

International law is organized horizontally, rather than vertically, as is most domestic law. This means that states often seek allies in order to advance their interests; they join forces with each other, with subnational components of states, and with non-governmental organizations (NGOs), private enterprises, and intergovernmental organizations both to shape and to carry out their obligations. It also means that international or cross-border regulation now may reach deeply into a state and directly affect the individuals in a country. But international law cannot do that without coordination or connection with national law and legal institutions. The Hague Convention on Child Abduction, for example, requires for its implementation that judges communicate directly with each other from the jurisdictions where the parents are located without going through separate diplomatic channels.

In this denser governing environment with multiple actors, where is the overarching logic to provide cohesion and coordination among governing units and processes? Such a non-hierarchical and partially institutionalized structure must find cohesion and coordination in a common and broad commitment to governance on the basis of respect for law—domestic, transnational, and international. The elements of such governance—the people, structures, and modes—already exist and are described below. Each is tied to an institutional framework, although not always an international one. The more institutionalized and formal framework may in fact be the national one working at the transnational or international level. At the same time, the transnational and international may offer the national something that it does not have operating alone—the ability to reach outside its borders in a sustainable and organized way. Given the globalized character of many regulatory problems today, the ability to reach beyond one's borders and to call on the assistance of counterparts in other countries is one of the incentives for cross-border cooperation.

This chapter will explore the changes required of three major groups of actors in the globalized environment—states, IOs, and NGOs. These groups are changed by the globalized environment, but also change the environment through their actions. This is one way the international system has developed to generate the capacity to govern in a dynamic environment.

The state as global actor

One feature of the state functioning as a global, rather than an international, actor is that it may govern through networks. Anne-Marie Slaughter describes this as:

> [A] world of governments, with all the different institutions that perform the basic functions of governments—legislation, adjudication, implementation—interacting both with each other domestically and also with their foreign and supranational counterparts. States still exist in this world; indeed, they are crucial actors. But they are "disaggregated." They relate to each other not only through the Foreign Office, but also through regulatory, judicial, and legislative channels.[1]

In this view, international institutions are the necessary partners of states in order to carry out their normative objectives and to pursue common interests. The complementarity principle provided for by Article 17 of the Statute of the International Criminal Court is an example of this, where the primary responsibility for prosecuting international crime is left with states.[2] However, should a state be unable or unwilling to discharge this obligation, the International Criminal Court will act.

We find another example of this in the success of the European Court of Human Rights institutionalizing its role as a well-recognized human rights court. In this case, the Court's success threatens to overwhelm it, with nearly 57,000 new applications reviewed in 2009 alone, compared to 8,400 in 1999. The Court's docket is now almost 120,000 cases. Council of Europe members recognize that one of the reasons for this growth is the failure of national authorities to implement the European Convention on Human Rights. There are a large number of repeat cases where the Court's jurisprudence is settled, but not yet implemented or reflected in national legal systems. To address the crisis, the Council of Europe met in February 2010 to urge action on its members. The Interlaken Declaration noted that the purpose of the High Level Conference was:

> [T]o achieve a balance between the number of judgments and decisions delivered by the Court and the number of incoming applications;
>   to enable the Court to reduce the backlog of cases and to adjudicate new cases within a reasonable time, particularly those concerning serious violations of human rights; and

to ensure the full and rapid execution of judgments of the Court and the effectiveness of its supervision by the Committee of Ministers.[3]

The Action Plan that the Interlaken conference produced emphasized implementation of the European Convention on Human Rights at the national level, including "introducing new remedies, whether they be of a specific nature or a general domestic remedy, [so] that any person with an arguable claim that their rights and freedoms as set forth in the Convention have been violated has available to them an effective remedy before a national authority providing adequate redress where appropriate."[4]

In this way, the European Court is evolving a relationship with its member countries to share the responsibilities of carrying out the decisions of the European Court of Human Rights. In cases where the European Court's jurisprudence is well established, the Council of Europe's plan is that national courts will apply those standards directly and lighten the European Court's docket. Where judgments exist, greater effort is being made by the Council to get countries to comply with them. These efforts are not only directed at judicial institutions, but also at political institutions, chiefly national legislatures. The UK Parliament's Joint Committee on Human Rights noted that:

> The Interlaken Declaration explicitly recognizes that Parliaments, as well as governments and courts, have a fundamental role to play in guaranteeing and protecting human rights at the national level. The role of national Parliaments has increasingly been recognized as crucial in achieving national implementation of the Convention. Traditionally, it was seen principally as the responsibility of the judiciary to remedy human rights violations at the national level. Today, however, it is increasingly seen as the shared responsibility of all branches of the state (the executive and parliament as well as the courts) to ensure effective national implementation of the Convention, both by preventing human rights violations and ensuring that remedies for them exist at the national level.[5]

Following the Interlaken Declaration's recommendation for a more active parliamentary role, this committee wrote to UK government departments calling their attention to European Court of Human Rights judgments and findings of incompatibility against the United Kingdom.[6] Although the United Kingdom remains among the top ten Council of Europe members in implementing European Court of Human Rights judgments, it has not carried out 13 judgments, some more than five years old. The failure of countries like the United Kingdom to carry out the court's judgments leads to erosion of the court's authority and institutional credibility to the detriment of the European human rights system. Parliament's plea has therefore been that the United Kingdom should lead by example and enforce the Court's judgments.

Principles such as subsidiarity within the European Union and the margin of appreciation in the European Court of Human Rights, all start from the premise that keeping governance as close to the people as possible is desirable, but that if local institutions are unable or unwilling to act, then international institutions offer another remedy.[7] Over time, as states act to meet their international obligations, they will meet the standard clearly envisaged by the countries endorsing the Interlaken Declaration and Plan of Action that places the primary responsibility for compliance on the national governments, leaving only the most serious or unsettled cases to the European Court. Theoretically, this is what the constructivist outlook predicts—that standards will shape as well as direct behavior by all who interact with a normative system or structure:

They [states] would each be operating both in the domestic and the international arenas, exercising their national authority to implement their transgovernmental and international obligations and representing the interests of their country while working with their foreign and supranational counterparts to disseminate and distill information, cooperate in enforcing national and international laws, harmonizing national laws and regulations, and addressing common problems.[8]

Networked governance provides a structure to address global issues and problems by building on one of the strongest political institutions in the international system, the state. It also provides a way to ensure that this key unit of global governance has the capacity to carry out its obligations through "government networks, technical assistance, benchmarks and standards, or other forms of cooperation."[9] The state, therefore, remains key even in the globalized politics of the twenty-first century. However, the state's relationship with the international arena has changed. Stemming from the accumulation of state actions over nearly a century in areas like human rights, the international system can now demand certain behavior from states and scrutinize state conduct even within a state's own territory.

For example, UN Security Council Resolution 1373, passed in the wake of the 11 September 2001 terrorist attacks, called for the *"domestic criminalization* of the financing of terrorism, freezing of terrorist assets by national authorities, use of domestic courts to bring to justice those involved in terrorist acts, and ratification by domestic authorities of relevant anti-terrorism conventions."[10] Resolution 1373 further provided for a familiar feature of international institutions—the requirement that states report to a newly created UN Counter-Terrorism Committee on steps taken to comply with the resolution. A similar approach was taken in efforts to strengthen non-proliferation. UN Security Council Resolution 1540 (28 April 2004) required states to "adopt national legislation prohibiting the manufacture or possession of weapons of mass destruction by non-state actors and to establish export control regulations and physical protection regimes for weapons and related technologies."[11]

Slaughter expands her view of the relationship between national states and international institutions by suggesting that the international system should provide the needed structure in cases where states are not able to govern themselves or to otherwise meet their obligations. This interim measure of international control and oversight would allow states to build the needed infrastructure to govern themselves. This recalls the League of Nations Mandate System in which territories were governed based on international standards until they were deemed able to function as independent states or until their status could be determined.[12] Anne-Marie Slaughter and William Burke-White see inadequate responses to transnational threats stemming from three causes: "a lack of domestic governance capacity, a lack of domestic will to act, and new problems that exceed the ordinary ability of states to address."[13] Because of technological and political developments over the last century, "the very concept of sovereignty will have to adapt to embrace, rather than reject, the influence of international rules and processes on domestic political processes."[14]

The domestic, however, is not a passive recipient of the international, but rather is a crucial part of the capacity of the international system to give effect to international obligations and standards. To effectively respond to new international threats, international legal rules must penetrate the surface of the sovereign state by requiring governments to take specific domestic actions to meet specified targets. Sometimes simple backstopping of national institutions may be sufficient to accomplish this task. In other circumstances, assistance and the bolstering of weak state capacity may be an essential prerequisite. At yet other times, international law may have to actively compel state action. When it does so, it once again seeks to alter the political choices of national governments and to compel states to utilize their national institutions in new ways.[15]

Another feature of the globalized governing environment is the deeper penetration of international law and obligations into national legal systems. Traditional conceptions of the international legal operating system rely on international institutions and processes to supervise norms. Yet, one of the adaptations to inadequacies in this system is to rely on *domestic* legal mechanisms to incorporate those norms. This transnational legal process is described by Harold Koh:

> Legal internalization occurs when an international norm is incorporated into the domestic legal system through executive action, judicial interpretation, legislative action, or some combination of the three. ... Judicial internalization can occur when domestic litigation provokes judicial incorporation of human rights norms either implicitly, by construing existing statutes consistently with international human rights norms, or explicitly, through what I have elsewhere called "transnational public law litigation". Legislative internalization occurs when domestic lobbying embeds international law norms into binding domestic legislation or even constitutional law that officials of a non-complying government must then obey as part of the domestic legal fabric.[16]

States use legal internalization to implement and enforce international norms for a variety of legal, political, social, or economic reasons. For example, states might prefer to deal with sensitive international norms through domestic processes, which are more malleable and reflective of national cultural practices. National legal systems may also demand national action to enforce international precepts. In Canada, depending on the subject matter, implementation of a treaty obligation will require action not only by the Federal Parliament, but also by individual provincial legislatures because of the division of legislative powers provided by Canada's Constitution.[17] Local actors then attain standing to press claims and seek redress in domestic courts.

The 2004 ruling by the Oklahoma Court of Criminal Appeals in *Osbaldo Torres v. the State of Oklahoma* provides an example of how domestic legal institutions are involved in giving effect to the decisions of the International Court of Justice—specifically the case of *Avena and other Mexican Nationals* regarding the imposition of the death penalty.[18] As a matter of criminal law, these issues fall largely within the jurisdiction of states in the US federal system, and the states necessarily must engage their legal institutions to implement obligations the United States has undertaken in international law. The *Avena* case was brought on behalf of the government of Mexico before the

International Court of Justice because of the failure of the United States to notify the Mexican government of the arrest and detention of more than 50 Mexican nationals in 10 different states of the United States. The Mexican nationals were subsequently tried and sentenced to death, but Mexico claimed relief for the failure of the United States to carry out its obligations under the Vienna Convention on Consular Relations to make available access to its nationals by appropriate consular officials.

In its decision, the International Court of Justice found that the United States had violated Article 36 of the Vienna Convention on Consular Relations and ruled that: "the appropriate reparation in this case consists in the obligation of the United States of America to provide by means of its own choosing, review and reconsideration of the convictions and sentences of the Mexican nationals. ... by taking account of the violation of the rights set forth in Article 36 of the Convention ... "[19] The judgment went on to specify what it considered to be appropriate review and reconsideration and further noted that "the clemency process, as currently practiced within the United States criminal justice system, does not appear to meet the requirements [of providing access to consuls during the overall judicial proceedings]."[20]

On receipt of this decision from the US Department of State, the Oklahoma Court of Criminal Appeals acknowledged that the United States was bound by treaties, in this case, the Vienna Convention on Consular Relations, and that:

> [a]s this Court is bound by the treaty itself, we are bound to give full faith and credit to the Avena decision. I am not suggesting that the International Court of Justice has jurisdiction over this Court—far from it. However, in these unusual circumstances the issue of whether this Court must abide by the court's opinion in Torres's case is not ours to determine.[21]

So, by virtue of the federal government's power to conclude treaties for the United States, the state of Oklahoma concluded that it would accept the International Court of Justice's judgment seeking a "review and reconsideration" of the death sentence of Osbaldo Torres. In this case, the sentence was commuted.

However, the existence and degree of legal internalization is always subject to the limits imposed by the national law in question. In the case of the United States, this means provisions of the US Constitution as well as relevant federal and state law and practices. For example, in the case of *Medellin v. Texas*, the US Supreme Court held in 2008 that

International Court of Justice (ICJ) decisions were not binding federal law and that ICJ judgments could not be enforced over state rulings and procedures—at least not in the death penalty and consular notification questions raised by the *Medellin* case. This was in contrast to the position taken by the state of Oklahoma in the case of Osbaldo Torres discussed above and shows the inconsistencies that federal systems can produce when applying international law. The US Congress could still pass legislation to give effect to the Vienna Convention on Consular Relations, but legal internalization is not automatic and may not be consistent, either with the adoption of the convention or through a ruling by the ICJ.

Despite its shortcomings, the incorporation of international norms into domestic legal processes has several advantages. Among the most notable is that the monitoring and enforcement of the law is invested in national legal operating systems, most of which are more developed institutionally than the international system. This means that norms violations are more likely to be detected and, most importantly, there are established mechanisms for dealing with such violations. Although there has been a significant increase over the last decade in the creation of international tribunals, the international court system is still quite weak and structurally limited when compared to its domestic counterparts, which remain the principal mode of holding those who have committed international crimes to account. Indeed, one might argue that legal internalization is, in some cases, superior to operating solely at the international level due to the more mature and better resourced criminal justice system at the domestic level.

Legal internalization, however, is not without its flaws or limitations. First, such internalization or incorporation will be subject to national and possibly sub-national interpretation. Application of international law will further depend on political considerations, including constitutional practices that affect a country's legal institutions. Second, the status of international law in a state's legal system differs from country to country. For example, in the United States international law depends on what Congress makes of it through legislation, although there is a presumption that Congress will not consciously act to violate international law. Despite differences in practice and interpretation, however, the benefits of legal internalization are significant. Incorporation legitimizes international law by implementing and interpreting it as part of domestic law.[22]

The strongest form of incorporation occurs when international law is given particular status in a country's constitution and international laws supersede national laws (e.g., Germany) as opposed to countries in which national and international law are co-equal (e.g., the United States). For internalization to be fully effective as an adaptation to international law's operating inadequacy, it must take place in over 190 different states. This is unlikely, but even if it occurred, there is no assurance that the implementation of such internalizations would always be consistent with the objects and purposes of the international norms. Indeed, the capacity of individual states to internalize international standards varies widely. A reliance on internalization could result in providing international protection only to those individuals living in the most advanced countries with the best developed domestic political processes and institutions.

Even if internalization were to occur universally, the lack of democratic processes and legal mechanisms in many states will prevent international norms from influencing the behavior of government officials. Authoritarian and oligarchic states are characterized by the lack of independent interest groups to press for norm compliance and by state officials who can subvert the legal process in order to avoid being held accountable for norm violations. To deal with states whose actions violate or fail to comply with international law, some national courts will accept claims based on actions that occurred outside the boundaries of that state. Belgium has enacted universal jurisdiction provisions with which it attempted to prosecute former Israeli Prime Minister Ariel Sharon for his actions during the 1982 invasion of Lebanon. Universal jurisdiction was also the basis for the detention of former Chilean President Augusto Pinochet in London in 1998, based on his indictment for human rights violations by a Spanish magistrate, Baltasar Garzon. The British government and courts allowed Pinochet to return to Chile after nearly two years under house arrest, and he was indicted in Chile for a number of crimes, but died before he could stand trial. Foreign plaintiffs have also relied on the 1789 Alien Tort Claims Act, to make claims for actions that did not occur in the United States and did not involve any US citizens.[23]

In the United States, the process of internalization is underway. And while controversy may simmer on the appropriate use of international law at the level of the US Supreme Court, the Chief Justice of the Supreme Court of Texas, Thomas R. Phillips, predicted that in the criminal and family law areas, international cases would increase, particularly for state courts, because those cases have traditionally been the province of state courts in the United States. At the same time, Justice Phillips noted that there may be an overall decline of international cases, as mediation and extra-judicial proceedings are used more frequently, even for family law and trade matters. But he concluded that as long as domestic courts retain a role in handling international matters, state courts in the United States will be among them:[24]

... both state courts and federal courts have, since the inception of the Republic, applied and developed international law. The constitutional framers could have structured the government so that most of this authority would lodge in the federal system, but they declined to do so. Congress could have used the jurisdictional grant in the Constitution to place most international questions in federal court, but it has likewise declined to do so.[25]

Chief Justice Philips therefore concluded that "state courts remain vital partners in the interpretation and application of both formal and customary international law."[26]

Global scripts and collective legitimation: states and international organizations

As domestic institutions figure more prominently in the international arena, IOs are also taking on expanded roles.

These roles come from their ability to frame issues, set agendas, legitimize action, and coordinate behavior through an accepted framework, script, or general principles. If compared to measures of domestic economic or military power, these roles may pale. Yet, they are important because they provide the means for states and other international actors to address new issues or conditions. The availability of forums and frameworks, familiar and accepted processes, and ready access to relevant players and to information are all assets when facing new situations.

Perhaps because IOs are thought to be the agents of their member states, they are often regarded as value-free as a political factor. In fact, we can see that the twentieth century development of IOs rested on certain assumptions that reflect liberal values. IOs were built on a belief:

[I]n the possibility, although not the inevitability, of progress; that modernization processes and interdependence (or, now, globalization) are transforming the character of global politics; that institutions can be established to help manage these changes; that democracy is a principled objective, as well as an issue of peace and security; and that states and IOs have an obligation to protect individuals, promote universal values, and create conditions that encourage political and economic freedom.[27]

Michael Barnett and Raymond Duvall have also usefully reminded us that IOs wield power, and that their power is used to pursue particular values and objectives that may be closer to the interests and outlooks of some states in the world than others. Not surprisingly, therefore, the values of today's IOs bear the heavy imprint of the powers that founded them—the United States, the countries of western Europe and of South and Central America, and the older former British Dominions, members of the Commonwealth such as Australia, Canada, and New Zealand.

IOs have acquired a legitimating function that makes possible actions that would not be accepted if done by a state on its own. Inis Claude explained in an early and classic study of the collective legitimization functions of the United Nations, that:

> [T]he world organization has come to be regarded, and used, as a dispenser of politically significant approval and disapproval of the claims, policies, and actions of states, including, but going far beyond, their claims to status as independent members of the international system.[28]

These actions taken by IOs are political determinations that facilitate the effective exercise of state power. But gaining international legitimacy comes at a price of relinquishing some of a state's historic independence and autonomy. Andrew Hurrell explains:

> The management of globalization necessarily involves the creation of deeply intrusive rules and institutions and debate on how different societies are to be organized domestically. This is a structural change. ... If you want to solve problems in a globalized world, you cannot simply persuade or bully governments into signing treaties, and are therefore inevitably drawn to become involved with how other people organize their own societies.[29]

While IOs were once regarded as apolitical by observers of international relations and value-free also because they were dealing with technical matters like postal and telecommunication standards, we can see examples of such intrusive behavior in the implementation of the structural adjustment requirements of the International Monetary Fund, the World Bank, and the Inter-American Development Bank. A particularly egregious example of where carrying out international requirements exacted a heavy toll on the local population occurred in Bolivia in 2000 when the structural adjustments imposed by the

International Monetary Fund (IMF), World Bank, and Inter-American Development Bank required it to privatize its water services.[30] To the extent decisions about allegedly that technical matters are based on an assumption that outcomes should support market-based economic development and individual freedoms, such IOs are advancing a particular world view.

The League of Nations and the post-First World War world order were built on an assumption that "the creation of more liberal states would help to produce a more stable international order."[31] IOs were initially given authority of their own in specific areas by member states. As these institutions matured, IOs began to strike out in new directions using their own political bases. IOs draw power from expertise because they appear apolitical, but neither domestically nor internationally is specialized knowledge value-free: "Deployment of specialized knowledge is central to the very rational-legal authority which constitutes bureaucracy in the first place since what makes such authority rational is, at least in part, the use of socially recognized relevant knowledge to carry out tasks."[32] See, for example, remarks by the UN's second Secretary-General, Dag Hammarskjöld, on the tenth anniversary of the founding of the UN in 1955: "It has rightly been said that the United Nations is what the Member nations make it. But it may likewise be said that, within the limits set by government action and government cooperation, much depends on what the Secretariat makes it."[33]

Michael Barnett and Martha Finnemore note that knowledge is not neutral and shapes both organizations and their work. This occurs because "the organization will not readily entertain policy options not supported by its expertise."[34]

The functionalist outlook assumed that "[g]iven the pressures to join IGOs, and the economic benefits presumably gained from membership and participation in them, states would be loathe to jeopardize these benefits by escalating interstate disagreements to violent conflicts that would inevitably destroy IGOs."[35] This depended on two assumptions: an increase in democratic participation in domestic political life that increased pressure on governments, "and that mass participation will make economic welfare the dominant concern of governments."[36]

All authorities draw on their ability to identify and solve problems as a source of power and influence, but this is particularly important for IOs because an IO can generate member state support for doing something about a problem and states will then often turn to that IO to come up with an action plan or solution. In a 1955 speech, Hammarskjöld said that the Secretariat "has creative capacity. It can introduce new ideas. It can in proper forms take initiatives. It can put before Member governments new findings which will influence their actions."[37] IOs have drawn criticism when the progress promised by their actions requires states to abandon long-standing practices, creating a situation where "individuals, peoples, and states all find it increasingly difficult to control their own fate."[38]

IOs "shape which activities in the international community [the IO] values and holds in high esteem."[39] This puts states in a position where progress may have to come at the price of the political autonomy that many struggled to win or an end to the traditional practices leaders relied on for power and privilege. The actions of IOs can place domestic governments in politically difficult positions if they are called upon to take unpopular measures like cutting social benefits in order to reduce government spending. The financial and monetary reforms required of states in order to receive assistance from international organizations during the 2010–2011 Greek and Irish financial crises or the earlier Asian financial crisis are examples of measures that created disquiet these states and popular discontent with the world view IOs were promoting.[40]

These concerns have led to increased questions about the accountability, transparency, and democratic deficit of IOs.[41] At an earlier stage in the development of the UN, US leaders raised similar concerns as the United States found itself increasingly in a voting minority in the 1960s. This criticism led, among other things, to the 1982 passage by Congress of a law requiring the US Secretary of State to report "to the Speaker of the House of Representatives and the Chairman of the Committee on Foreign Relations of the Senate a full and complete annual report [on] the voting practices of the governments of [member] countries at the United Nations, and which evaluates the General Assembly and Security Council actions and the responsiveness of those governments to United States policy on issues of special importance to the United States."[42] But while states naturally will assess IOs in connection with how well their interests align with policies espoused by the IOs, state interests today include having access to the forums and frameworks of IOs, not just how frequently they find themselves part of a voting majority.

As IOs have moved into operations, their need to meet standards of accountability and responsibility has also changed. An example is in the area of peacekeeping operations and the conduct of soldiers in the field. Prior to 1999, the UN did not regard those serving in UN peace support operations as bound by international humanitarian law because it maintained that "the UN is unsuited for carrying out most of the obligations in the [Geneva] [C]onventions, because it lacks the administrative organs with which states are endowed."[43] Soldiers serving in UN operations were therefore assumed to be bound to international humanitarian law only through their national systems. This meant that any disciplinary action had to be taken by the national command systems of each troop contributing state. This changed in 1999 with the issuance of the UN Secretary-General's Bulletin on "Observance by United Nations Forces of International Humanitarian Law" that requires the UN to take responsibility for the actions of its troops, including any disciplinary action.[44] Since the UN does not have troops of its own, it must always work in concert with national military authorities to command and to control troops. This means that troops serving in UN operations are subject to a system of blended accountability where they are accountable to their own national authorities as well as to UN authorities.

Applying such standards is complicated in the difficult environment of many peace operations, where a variety of personnel are held accountable to different authorities and answer to different mandates, as may be the case with NGO relief workers, contractors, and the military. Where misconduct occurred in the 1990s, the lack of a functioning judicial system on the ground and the UN's inability to undertake a proper investigation that could be used in a national legal system also hampered efforts to hold individual soldiers accountable.[45]

The revelation in 2004 of sexual exploitation and abuse by peacekeeping personnel in the UN Organization Mission in the Democratic Republic of the Congo (MONUC) led to a major UN effort to ensure accountability for individual actions at the international level. Problems of sexual abuse and exploitation by UN peacekeepers did not start in the Congo, but had also been documented in Bosnia and Herzegovina, Kosovo, Cambodia, and Timor-Leste in the 1990s and in West Africa in 2002.[46] In response to these problems, the UN Secretary-General in 2003 issued a bulletin[47] on special measures for protection from sexual exploitation and sexual abuse that applies to all UN peacekeeping personnel, including civilian police, military observers, members of national contingents, UN volunteers, consultants, and individual contractors. The UN General Assembly approved "Ten Rules: Code of Personal Conduct for Blue Helmets" and "We Are United Nations Peacekeepers," with a recommendation that all UN agreements with troop-contributing states include this code and provide the UN assurance that national authorities will hold their military contingents to that standard and to account, if the standard is not met.[48]

These recommendations are the latest steps taken by the UN to provide accountability for sexual misdeeds that take place while individuals are on UN missions. The General Assembly's 2005 report acknowledges that the UN is ultimately accountable for actions taken by participants in peacekeeping operations. To discharge this responsibility, the UN has instituted procedures to address problems as soon as they arise and to take appropriate measures against those involved, including through international institutions and international law, if national systems are not available to address abuses. These developments are further contributing to a system of blended accountability between international and national authorities in implementing international mandates that involve the use of military forces from contributing nations.[49]

To the extent that governments are moving toward some form of performance-based standard as measured by their publics, IOs have a similar challenge as they consider their future. The balance that needs to be struck is between following the values and interests of the member states whose financial resources support IOs with that of the role of giving voice to the otherwise unrepresented. Hammarskjöld described this in his 1962 Annual Report to the UN General Assembly: "The United Nations has increasingly become the main platform—and the main protector of the interests—of those many nations who feel themselves strong as members of the international family but who are weak in isolation."[50]

The alleged imbalance in the ability of states to maintain their autonomy in the face of the growing power of IOs, however, may not be as great in practice when viewed in terms of implementation or a performance-based evaluation. States continue to play crucial roles in the implementation of international projects and standards. See, for example, the work of Terence Halliday and Bruce Carruthers analyzing the efforts made by Korea, Indonesia, and China to respond to the 1997 global financial crisis and the changes these countries made to meet international structural adjustment requirements in the area of bankruptcy. Halliday and Carruthers identified a pattern of recursivity.[51] This concept, as applied to the globalization of bankruptcy law, can be broken down into three cycles: at the national level through recursive cycles of *lawmaking*, at the global level through iterative cycles of *norm* making, and at the intersection of the two where a variable and uneven balance exists in which national experiences influence global norm making and global norms constrain national lawmaking.[52] As they concluded,"[a]n asymmetry of knowledge and power exists in which global actors can more strongly influence enactment, while national actors more effectively control implementation."[53]

This pattern seems inevitable in any long-term effective change, since change requires buy-in from those most directly affected as well as the capacity to carry out the changes. While forces outside of states can provide some of this, they usually cannot do so over the long-run without local support and cooperation. And while outside forces can change priorities and focus activity, they can also open local rivalries, including professional ones. For example, in the case of the 1997 bankruptcy reforms in South Korea, lawyers and economists disagreed about the proper criteria to apply as a check on judicial discretion and independence which were key international requirements set by the IMF in order for South Korea to receive assistance. At the same time, adopting the global standard may be desirable to facilitate access to global financial markets and to legitimate the consideration and undertaking of reforms.[54]

This same phenomenon exists in other developed countries with a well-established regulatory infrastructure. In fact, Kal Raustiala notes that "long-standing domestic institutions can act as an impediment to the implementation of new global regulations," since the cost of change where established procedures and regulations are in place may be greater.[55] Furthermore, Daniel Drezner finds that:

> The key variable affecting global regulatory outcomes is the distribution of interests among great powers. A great power concert is a necessary and sufficient condition for effective global governance over any transnational issue. Without such a concert, government attempts at regulatory coordination will be incomplete, and non-state attempts will prove to be a poor substitute.[56]

Similar findings were reported by Harold Jacobson and Edith Brown Weiss in their 1998 study of compliance with and implementation of five international environmental treaties in nine countries. Jacobson and Brown Weiss note that "there are reasons to believe that national implementation of and compliance with international accords is not only imperfect but often inadequate, and that such implementation as takes place varies significantly among countries."[57] Jacobson and Brown Weiss looked at several specific factors to determine the level of compliance: international public support and the level of NGO activity; in-country leadership and commitment to the obligation or buy-in; transparency, including the openness of a society; and administrative and bureaucratic capacity.[58]

The study concluded that there were institutional arrangements associated with each of the five treaties studied that could help to encourage implementation and strengthen compliance. Many of these arrangements involve international institutions and thus reinforce the influence and power of international institutions in international relations as they shape the framework within which states work to achieve the treaty's common objectives. Such institutions not only offer regular points of contact between national and international bureaucracies, they provide technical assistance to encourage compliance, maintain ongoing scientific assessments of perceived problems, and build local capacity to comply with environmental accords. Foreshadowing the findings of Halliday and Carruthers, Jacobson and Brown Weiss concluded that "[a] strategy of compliance must look beyond governments to provide incentives and pressures for all relevant actors to comply with the environmental accords. ... Engaging states and all relevant actors from the beginning and keeping them engaged are the essential steps that must be taken to strengthen national compliance with international environmental accords."[59]

Another area where IOs and individual states have established an uneasy partnership is in the authorization to use military force. Although the UN system has not stamped out the unilateral use of force, the UN security system has achieved a status whereby most states would prefer to go to war or use military force with a UN or other multilateral organization mandate than not. This is the case even for the strongest military powers like the United States. UN authorization is a form of legitimacy that is important in winning and maintaining public support for the use of force as well as in building alliances among countries contributing troops and other resources.[60]

A collective security system assumes that states that have committed themselves to use military force in specific situations will do so automatically without further domestic debate. The executive of the state will participate in the international collective decision-making process, but the basic decision to use force will result from the determination by an international institution that a state's action constituted aggression or a threat to the peace, warranting a collective response. This determination has become more difficult when the trigger is not a cross-border invasion, but stems from gross violations of a group's human rights in places like Kosovo and Rwanda that may nevertheless require an international response. Furthermore, the reality is that states will not be able to maintain military readiness or public willingness to respond to crises in any part of the world without establishing some priorities. These priorities will reflect the strategic interests of those states that will carry the burden of these military operations and not just those of the authorizing organizations.

There is an inherent tension between the expectations of collective security and the demand for democratic accountability with respect to decisions to deploy and use military forces. This tension has been evident whenever international institutions have been called upon to take action involving the military forces of member states. Different uses of military forces raise different issues of accountability. When the risks associated with military actions are great, but the immediate interests of the states asked to provide military forces are unclear, and the international legal basis for action is ambiguous, in democratically governed states, the executive will be held accountable domestically for any decision to use military force. Intervention in internal conflicts to avoid humanitarian disasters has been particularly problematic. Following the North Atlantic Treaty Organization's (NATO's) action in the former Yugoslavia to safeguard the Kosovar population, parliamentary inquiries were launched in the United Kingdom and the Netherlands, to ensure that the executive branch could not take their countries to war without consultation with the legislative branch, the international mandate notwithstanding.

Decisions to use military forces remain with national authorities and must follow relevant national procedures. We can, nevertheless, see the influence of international mandates on domestic decision-making. Because the twentieth century succeeded in making the legitimacy and the legality of the use of force subject to international review, each country will build its case for using force with as many tools as possible. In taking any coercive actions, authorization by the UN Security Council is the most desirable.

In the United Kingdom, international mandates not only provide a basis for deploying military forces, but have enabled the executive to bypass parliamentary review of the decisions to deploy those forces. This has extended to preclude domestic judicial review of the executive's actions and demonstrates the complex interplay between international and domestic institutions and standards:

> By consistently arguing that a combination of articles 25 and 103 of the UN Charter which between them provide that binding decisions of the Council prevail over any other inconsistent treaty obligations, the UK government has argued on a number of occasions, before domestic courts and regional courts as well as the International Court [of Justice], that this means that it cannot be held to account for violations of its treaty obligations, including those arising under human rights covenants.[61]

Compliance with international law when carrying out a UN Security Council mandate is more likely to occur when it is compatible with the relevant domestic decision-making process. In the case of the use of military forces, such compliance would include a review of the international legal basis for such use. As part of efforts underway in countries like the United Kingdom to restrain the power of the executive to send troops to war, there are increased moves towards requiring consultation with the legislature prior to any deployment. In the cases where legislative consultation is undertaken, international authorization plays an important role in helping the executive secure backing for a decision to use military forces.[62]

Almost all reviews of executive decisions to use force have been undertaken after the decision to go to war has been implemented. See, for example, the finding of the independent Dutch Commission of Investigation of Decision Making on Iraq chaired by Willibrord Davids, former head of the Dutch Supreme Court, released in January 2010. The report examined UN Security Council actions in the run-up to the 2003 war in Iraq and found that "the military action had no sound mandate under international law."[63] The Commission also found that requirements for consultation between the executive and the legislature were not clear, especially about whether the latter had to approve the possible involvement of the Dutch military in Iraq.[64]

The developing relationship between states and IOs is complex. States, for their part, seek the legitimacy that IOs provide. At the same time, IOs continue to rely on states to carry out decisions or mandates. States seek to enhance their ability to govern with the help of IOs. However, as IOs have matured, they are no longer simply agents of their state masters, but increasingly have their own identity and political constituencies. As such, they can and do strike out on their own without specific member state direction. The more IOs have become operational and the more independent they have become, the more questions of their accountability and responsibility have been raised by member states and the people in those states whose lives are affected by the actions of IOs.

The 1949 International Court of Justice Advisory Opinion on the *Reparation for Injuries Suffered in the Service of the United Nations*, "acknowledged that its members, by entrusting certain functions to it [the United Nations], with the attendant duties and responsibilities, have clothed it with the competence required to enable those functions to be effectively discharged."[65]

As the range of IO activity has grown, so has the functional basis from which IOs derive their legal responsibility and need for accountability. This was the subject of an International Law Association (ILA) study released in 2004 that expanded the earlier understanding of the legal status of IOs as articulated above by the ICJ. IOs can be held accountable where they have some measure of autonomy or *volonté distincte.* The legal capacities of an IO as a subject of international law are limited by the powers and functions it has been entrusted with [by member states], together with any necessary consequential powers deemed incidental to or implied by such express powers in relation to the functions prescribed for the IO. The expansion in the activities of IOs widens the range of substantive primary rules of international law applicable to IOs, but this has not been accompanied by a parallel development in legal theory concerning the international legal responsibility of IOs.[66] The ILA report further acknowledged the work of the International Law Commission in the area of responsibility, including the important distinction that, while IOs may be legally responsible, their responsibility may not necessarily be governed by the same rules as those governing state responsibility.[67]

We see from the above that IOs can create and enforce global scripts—common texts, platforms for action, and guiding principles that seek to change international behavior through coordination and harmonization of state actions, but compliance is not automatic and implementation gaps remain. Yet, IOs increasingly provide the kind of legitimacy that suggests widespread acceptance of their authority to address particular issues. In the case of the UN, authority stems from the UN Charter, and the particular issues in its competence include those of peace, security, and human rights. As the links between poverty, disease, and other social conditions and security have been recognized, states seek the stamp of UN Security Council legitimacy to generate action, but in doing so, they have complicated the dynamics of legitimation and governance:

> The strong must delegate some symbol-making power to others, they must back up the symbols with promises to behave a certain way, and they must trust in the symbols to achieve what force might otherwise have done. This creates an opening for the weaker agents to appropriate, manipulate, and perhaps subvert the meaning of the symbols and alter the path of the society. That legitimacy is the source of the Council's authority may therefore sometimes be a source of power to the rest of the UN membership.[68]

By shifting the legitimacy states once monopolized in certain areas to IOs, states have also shifted to them some of their power and authority, thus changing the power dynamics of international relations. A state's military power today no longer depends only on the numbers of its soldiers and weapons, but also on its ability to secure international legitimacy from an international authority empowered to mandate the use of force.[69] No state can ignore the role of IOs in the governing environment today.

NGOs and global politics

Although the prominence of NGOs in international activity is normally associated with the last 100 years, NGOs have been active for centuries. Jacobson identifies the first NGO as the Rosicrucian Order, an educational fraternal order founded in the seventeenth century.[70] As early as the Congress of Vienna in 1814–15, private actors lobbied governments on issues of the slave trade, religious freedom, and intellectual property. The First Hague Peace Conference in 1899 saw the convening of the first parallel conference of "voluntary associations." Steve Charnovitz identifies the 1923 League Conference on the Convention Relating to the Simplification of Customs Formalities as one of the first intergovernmental conferences that accredited NGO participation—in this case, the International Chamber of Commerce.[71]

NGOs represent a political impulse among people to band together in some organized fashion in order to call attention to their concerns, raise awareness of an issue, and promote change. Non-governmental organization is the term used in Article 71 of the UN Charter and is therefore used throughout the UN system. Article 71 provides that: "The Economic and Social Council may make suitable arrangements for consultation with non-governmental organizations which are concerned with matters within its competence." Charnovitz traces the lineage of the term to 1919 and a book by US diplomat and politician, Dwight Morrow, *The Society of Free States*, that "contrasted 'non-governmental organizations' with organizations composed of sovereign states."[72] If one includes faith-based efforts as part of world-wide NGO activity, then the schools, social services, and medical facilities associated with missionaries would expand the pool and history of NGO programs further.

As a factor in the development of international law, NGO presence was recognized a century ago in the pages of an early *American Journal of International Law*. Elihu Root noted the work of the Institute of International Law, established in Ghent in 1873, the Association for the Reform and Codification of the Law of Nations, also organized in 1873, and the Central Office of International Institutions established in Brussels in 1910. The Central Office convened a congress of representatives from international associations, 134 of which were represented out of some 300 the Central Office had listed. Not unlike today, Root noted that these 300 or so private organizations were often "quite ignorant of each other's existence." He continued:

Most of them are not consciously endeavoring to develop international law, but they are building up customs of private international action. They are establishing precedents, formulating rules for their own guidance, many of them pressing for uniformity of national legislation and many of them urging treaties and conventions for the furtherance of their common purposes.[73]

Charnovitz noted that these organizations moved beyond indirect advocacy, working through states, and took up direct advocacy by "attach[ing] themselves to IOs and being present at international negotiations in order to lobby for manifold causes."[74]

Charnovitz also references the 1908 Nobel Peace Prize lecture given by Fredrik Bajer that "likened the 'organization of peace' to a 'house of three stories,' including on the first story the peace associations; on the second story, the interparliamentary conferences; and on the third story, the intergovernmental Hague Peace conferences."[75] These Hague conferences attracted NGO attention because of the number of high-profile individuals in attendance, the opportunity to reach a large number of influential individuals in one place, and agendas that frequently touched on broad world order issues.[76] The conferences differed from state to state bilateral negotiations. These discussions could more easily be held out of the public eye and with an agenda more focused on specific interests of states. The move towards public participation in international gatherings was given an important push when one of Woodrow Wilson's Fourteen Points called for "open covenants openly arrived at."

NGOs are an attractive political form because they can be flexible and responsive to specific needs. At the same time, their effectiveness at maintaining public support and their existence over the long-term may be limited by the appeal of their message and goal. Their "[i]nfluence must constantly be earned."[77] Nevertheless, NGOs have become an important factor in advancing international law, particularly in areas that relate to the well-being and protection of the individual. They can serve to provide a degree of legitimacy by lending a measure of public support to advance particular issues or sets of norms both at the international level and within domestic politics.[78]

NGO influence stems from the coherence of the NGO message and effectiveness of NGO advocacy, but also comes from alliances with other NGOs, states, and staffs of international organizations. Support for an issue, even from established NGOs, is unlikely to assure success without a broad base of state support. For example, the Landmines Coalition overcame the objections of the United States to ban the use of anti-personnel landmines in 1998, but it did so in the context of a multilateral convention signed and agreed to by 133 states. Nevertheless, the "naming and shaming" that NGOs undertake raised awareness and built political momentum to support strong international action.[79]

One of the challenges in understanding NGOs is that there is no single widely used definition of them. One definition adapted from Article 2 of a resolution adopted by the Institute of International Law[80] in 1951 describes persons or societies "freely created by private initiative, that pursue an interest in matters that cross or transcend national borders and are not profit seeking."[81] Of course, there are domestic NGOs whose work does not cross any border, so they are far from an exclusively international or transnational phenomenon. The League of Nations referred to "unofficial, nonpublic, voluntary, or private organizations."[82] The United Nations Department of Economic and Social Affairs maintains information on nearly 14,000 NGOs.[83]

The nature of NGO members varies widely—to the extent that the organizations have members. Membership of the International Union for the Conservation of Nature consists of states, governmental agencies, and several hundred NGOs.[84] Public officials can form private associations like the Parliamentarians for Global Action[85]; municipal officials are members of United Cities and Local Governments.[86] And, within international organizations created by treaty, NGOs can have designated roles as part of the governance of the organization. The International Labor Organization and the World Tourism Organization both give NGOs specific governance roles.[87] Although NGOs are often thought to be a North American and European phenomenon, UN data show that the rest of the world may be catching up in the number of NGOs. Nearly identical numbers of organizations are now based in Africa (2,361), Asia (2,416), Europe (2,894), and North America (2,618). Latin America is credited with 1,182 organizations and in the UN database, 5,200 NGOs did not have any specific geographic base.[88]

The explosive growth of NGOs has generated a rich literature. Although the character of their long-term influence is not yet fully understood, there is little disagreement that since the founding of the League of Nations, NGOs have become a permanent feature of the international political landscape.[89] The scale of NGO involvement and participation in international meetings and politics differs from that of previous eras.[90] Fewer than 300 NGOs were represented at the 1972 UN Environment Conference in Stockholm. At the Mexico City UN Women's Conference in 1975, 6,000 people attended the NGO forum. In 1985, there were 13,500 individuals registered for the Nairobi UN

Women's Conference. And at the 1995 UN Women's Conference in Beijing, over 300,000 individuals attended.[91] NGOs typically contribute to the development of international law by providing specialized or technical knowledge, information, and expertise. They influence the law-making process by offering draft agreements, preparing position papers, monitoring, filing friend of the court amicus briefs, and even through limited direct participation in international judicial proceedings.[92] For example, the International Union for the Conservation of Nature helped to draft portions of the Convention on the International Trade of Endangered Species (CITES) and the World Heritage Convention.[93] Raustiala concludes that: "[t]he chief result of the plethora of NGOs providing policy information and evaluation is that states can maximize their policy information and research and minimize their resource expenditures devoted to policy development."[94] This closing of the information gap is an important one that enables less wealthy states to participate fully and actively in these international conferences.

NGOs provide perspectives and ideas that may not have emerged from a bureaucratic review process. This is particularly important for developing countries, which often lack not only the resources but the intellectual infrastructure and expertise to allow adequate policy evaluation and creation.[95] In countries with more developed political processes and domestic civil society, government failure to pay due regard to the views of particular NGOs can reap negative consequences in domestic electoral politics.[96]

NGOs have been active in assisting in individual complaints and communications procedures of regional and universal human rights systems. This includes individual communications about human rights violations to the UN Human Rights Commission (predecessor to the UN Human Rights Council), the International Labor Organization, the Inter-American Commission on Human Rights and the European Commission on Human Rights. The African Commission on Human and People's Rights also allows NGOs to submit communications to the Commission, and the European Court of Human Rights allows NGOs to bring a case if the NGO itself claims to be a victim.[97] NGOs have also been active in submitting oral and written communications to a variety of UN bodies, including the Trusteeship Council, the Special Committee on Apartheid, and the Special Committee on the Situation with Regard to the Implementation of the Declaration on the Granting of Independence to Colonial Countries and Peoples. NGOs provide assistance to UN Special Representatives who often lack staff and resources to produce systematic reviews and recommendations about specific human rights issues.

Christine Chinkin explains:

> NGOs have explored their potential through identifying appropriate claims, supporting individual complainants, and submitting their own arguments. By initiating some complaints of human rights violations, NGOs have been able to ensure that cases have been presented in their terms and that States have been forced to respond rather than the other way round. Through the submission of arguments as amici curiae, non-State actors have been able to extend the scope of argumentation before various tribunals. The indeterminate and imprecise language of human rights treaties has allowed innovative claims that have led to interpretations that encompass people and groups previously excluded in ways that were not necessarily envisaged when the treaties were first drafted.[98]

Chinkin, however, cautions that the same open environment that permits NGO participation can be co-opted by the more powerful and privileged NGOs at the expense of the individuals whose causes are advanced by less well-funded NGOs. In the 1996 ICJ Advisory Opinion on the use of nuclear weapons, Judges Gilbert Guillaume and Shigeru Oda expressed concern at what they saw as inappropriate NGO influence over states. Judge Guillaume, for example, noted in a separate opinion that the requests to the Court for an advisory opinion by the UN General Assembly and the World Health Organization (WHO) should have been dismissed as inadmissible because they had "originated in a campaign conducted by associations and groups."[99]

Transnational networks and epistemic communities work with both NGOs and IOs. These are networks of individuals who share particular expertise in an issue area and who coordinate actions and policy advice to promote specific normative goals.[100] The networked approach, in which NGOs group together to follow particular treaty negotiations, can be very effective, as demonstrated by the experience of drafting the Statute of the International Criminal Court. Working through the self-created Coalition for an International Criminal Court (CICC), NGOs at the Rome Conference achieved "an unprecedented level of participation by civil society in a law-making conference."[101] The CICC had a more visible presence at the conference than 800 small separate organizations would have had. As the "go to" place for information and resources, the CICC assisted state delegations that were understaffed or under-resourced to participate more fully in the conference.[102]

The 1984 Torture Convention that was spearheaded by Amnesty International has been described as "one of the most successful initiatives ever undertaken by an NGO."[103] Amnesty did this by calling attention to the problem of torture and by working with government officials, including the police, on the problem. It did so through a variety of techniques—urgent action campaigns, publicity, petitions, focused country campaigns, and "bombardment" of the UN with reports and accounts of torture.[104] The Landmines Convention is another example of a normative agenda pushed by NGOs—in this case a coalition of 1,200 NGOs across 60 countries forming an International Coalition to Ban Landmines (ICBL). Apart from the strong political constituencies represented in the coalition (veterans' groups, health workers, development specialists), the government of Canada pressured its negotiating partners in the Review Conference of the Convention Prohibiting the Use of Certain Weapons to complete a Landmines Convention in 1996. This is an example of an effective partnership between private NGO efforts and those of a government working through a traditional multilateral negotiating forum.

The prominence of women's issues on the international agenda today is another example of strategic NGO-state alliances that resulted from highly effective NGO political lobbying.[105] Chinkin writes:

> Through the experience gained at successive summits, women's NGOs have developed ways of maximizing their impact upon diplomatic negotiations, either directly through the inclusion of their representatives in State delegations or indirectly through consciousness-raising activities, intensive and careful work on draft texts, campaigning at the national, regional, and international levels, and the formation of caucuses and international coalitions.[106]

Women have continued to press awareness of the "gendered dimension" of all issues, including environmental protection, and achieved some recognition of these issues in the UN Secretary-General's 1998 report on "The Question of Integrating the Human Rights of Women throughout the United Nations System."[107]

NGOs may also provide the means for individuals with special interests to be present at forums and discussions to which they would not otherwise have access. At the Rome Conference, for example, the CICC organized meetings between specific NGOs and state delegations on particular issues.[108] The high-quality information that the Coalition provided gained it credibility with states participating in the Rome Conference, increasing its influence and allowing it to reach more and more of the conference's official delegates and staff. The Coalition has remained active since the creation of the International Criminal Court by monitoring the development of national legislation to implement the provisions of the ICC Statute.[109] Through such monitoring, NGOs are increasingly able to provide information about local conditions that would otherwise be unavailable both to international and domestic authorities. The Coalition for the International Criminal Court's self-proclaimed goal is: "Together for Justice: Civil Society in 150 countries advocating for a fair, effective, and independent ICC."[110]

NGO involvement and monitoring can, of course, provide a check as governments report on their compliance with international obligations. But of growing importance is the operational as well as the monitoring role of NGOs. This has particularly been the case since UN officials became targets of hostile state and non-state actors, most notably in Baghdad in 2003. The bombing of the UN's headquarters killed several senior UN officials, including the UN's top envoy in Iraq, Sergio Vieira de Mello, and crippled at least temporarily the development of IO capabilities in conflict zones.[111] NGOs filled the void. Operational NGOs that work closely with the UN to provide humanitarian relief include the International Committee of the Red Cross, CARE, Save the Children, and Catholic Relief.

In the human rights area, domestic authorities may have little incentive to document and report human rights abuses, so that such conditions often come to light only when reported by victims themselves and picked up by NGOs outside the country. See, for example, the case of the Nigerian Civil Liberties Organization founded in 1987 to represent prisoners held without charges or trial for extended periods. Led by two Nigerian lawyers, volunteers and staff of the Civil Liberties Organization visited 56 Nigerian prisons and produced a report, *Behind the Wall*, on Nigerian prison conditions. The report's findings were based on relevant provisions of the Universal Declaration of Human Rights, the International Covenant on Civil and Political Rights, the UN Standard Minimum Rule for the Treatment of Prisoners, and the Body of Principles for the Protection of All Persons under any Form of Detention or Imprisonment. The report received wide publicity in the Nigerian press, caught the attention of the international human rights network, and helped to bring about prison reforms, including the granting of amnesty to 5,300 prisoners.[112]

Major NGOs like Amnesty International rely on the success of their domestic affiliates to help establish their worldwide standing and credibility. In turn, the domestic affiliates capitalize on Amnesty International's and other NGOs' worldwide network to make known the needs of prisoners of conscience.[113] In 1999, the UN General Assembly approved a Declaration on the Right and Responsibility of Individuals,

Groups and Organs of Society to Promote and Protect Universally Recognized Human Rights and Fundamental Freedoms. It provided that "everyone has the right, individually and in association with others, at the national and international levels ... to communicate with non-governmental or intergovernmental organizations."[114] Traditionally, NGOs were involved in consciousness-raising and norm creation. Elimination of the slave trade, worker protection, women's rights, and international peace have all been subjects of private advocacy since the nineteenth century. We can see the agenda of the League of Nations in the plans and manifestos of its antecedents, earlier private organizations. See, for example, the US League to Enforce Peace, founded in 1915 by 100 prominent Americans, including former US President William Howard Taft, Harvard President A. Lawrence Lowell, US Chamber of Commerce President Edward Filene, Alexander Graham Bell, and James Cardinal Gibbons of Baltimore. Convened by Taft, they adopted a resolution that included a recommendation to governments to "jointly use their economic and military force against any one of their number that goes to war or commits acts of hostility against another."[115]

Such private efforts starting in the mid-nineteenth century created the momentum to establish a permanent institution for the settlement of disputes.[116] The American peace movements, in particular, took as their model the role played by the US Supreme Court, "which in the nineteenth century was viewed as an institutional innovation that had bridged the transition from the Articles of Confederation to the Constitution by serving as arbiter between the states."[117] NGO influence can be seen in cases like Germany's acceptance of a permanent court of arbitration. Germany initially opposed the creation of such an institution, but changed its position after advocates pointed to "organized public opinion" in favor of such a court.[118]

More recently, private advocacy has worked to advance the creation of dedicated international institutions focusing on specific areas of international concern, including environmental protection, peace and security, women's rights, and human rights.[119] NGOs' influence has grown as IGOs designate roles for them in the implementation of norms, particularly in the monitoring and implementation of legal instruments.[120] See, for example, Article 45(a) of the Convention on the Rights of the Child that allows the UN Committee on the Rights of the Child to invite "competent bodies to provide expert advice on the implementation of the Convention."[121] The Global Environmental Facility (GEF), created in 1991 with funding from the World Bank, helps to finance projects to protect the environment and to promote sustainable development. It provides for the rotation of five NGOs, as selected by the GEF NGO network, to take part in GEF Council meetings.[122]

This is not an entirely new phenomenon, as the International Committee of the Red Cross has performed such monitoring and review functions in the area of international humanitarian law since 1863.[123] The difference today is that more organizations are performing such functions in a larger number of issue areas that reach more deeply into a state's life. As to the ability of NGOs to wield influence, Peter Willets finds that "the smaller the decision-making body, the lower its public profile, the more technical the subject matter, and the more experienced the NGO representatives, the more likely it becomes that the NGOs can take a full part in the discussions and exercise significant influence."[124] This conclusion further suggests that the working group model is one where NGOs can have the greatest impact in norm development and implementation.

The environmental law area is particularly open to NGO participation. Decades ago, the 1933 International Convention for the Protection of Fauna and Flora and the 1946 International Convention for the Regulation of Whaling included NGO input. The 1987 Montreal Protocol on Substances That Deplete the Ozone Layer, the Framework Convention on Climate Change, the Convention on Biological Diversity, the Convention on International Trade in Endangered Species, and the Basel Convention on the Control of Transboundary Movements of Hazardous Wastes and Their Disposal, all provide opportunities for NGO participation in matters covered by those conventions.[125] At the 2010 Copenhagen Conference of the Parties (COP) of the Kyoto Protocol on Climate Change in 2010, also in addition to the national delegations taking part, there were 15,000 individuals and 2,000 journalists present. The purpose of NGO participation was "to bring the general population's concerns and ideas to the attention of world leaders."[126]

Developments in technology have also "broken governments' monopoly on the collection and management of large amounts of information."[127] Technical experts, such as climatologists with respect to environmental agreements, can offer professional evaluations on meeting treaty standards as well as assist in designing new mechanisms for compliance.[128] The ban on the use of anti-personnel landmines (Ottawa Convention, 1997) provided an example of the new power that individuals linked by technology, organized into a political network, and working in alliance with governments can wield.[129] This influence can be especially strong if the group is allied with states that are important either to the creation or the implementation of a particular norm. We can see a similar phenomenon in the work of the International Whaling Commission (IWC) where private groups such as cetologists, whaling managers, and environmentalists promoted their views and positions with regard to the killing of whales through sympathetic government representatives at the IWC's regularly scheduled annual meetings.[130]

NGOs can supplement government and IGO capacity in helping them keep abreast of specific issue areas and assuring that certain obligations are met. Again, the work of the WHO provides an example. WHO Legal Counsel Gian Luca Burci reports that the "[m]ost relevant information comes to WHO from third parties, be they international agencies, NGOs or even individuals in the countries concerned."[131] WHO then contacts the government of the affected country to seek confirmation. This NGO involvement is important, since even the most well-staffed government agencies may not be able to monitor compliance or respond quickly to changing circumstances.

Despite concerns about NGO accountability and responsibility, scholars acknowledge the positive influence that NGOs and transnational networks have had on contemporary international law in areas such as the well being of individuals, human rights, gender and race equality, environmental protection, sustainable development, indigenous rights, non-violent conflict resolution, participatory democracy, social diversity, and social and economic justice.[132] Effective governance requires sustained attention to these issues and the political and financial mobilization of resources at all levels from local to global. The voluntary, local, and issue-specific character of NGOs and transnational networks makes them indispensable to a system of global governance that links sub-national and local interests and capacities to those at the national and international levels.

By providing this connection, NGOs and transnational networks supplement the human and financial resources of governments, IGOs, and other elements of the legal operating system. NGOs also connect states and IOs to the public in a way that governments historically have not. Finally, NGOs are able to mobilize the public to shape laws and regulations both nationally and internationally. In the United States, administrative law provided the model, based on the premise that "people should have a chance to say what kind of law they want before it is made."[133] Starting with the Administrative Procedures Act of 1946, the United States embarked on a course of rule and law-making with "a wide scope for public participation in the process of creating, monitoring, and enforcing regulatory laws."[134] Another example of such input is the Environmental Impact Statement preparation and review process required by the 1970 US National Environmental Protection Act.[135]

NGO participation in setting international norms and standards can help states clarify and develop their policy positions.[136] The future role of NGOs will depend on the opportunities that states and state institutions (including intergovernmental conferences) provide for direct or parallel activities by NGOs and how able NGOs are to seize these opportunities and to create additional ones. This includes the ability of NGOs to maintain their existence with adequate financial and other resources to continue their work. With nearly 100 years of IO and NGO activity to review, we can see how NGOs have become sophisticated organizations, able to participate effectively in international treaty-making and political activity. From an initial consultative role at state initiative, NGOs have become active partners with states in governance areas like human rights and the environment. The most striking aspect of NGO activity in a system of global governance is that they play roles previously reserved to public governmental authorities. By doing so, they have created an important pathway to connect individuals to the otherwise distant decision and policy-making organs of national governments and of international institutions.

The present acceptance of NGO activism stems from their success in advancing particular normative projects. Voluntary networks have also demonstrated their power to influence states by monitoring state conduct in the treatment of their own citizens. "Principled issue networks" built on the activities of international and regional intergovernmental organizations, and private foundations have emerged, and "are driven primarily by shared values or principled ideas—ideas about what is right and wrong—rather than shared causal ideas or instrumental goals."[137] These networks offer denser interactions and exchanges of information and have proven to be increasingly effective agents for change in state behavior and international standards. Made possible through resources provided by private foundations, spurred on by the commitment of individuals, and held together by new technologies, these transnationally linked organizations have had some notable achievements, particularly in the protection of human rights.

NGOs have become adept at leveraging state power and international institutions to advance specific agendas. The issue cohesion, focus, expertise, resources, and connection to people that NGOs provide have filled a void in an international system that has struggled with building political consensus on bases other than military power. The political energy that NGOs can now muster and generate has changed the power balance in normative development and created a more intense and complex normative and governing environment. NGO networks play a growing role in promoting specific agendas, but are not in a position to govern. The result has been an increase in the obligations and responsibilities of states and international institutions without necessarily an increase in the resources available to discharge these new duties. NGOs have connected individuals to the bases of global power, but have only begun to facilitate the creation of resources to operationalize their normative achievements.

Summing up

States no longer govern alone in the global environment; they are assisted by IOs and NGOs in discharging their responsibilities. In fact, the global governing environment is one where major actors work together to leverage their capacities by working with other actors— even actors quite different from themselves. In this way, we see an expansion of the idea of mutual empowerment where actors are no longer content simply to replicate themselves, but actively seek partnerships to maintain their viability.

The discussion in this chapter began with the continued reliance on the state to carry out international obligations and to implement the decisions of international institutions. This reliance is inevitable, not only because states remain principally responsible for their populations and territory, but also because they are organized to reach the people they govern and to manage that territory in ways that no other entity can yet match. Since it remains the primary responsibility of states to govern their people and territory, states generally can call on greater resources to carry out these functions. Despite their increased cross-border needs, states are far from passive partners when working with IOs or other partners. Without sound national governments and institutions, IOs could do little to meet their goals and objectives.

IOs, at the same time, are finding that increased operations change the character of their institutions and raise issues of accountability, responsibility, and liability once only applied to states. In the decades since their founding, IOs have become increasingly active in areas where some states have been unable to govern or to manage a situation. And finally, NGOs have become global actors because, like IOs, they fill a gap—a political and information gap. Through NGOs, individuals engage international issues and participate in international activity without going through their own states. The expertise and focus of NGOs have allowed both states and IOs to tackle new issues with minimal start-up costs by providing information that states and IOs needed without drawing on their resources.

The global political and governing environment is therefore one that involves multiple levels of governing institutions and officials. It is further an environment characterized by issues that do not fit neatly into the classic categories of international activity. For example, the UN Charter separated security issues from those of human rights. Yet, seven decades later, the UN cannot escape dealing with concepts like human security and the responsibility to protect that put individuals and human rights at the center of international security discussions and decisions.

This chapter provided an indication of how states, IOs, and NGOs work together to enhance their own roles as well as to support and to complement each other. In this complex governing environment, each actor can draw from an expanded number of resources in order to carry out its own responsibilities while simultaneously creating a more orderly system that draws on the strengths of each major group of actors: the resources and settled order of the state; the focal point for discussion and norm creation that IOs provide; the legitimacy that can come from their mandates; and the flexibility, expertise, and direct link to people that typify NGOs. The state is important in the shaping and implementation of international obligations; the IO is important to provide legitimacy and a generally accessible and broad-based forum for debate and consultation; and the NGO can bring international activity in direct contact with people and provide them a voice, shaping the future normative and legal order.

This symbiotic relationship is creating a pattern of behavior that is widely accepted and practiced by all political actors on the international stage. In the future, these actors will increasingly find effective modes of participation and voice in the expanded global political and juridical space.

5 International law in the global environment[1]

- **Soft law and the dynamics of legal development**
- **Standards, codes, and global administrative law**
- **Summing up**

On the eve of the new millennium, United Nations (UN) Secretary-General Kofi Annan wrote in *We the Peoples: The Role of the United Nations in the 21st Century*, that:

> ... while the post-war multilateral system made it possible for the new globalization to emerge and flourish, globalization, in turn, has progressively rendered its designs antiquated. Simply put, our post-war institutions were built for an inter-national world, but we now live in a *global* world.[2]

The actors and the relationships that provided the basis for governance for nearly 400 years are changing. States no longer function alone as the only authoritative actors in the international sphere. International organizations (IOs), non-state actors—including private enterprises, non-governmental organizations, and individuals have joined states as part of the governance landscape. In doing so, they have changed the relationships that historically undergirded the making and implementation of international law.

Diplomacy is a routine part of a state's activities and includes negotiation and treaty-making. We have forgotten the extraordinary character of such interstate interaction in ancient times when an envoy was sent into hostile or foreign territory only under the most exceptional of circumstances.[3] As part of modern diplomacy, multilateral treaty-making is an even newer phenomenon. As Douglas Johnston writes: "Before the outbreak of World War I ... the shape and scale of future multilateral diplomacy were barely discernible in the first treaties concerned with the protection of plant and wildlife and disease control, or even in the turn-of-the-century consolidation of the law of war and related areas of international law."[4]

Historically, international law functioned between states. As such, it reflected the interests and values of the states involved. Obligations were undertaken only through an expression of state consent. Enforcement of the obligations, if necessary, was based on self-help, with reciprocity serving as both carrot and stick. Where disputes occurred, they might be referred for resolution to a fellow sovereign or other mutually acceptable third party like the Pope. Failure of a state to perform could trigger some form of retaliation on the part of the allegedly injured state, if it had the capability to do so. As international society and international life have become more complicated, international law is also more complex. Its present scope reflects the reality that states' responsibilities are now more extensive than they were even in the middle of the twentieth century.

Today, states are expected to provide for their people, safeguard their environment, and generally enhance well-being through productive interactions within their own societies and transnationally across borders. As governments have become involved in more aspects of life and responsible for more tasks, the apparatus of government has grown, with an increasing number of cabinet-level ministries and offices reflecting new tasks that citizens expect them to accomplish. Governments have also developed a variety of legal forms to carry out their responsibilities. These include regulation, administrative law, standards, impact statements, and best practices. Note, for example, the growth of the *Federal Register*, the official journal of the US government. Started in 1936, the *Federal Register* took 1,500 pages to cover its first six months. In 2004, it published 75,675 pages, and in 2008, 80,700 pages.[5] Note also the creation of the Environmental Protection Agency in the United States in 1970—at the time it was the only national level office in the world dedicated to coordinating the complex issues related to protecting the environment. Today, there are more than 100 governmental agencies charged with national development and oversight of environmental policy.[6]

The nature of the issues and the variety of people and institutions that are now affected by and crucial to its effective functioning have profoundly changed international law. It is now a dense system of legal interactions with connections to national and sub-national institutions, IOs, non-state actors, and individuals. This system now functions in forms and ways that would have been unimaginable even several decades ago. International law's ability to adapt and to change is widely celebrated as an indication of its importance and vibrancy. Yet, its many forms and modes of operation have raised questions about its overall coherence and ability to function as a unified system of law. One way to evaluate international law's efficacy and performance in this new environment is to understand its functions. Saskia Sassen observed that "old capabilities are critical in the constitution of the new order."[7] These capabilities take on new functions within the established order, even as the new practices emerge that will be pillars of the new governing order. Sassen calls this a "process of switching," and suggests that there is a period during which old capabilities perform a mediating function between the old and the new prior to becoming part of a new ordering system.[8] The rich period of international norm-creation and institution-building that began at the dawn of the twentieth century and intensified in the last half of the century provides an opportunity to observe such switching. But, how can we know that switching is taking place in the case of international law? One way is to observe areas where the capacity of international law to meet its normative objectives seems insufficient or inadequate.

We can identify such inadequacies or insufficiencies by locating instances of imbalance between what Paul Diehl and I have called the operating and normative systems of international law.[9] We developed this analytical framework for three reasons:

To understand the capacity of the international legal system to give effect to norms and the conditions that trigger adaptation and give rise to system-wide change;

To recognize the multilevel character of the contemporary international legal system and how practices at different levels of the legal system—international, national, sub-national, and non-state—fill gaps to give norms effect and to produce sustained change in both the operating and normative systems; and

To capture the cumulative effect of system-wide changes that enable the international legal system to meet the new demands and requirements of global governance.

The starting point for the analysis is the view that the international legal system divides into two inter-related sub-system components: the operating and normative systems. The former signifies legal rules that deal with how international law functions, specifically laying out the sources of laws, rights and obligations of actors, jurisdictional delineation, and mechanisms for dispute resolution. The latter subsystem deals with issue-specific prescriptions and prohibitions involving topics such as human rights and the use of force. Over the past century, the breadth of both subsystems has increased dramatically. The number and character of forums for dispute resolution have expanded, even in the private realm; for example, international commercial arbitration has developed to allow for the settlement of investor-state disputes. Most notably, the types of actors and their accompanying rights and obligations have dramatically changed in the last century.

The operating system now includes the recognition of individuals as actors within the international legal system both in human rights and in international investments. Similarly, IOs have become complex norm-generating systems of their own. They began by governing their own internal affairs, such as personnel, and moved to implement state-sanctioned mandates; then they brought attention to particular issue areas and subsequently facilitated the drafting of legal instruments to address those areas.[10] This has led writers such as Jonathan Charney to recognize such forums as the UN General Assembly as having a special role to "advance and formalize the international lawmaking process."[11] The broader application of universal jurisdiction is also consistent with the expansion of the operating system. Similarly, the normative system has deepened and expanded its boundaries. With respect to the latter, international law now covers new areas, such as governance of cyberspace, and includes such related issues as the protection of software licenses. Furthermore, the legal rules in established areas such as human rights and the environment are now more numerous and detailed than only a few decades ago.

The operating and normative systems work together to give us international law, but may develop at different rates. Actors often seek to pursue objectives beyond those provided for in existing norms. The development of human rights law is an example. States initially set out to achieve acknowledgment that human rights, such as those enumerated in international instruments like the International Covenant for Civil and Political Rights, existed and should be protected. States then moved further into authorizing IOs to monitor the behavior of those states accepting these obligations through regular reporting, and the Human Rights Committee was set up to receive and to review these reports.[12] The review function subsequently became an interpretive one that clarified ambiguities in the International Convention on Civil and Political Rights (ICCPR). In addition, for states that accept the provisions of Optional Protocol I to the ICCPR, the Human Rights Committee can receive complaints from individuals in those states alleging a violation of their ICCPR rights. Initially, monitoring and sanctioning of human rights violations were largely left in the hands of states. This gap between the capacity to perform and the normative expectation has been narrowed outside the legal system by the ongoing monitoring work of non-governmental organizations, acting with IO secretariats, and the adoption of national laws that incorporate international standards.

When the operating and normative systems are not aligned, an imbalance occurs. The international legal system then functions suboptimally, but nevertheless functions, even during periods of imbalance when norms are not effectively implemented or monitored and operating system provisions are underused such as in certain adjudicatory forums. Such suboptimal conditions can remain for long periods of time before a permanent change occurs. The imbalance may persist even after operating systems change, as alterations may not be fully effective or adequately extensive. This often leads to adaptations outside the formal legal system to redress the gaps created by the imbalance between the two systems. The international political system and its constituent actors move to make international law more effective by substituting for inadequate or non-existent capacity in the operating system. They do this by creating rules in different forums and venues that serve to promote new international legal norms as in the human rights case noted above.

Finally, we can reverse the causal arrow and examine how the operating system influences change in the normative system. While state influence, power, and interests affect which norms are adopted and their configuration, there are also subtle ways in which the operating system itself affects normative change:

It sets the parameters of acceptability by limiting the scope and direction of normative change, including excluding certain options.

It clarifies credible commitment by enhancing or undermining faith that possible agreements might be observed, thereby affecting the probability that such agreements will be adopted.

It provides flexibility by permitting some maneuvering room—for example through reservations or withdrawal clauses—that increases the likelihood that hesitant states will come to agreement, as well as providing the means for states to indicate the degree to which they are willing to be bound.

It specifies the actors, including the rights, obligations, and identities of players, in the formulation of normative rules that will shape the content of those rules.

It specifies the forums in which the normative rules are drafted, which will affect the content of those rules.

It can directly make law in areas where institutions of the operating system can create normative rules.

It can shape the identities and interests of the actors in a system and ultimately the system itself.

International law is a system that is characterized by stability, but punctuated by infrequent, rapid, and dramatic change. The internal processes of both the operating and normative systems are influenced by external actors and national processes as the systems' borders become increasingly permeable. It is therefore in the realm of international law's system adaptations that we can find elements of a future governing order and see where capacities for the new order are being developed. However, formal acceptance of the new order may require a profound event, historically a major war or world crisis, that is recognized widely by states as altering the assumptions and structure of the prevailing governing order.

Critics who fail to pay attention to the broader context in which international law functions often allege that it is doomed to perform suboptimally. In a *closed* system, all interactions are endogenous and any regulation must come from interactions inside the system. Such systems often have little adaptive ability, at least in the short term, because they cannot draw upon external resources or mechanisms when things go wrong. For example, computer software and platforms without the capacity for data sharing have largely atrophied in favor of more permeable systems. But we know that the international legal system and its component parts are embedded in the broader international relations system. Accordingly, this *open* system is subject to influence from external forces; indeed, the political shocks necessary to systemic change are just one example of how external factors influence international law. Those influences prompt change in both the operating and normative systems. External factors affect the implementation of the normative proscriptions and prescriptions and by doing so, provide the international legal system with added adaptive capacity.

Because the international legal system is not perfectly self-regulating and imbalances between the operating and normative systems occur, various actors may undertake actions that are outside the formal legal operating system in order to fill some of the gaps left by the suboptimal operating arrangements. Before describing the forms of extra-systemic adaptations, it is worth discussing the context within which they occur. Unlike biological systems, which may be inherently adaptive, the international legal system requires some agency to achieve change. Actors outside or inside of the legal operating system must observe the imbalance and have incentives and capacity to redress it. Even those actors (e.g., states) that are central to the international legal system might operate outside its confines when acting to deal with the imbalance of the two systems; the actions occur outside the operating system because the actor has a special reason for going outside that system or the actor has failed to achieve change within the system. A variety of actors can be involved in these extra-systemic changes, ranging from states to international organizations—intergovernmental and non-governmental, private enterprises, and even individuals.

Most often, these actors are those that are willing *and* able to supply the mechanisms needed to ensure norm compliance. A variety of actors may have a strong preference for the norm involved, but not have the capacity to take the action necessary to redress the deficiencies of the operating system. In other cases, actors may have the desire to see norm compliance and the necessary resources, but choose not to provide them for a variety of reasons: efficiency, budget constraints, or other priorities. The ability of actors to effect adaptations is not equal across the different components of the operating system. Outside of the system, there is little that non-state actors can do to affect the rights of parties to make international law or to confer legal personality on international actors; these decisions are endogenous to the international legal system although astute political lobbying and violence (e.g., national liberation movements) have secured influence for non-state actors. Since there is little that can be done external to the operating system to change the *international* subjects of *international* law, change in the normative system emanates from changes to the operating system as well as from extra-systemic adaptations that compensate for deficiencies in the law.

The expanding rights and obligations of actors in national legal systems may reflect an international norm in transition. One can find such an example in the adoption of international human rights standards as part of some national constitutions.[13] This has the effect of giving individuals legal standing in domestic courts to protect rights given to them by international instruments; the state grafts the international obligation onto its national system for implementation. When actors can't change what constitutes international law through internal mechanisms like treaties and custom, they can pursue alternative mechanisms (see discussion of soft law below) that achieve many of the same objectives as international treaties and custom. Indeed, observers like Johnston have concluded that informal agreements exceed the number of formal, legally internally binding agreements possibly by a ratio of 7:2.[14]

In the absence of a world government, international institutions like the UN play important roles in international law-making. The importance of the UN stems from the near universal representation of states in its membership, reasonably open proceedings, and opportunities to participate in debate and decision-making. Debates are recorded in written records that can then be digested and consulted and provide a form of legislative history to support the development of particular international norms. Established by a multilateral treaty—the UN Charter, the UN's authority and methods are the product of state practice and the reflection of state interests and values.

José Alvarez notes that from 1970 through 1997, the number of international treaties more than tripled. He further notes that: "The age of global compacts is not coincidentally the age of IOs."[15] Alvarez concludes that activism by IOs has "changed the landscape of treaty-making" in important ways. It has made possible participation by a much wider array of actors—smaller states, international civil servants, non-governmental organizations, and non-state actors, including the private sector. There are now multiple venues for treaty-making that can determine the scope and content of an agreement. State power is altered in these settings.[16] An example is the third United Nations Conference on the Law of the Sea, initiated by Malta, with its representative, Arvid Pardo, coining the phrase, "common heritage of mankind," that appears in Article 136 of the 1982 United Nations Convention on the Law of the Sea. An equally significant move made in the UN General Assembly by Trinidad and Tobago in 1989 led to efforts in 1990 to establish an International Criminal Court. These efforts culminated in the signing of the Rome Statute of the International Criminal Court in July 1998.[17]

IOs usually provide publicly accessible venues with copious amounts of information available to those interested in initiating a treaty or in participating in the treaty-making process. Alvarez reported that the 1998 Rome Conference that completed the Statute of the International Criminal Court recorded participation from representatives from 160 states, 33 international organizations, over 200 non-governmental organizations, and more than 400 journalists. Contrast this with the 1899 Hague Peace Conference that included 100 delegates from 24 countries with little press access to the delegates, even though journalists were in attendance and there was great public interest in the Conference proceedings.[18] The existence of IOs can lower the costs of undertaking international treaty-making because the mechanisms, structures, and personnel needed to support such efforts are now permanently available through UN organs and those of the UN specialized agencies, as well as regional organizations.[19] In areas like protection of the environment, the number of treaties has raised concerns that "treaty congestion" places strain on national resources to carry out the reporting and monitoring requirements of each treaty, which leads to "operational inefficiency."[20]

The practice of using the infrastructure, staff, and know-how of international organizations to facilitate treaty-making and the number of multilateral treaties that have now been concluded under the auspices of IOs have provided IOs with a stature and possibly even authority that states did not foresee at their founding. As Charney put it, "[international organizations] contribute to the coordination and facilitation of contemporary international relations on the basis of legal principles."[21] They do so by providing an established venue to take decisions that may have legal effect. In doing so, they supplement the traditional modes of international law-making, state practice, and *ad hoc* bilateral and multilateral negotiations, and provide the secondary rules of recognition that international law is said by some to lack.[23]

IOs therefore play an important law-making role even though they generally do not have independent legislative authority. Charney wrote:

> ... the products of multilateral forums substantially advance and formalize the international lawmaking process. They make possible the rapid and unquestionable entry into force of normative rules if the support expressed in the forum is confirmed. Decisions taken at such a forum, support for the generally applicable rule, publication of the proposed rule in written form and notice to the international legal system call for an early response. If the response is affirmative (even if tacit), the rule may enter into law. This process avoids some of the mysteries of customary lawmaking. It also permits broader and more effective participation by all states and other interested groups and allows a tacit consent system to operate legitimately.[23]

Reflecting on the rapid development of the law of the sea, including recognition of the exclusive economic zone, international environmental law, and human rights, we can appreciate the power of such standing multilateral forums as the UN General Assembly. To use the operating and normative system framework, IO organs play a facilitative role that adds to the operating system capacity of international law in the area of law-making.

Soft law and the dynamics of legal development

One of the most widely used, but perhaps least understood, forms of adaptation is "soft law." Part of the confusion stems from the lack of agreement as to what soft law includes and precisely how it relates to hard law, or where hard law leaves off and soft law begins, and vice versa. As Dinah Shelton notes: "Traditional international law clearly distinguished between binding and non-binding instruments, but the distinction may be blurring."[24] She continues:

Treaty mechanisms are including more "soft" obligations, such as undertakings to endeavor to strive to cooperate. Non-binding instruments in turn are incorporating supervisory mechanisms traditionally found in hard law texts. Both types of instrument may have compliance procedures that range from soft to hard. The result seems to be a dynamic interplay between soft and hard obligations similar to that which exists between international and national law. In fact, it is rare to find soft law standing in isolation; instead, it is used most frequently either as a precursor to hard law or as a supplement to a hard law instrument. Soft law instruments often serve to allow treaty parties to authoritatively resolve ambiguities in the text or fill in gaps. This is part of an increasingly complex international system with variations in forms of instruments, means, and standards of measurement that interact intensely and frequently, with the common purpose of regulating behavior within a rule of law framework.[25]

Christine Chinkin points out the wide range of forms in which we find soft law.[26] These include political instruments like the 1945 Yalta Agreement or the 1975 Conference on Security and Cooperation in Europe Final Act. As noted in earlier chapters, the importance of the Helsinki Final Act came from its provisions that enabled non-state actors to function within the Conference on Security and Cooperation in Europe (CSCE) framework. Follow-up activities provided for by framework conventions like Helsinki include monitoring and implementation procedures, exchange of data and information, and further scientific research. This package of a hard agreement combined with soft follow-up obligations was used throughout the 1970s in the Organization for Economic Cooperation and Development (OECD) and by the North Atlantic Treaty Organization's (NATO's) Committee on the Challenges to Modern Society (CCMS) in the areas of science and environment.[27] More recent examples are the 1985 Vienna Convention for the Protection of the Ozone Layer, the 1992 Convention on Climate Change, and the 1992 Convention on Biodiversity.

Statements or practices undertaken to supplement or to correct a treaty are another form of soft law. The 1987 Montreal Protocol to the

1985 Vienna Convention for the Protection of the Ozone Layer provides an example of details for a non-compliance procedure prepared by a working party and adopted by a meeting of the parties to the Protocol in 1992. Resolutions, declarations, codes of conduct, and guidelines of IOs, including the World Bank's operational guidelines, are yet another form of soft law, as are world conference declarations, agendas, programs, and platforms for action.[28] Norm-making also occurs through such initiatives as the MacBride and Sullivan Principles, that are "statements of principles from individuals in a non-governmental capacity, texts prepared by expert groups, the establishment of 'peoples' tribunals, and self-regulating codes of conduct for networks of professional peoples and multinational corporations."[29]

A growing body of empirical work shows that such informal mechanisms do influence state behavior.[30] Of further relevance is work showing that norms have influence if the organizational culture at both the national and international levels supports them. As described by Jeffrey Legro, this approach "focuses on the way that the pattern of assumptions, ideas, and beliefs that prescribes how a group should adapt to its external environment and manage its internal affairs influences calculations and actions."[31] In this formulation, compliance can be achieved regardless of whether the norm is hard or soft as long as there is a culture that encourages adherence to the norm. Legro concluded from his case studies that the "organizational culture perspective matched the outcome [or actual behavior] more consistently than predictions from a norm perspective."[32]

Soft law fills a gap when it provides for both norm creation and implementation when formal agreements are not possible, perhaps because an issue is regarded by some states as a matter of domestic concern. Indeed, the executive can sometimes circumvent a disagreement with the state's legislative or judicial branch through soft international law. For example, entering commodity agreements, including those on the marketing of specific products such as breast milk substitutes, provides a way to monitor and regulate domestic behavior of international concern without resorting to a treaty.[33] Similarly, soft law is a vehicle to link international law to private entities regulated principally by domestic law, such as individuals and transnational corporations. The codes of practice of corporate social responsibility are an example of how corporations doing business across borders adhere to good labor practices and environmental protection by complying with domestic law in their worldwide operations.[34] Finally, as already discussed, soft law can supplement traditional operating system forms like treaties, as in the case of the 1987 Montreal Protocol to the Vienna Convention for the Protection of the Ozone Layer.

Why would actors choose to rely on soft law, given its ambiguity and potential to create multiple legal regimes? Kenneth Abbott and Duncan Snidal identify a number of advantages of soft law. These include lower contracting and negotiating costs, in comparison to the long and detailed process required to produce such legal agreements as those negotiated under the auspices of the World Trade Organization (WTO). There is also the extended period prior to a treaty's entry into force experienced by such major international instruments as the Third United Nations Convention on the Law of the Sea.[35] Soft law entails fewer sovereignty costs, something that states reluctantly bear when signing hard legal agreements.

States adopt soft international law provisions in areas where they have failed to produce hard law.[36] Soft law guidelines may later be the basis for hard law, but in the interim may function much as hard law does, albeit without the same obligations for compliance. A good example of this is preservation of the world's forests through the Forest Stewardship Council (FSC). Formed in 1993 by loggers, foresters, environmentalists, and sociologists, its purpose is to provide an international forum for dialogue on what constitutes a sustainable forest and to set forth principles and standards to guide "forest management towards sustainable outcomes." FSC standards are in use in over 57 countries around the world, including the United States.[37] Such soft law provides states greater flexibility, as they do not risk creating operating system institutions that turn out to be costly and possibly inappropriate, ineffective, or difficult to adapt or eliminate over time.[38] Soft law also allows the executive to avoid problematic domestic political constraints and ratification procedures that could block the adoption of hard law.[39] Soft law institutions and processes can enable states to work on "compliance first" and to develop an appreciation of the costs and benefits of creating formal operating system mechanisms before entering any agreement in the future.[40]

Chinkin observes that soft law is a phenomenon that is here to stay because the number and scope of international issues have outpaced the capabilities of traditional state negotiations. She argues that norm creation must occur "through international organizations, specialized agencies, programmes, and private bodies that do not fit the paradigm of Article 38(1) of the Statute of the ICJ."[41] Xinyuan Dai finds that soft law can have particular influence because of "its potential ability to empower domestic constituents, who directly impact a government's rational self-interests."[42] As Shelton concludes, the contemporary international legal system is "a complex, dynamic web of interrelationships, between hard and soft law, national and international regulation, and various institutions that seek to promote the rule of law."[43]

The present globalized legal environment provides an opportunity for national and international activity to draw on the strongest operating capacity, whether that is national or international. International soft law can draw on hard national institutions to strengthen it, and soft private sector practices might harden by virtue of their incorporation into a hard law international instrument like a treaty. The key is that global actors seek to promote orderly and reliable behavior, and that they look to law and legal institutions to help shape those expectations. This has enriched international law's capacity to address global needs, but the resulting complexity in its normative and institutional structure has not yet been fully appreciated by critics of international law at the national level.

Two examples of where soft law linked to hard law became an important part of governance can be found in the Operational Standards of the World Bank and the Recommendations made by the International Labour Organization (ILO). World Bank Operational Standards are administrative guidelines developed for staff use, but they have taken on a harder legal character as part of the loan and credit agreements that are concluded between the Bank and states. Laurence Boisson de Chazournes explains:

> Operational Standards create normative and procedural expectations for the staff and partners of the Bank and contribute in many ways to forging and developing accepted practices under international law. In addition, their incorporation in loan and credit agreements negotiated between the Bank and the borrowers enables them to become binding under international treaty law. By entering into an agreement with the World Bank, a borrowing state is placed under an obligation to take the measures necessary to comply with its contractual obligations. These obligations may in some cases include references to policy requirements, causing the latter to become part of the contractual terms. This practice progressively has gained acceptance with respect to environmental and social policy requirements.[44]

Founded in 1919, the ILO is organized on a tripartite model in which governments, employers, and union representatives together take part in the International Labour Conference. The organization decided in the late 1990s to move away from its complicated convention-making procedures to adopting recommendations to expedite the promulgation of labor standards and to increase compliance by member states. In 1997, the Director-General of the ILO suggested that ILO Recommendations might have the same effect as an unratified convention.[45]

Whether an ILO convention or recommendation, implementation relies on national legislative or administrative action to turn soft international law—in the case of Recommendations—into something hard. Some ILO standards, like those on maternity protection, have been incorporated into many national constitutions and legislation, so that the international status of a standard as either convention or recommendation is less important than its broad acceptance and recognition throughout the world as reflected in domestic legislation. The ILO tries to assess the level of national compliance through a long-standing reporting and survey mechanism, but there are limits to this method; reporting rates remain low given the administrative burden involved with filling out one of its surveys. It is also hard to verify the data reported.[46]

Reciprocally, domestic legislation influences the development of ILO standards when there are widely accepted existing national standards and practices, as found, for example in the member states of the EU. The ILO will take domestic standards into account when developing its own, and it provides technical assistance to help member states draft legislation based on relevant international conventions and recommendations.[47] This system, however, can only work when governments have adequate institutional capacity to put ILO conventions and recommendations into place.

Soft law is also important in developing normative frameworks to address particular areas of international concern, notably the Guiding Principles on Internal Displacement and the principle of a "Responsibility to Protect." Starting in 1995, the Representative of the UN Secretary-General on Internally Displaced Persons, Dr. Francis Deng, led an effort to develop a normative framework to address the legal status and needs of the internally displaced. A "Compilation and Analysis of Legal Norms"[48] pertaining to internally displaced persons was prepared by the Representative in consultation with legal experts convened by the American Society of International Law and other non-governmental and governmental groups. They concluded that, "while existing law provides substantial coverage for the internally displaced, there are significant areas in which it fails to provide an adequate basis for their protection and assistance."[49] The Representative was asked by the UN Human Rights Commission and the General Assembly to prepare a normative framework that would address those gaps.

Drafted over a two-year period "in a broad-based process that brought together international legal experts from different parts of the world, including representatives of international organizations and research institutions," the Guiding Principles were presented to the Human Rights Commission by Dr. Deng in 1998.[50] According to

Walter Kälin, "although they do not constitute a binding instrument like a treaty, they reflect and are consistent with international human rights law and humanitarian law."[51] The Principles were prepared to "offer guidance to governments" in their work with internally displaced persons. They are based on three basic ideas: 1) although internally displaced persons have departed from their homes, unlike refugees, they have not left their country of origin; 2) internally displaced persons experience a special factual and legal situation and therefore have special needs; and 3) legal provisions which respond to the specific needs of internally displaced persons must be restated in more detail in order to clarify their applicability in situations of internal displacement.[52]

The Guiding Principles have normative momentum because they are based on existing international humanitarian and human rights law. They have been adopted by the UN Human Rights Commission, the UN General Assembly, and regional organizations, including the Organization of American States, the African Union, and the Economic Community of West African States. The Organization on Security and Cooperation in Europe (OSCE) has been most active in using the Guiding Principles. It convened a meeting on internal displacement in 2000, urging member states to use the Principles as a framework for their humanitarian activities.

Many states have accepted the authoritative character of the Guiding Principles and worked to comply with their framework both in practice and in law. Colombia, Burundi, Uganda, the Philippines, and Sri Lanka have all applied the Guiding Principles. The governments of Armenia, Azerbaijan, and Georgia reviewed their domestic legislation and administrative procedures to ensure compliance with them. The cumulative effect of these actions has made the Guiding Principles:

> an important tool that provides sound and authoritative guidance to governments, international agencies, regional organizations, and NGOs. At the same time, more and more displaced populations see them as a document that empowers them when facing the multiple problems affecting them as a consequence of their displacement. Without a doubt, their continued usage will serve to enhance legal and practical protection for internally displaced persons all over the world.[53]

In like manner, an effort was undertaken by the non-governmental International Commission on Intervention and State Sovereignty in 2001. This panel of prominent international representatives acting as individuals examined existing international law to establish a legal basis for international action against genocide, ethnic cleansing, and crimes against humanity. They faced a twofold problem: first, to identify a commonly agreed basis of when a state's prerogative to be left alone gives way to the need to protect individuals subjected to mass crimes; and, second, to compel international action in response to an unfolding or impending crisis.

The Commission had to deal with the dichotomy left by UN Charter Article 2(7) that stipulates: "Nothing contained in the present Charter shall authorize the United Nations to intervene in matters which are essentially within the domestic jurisdiction of any state or shall require the Members to submit such matters to settlement under the present Charter ...," and the desire to address situations where mass violence was threatened or directed against substantial portions of a country's population. A legal concept of humanitarian intervention was rejected as too corrupted by the potential for self-judging use, particularly by the world's strongest military powers. Instead, the Commission identified a "responsibility to protect" in situations "where a population is suffering serious harm, as a result of internal war, insurgency, repression or state failure, and the state in question is unwilling or unable to halt or avert it." In such cases, "it becomes the responsibility of the international community to act in its place and the principle of non-intervention yields to the international responsibility to protect."[54]

The interest of many states and non-governmental organizations in the 1990s to compel action in cases of humanitarian emergencies was pushed aside following the September 2001 terrorist attacks on the United States. The international community shifted its attention to the question of whether the UN security system was adequately equipped to handle the new security threats of the twenty-first century, in response to the insistence of the United States that it had a right to go to war in 2003 to topple the government of Saddam Hussein in Iraq. To address these issues, UN Secretary-General Kofi Annan convened a High-level Panel on Threats, Challenges and Change. The Panel released its report, *A More Secure World: Our Shared Responsibility*, in 2004. The report began by describing the new security environment:

> ... we know all too well that the biggest security threats we face now, and in the decades ahead, go far beyond States waging aggressive war. They extend to poverty, infectious disease and environmental degradation; war and violence within States; the spread and possible use of nuclear, radiological, chemical and biological weapons; terrorism; and transnational organized crime. The threats are from non-State actors as well as States, and to human security as well as to State security.[55]

The report concluded that collective security must be based on the recognition that first, today's threats know no national boundaries, are connected, and must be addressed at the global and regional as well as national levels; second, that no State, no matter how powerful, can by its own efforts alone make itself invulnerable to today's threats; and finally, that it cannot be assumed that every State will always be able, or willing, to meet its *responsibility to protect* its own peoples and not to harm its neighbors.[56]

UN Secretary-General Kofi Annan released a further report of his own in 2005, *In Larger Freedom: Towards Development, Security and Human Rights for All*, that called on governments to implement the responsibility to protect through a range of measures that could include the use of military force as a last resort. At the regional level, the new African Union adopted an earlier expression of the responsibility to protect in its 1999 Constitutive Act in Article 4(h), stating that "it is the right of the Union to intervene in a Member State pursuant to a decision of the Assembly in respect of grave circumstances, namely war crimes, genocide and crimes against humanity."[57] The 2005 World Summit that reformed the UN human rights system included a commitment to the responsibility to protect spearheaded by Argentina, Chile, Guatemala, Mexico, Rwanda, and South Africa. Paragraph 138 of the World Summit Outcome Document stated: "That each individual state has the primary responsibility to protect its populations from genocide, war crimes, crimes against humanity and ethnic cleansing. And it also has a responsibility for prevention of these crimes."[58]

The Security Council added authority to the concept in 2006 when it unanimously passed United Nations Security Council (UNSC) Resolution 1674 on the Protection of Civilians in Armed Conflict, including a reference to the responsibility to protect. Secretary-General Ban Ki-moon issued a report in January 2009 on implementing the responsibility to protect that examined ways to help states exercise their responsibility and build capacities to protect their populations. The report started with the three-pillar strategy adopted by the 2005 World Summit: the protection responsibilities of the State; the need for international assistance and capacity-building; and timely and decisive response by the international community.[59] The Secretary-General had also appointed in 2008 a Special Advisor, Edward Luck, to further the conceptual development and consensus-building through broad consultation among UN members responsibility to protect populations from genocide, ethnic cleansing, war crimes and crimes against humanity.[60]

The basis in existing law of the responsibility to protect was not as deep as that underlying the Guiding Principles on Internal Displacement.

Implementing the responsibility to protect requires a wider range of possible actions, from diplomatic initiatives through the use of major combat operations by intervening states. The responsibility to protect may "be seen less as a normative vocabulary that can catalyze action, and more as a policy agenda in need of implementation."[61] Comparing the responsibility to protect and the Guiding Principles on Internal Displacement, we can see that two similar efforts to address gaps in existing international law developed in quite different ways. Reasons for this include:

- specificity of the initial concern—quite specific in the case of internal displacement, much broader in the case of the responsibility to protect;
- the availability of an institutional infrastructure to carry out the Guiding Principles—though not perfect, in the case of internal displacement, there was an assumed reliance on national governments that would be assisted by international public and private aid organizations;
- the range of responses was larger, in the case of the responsibility to protect, but the capacity of states and international institutions, including regional organizations to respond was smaller.

The gap between needs and available resources to respond to intervene in the responsibility to protect and humanitarian emergencies remains large, with states with the greatest capacity increasingly reluctant to contribute in the face of competing demands—including their own domestic needs; and the continued absence of automatic and broad support and capacity to drive collective action when humanitarian crises are identified.

Despite their uneven effects on resolving the problems they set out to address, both the Guiding Principles on Internal Displacement and the responsibility to protect provide a global framework for states and other actors to follow when dealing with two major issues of international concern. The two frameworks may be authoritative, but a combination of legal, political, social, and other factors will determine how quickly and fully states implement them. Uncertainty will continue until a sufficiently shocking event occurs to clarify state behavior and usher in broader systemic change. The value of having such principles in place is that they contribute to the development of a future norm of international law and to the capacity of the governance system by identifying inadequacies in the present system and changes that need to be made.

As we have seen, soft law may contribute to governance by attaching itself to domestic or international hard law or institutions. It may also serve as a bellwether for needed change and provide some indication of what the normative change will look like prior to its adoption as law. Soft law decreases the time and transaction costs to adopt a hard law obligation once the political will is generated to make a major change. And, soft law may harden when referenced in judicial or quasi-judicial proceedings.

Moreover, if we see the value of international law in providing a global operating and normative framework, this role may be even more significant for soft international law. Abbott and Snidal conclude that: "Soft law if valuable on its own, is not just a stepping-stone to hard law. Soft law provides a basis for efficient international 'contracts,' and it helps create normative 'covenants' and discourses that can reshape international politics."[62] Shelton even contends that "stronger monitoring mechanisms exist in soft law precisely because it is non-binding and states are therefore more willing to accept the scrutiny they would reject in a binding text."[63]

Lesley Wexler has demonstrated the importance of the consciousness-raising that the Landmines Coalition did in preparing the political ground for the treaty to ban landmines. This was the classic non-governmental organization role of providing information and expertise; however, when linked with the hard law-making process, the "shaming" that the Coalition undertook brought about state compliance—even for states like the United States that refused to sign the Ottawa Convention to Ban Anti-Personnel Landmines. The US did so through:

(1) increased domestic funding for global demining efforts; (2) promotion of international landmine regulations; (3) adherence to a unilateral moratorium on landmine use; and (4) research on feasible replacement weapons.[64]

Standards, codes, and global administrative law

Consistent with the need states feel to deal with increased cross-border activity and to enhance the well-being of their own people, IOs—and particularly the UN specialized agencies—have sought to regulate and to standardize a wide range of social and economic practices. As José Alvarez concludes in this area, the impact of IOs "on law is multifaceted and 'de-formalized.'"[65] Although not formal norms of international law, with such actions of international organizations are important because of their ability to influence state behavior. As Frederic Kirgis has written: "[international organizations] have the capacity to channel the conduct of members in ways that are designed to advance, or at least not impede, an organization's attempts to achieve its stated goals. Regulations and standards are promulgated or established by bodies recognized as legitimate by the members, and as a result, they command the respect, even if not always the strict obedience, of decision-makers in national governments."[66]

The influence of these actions by IOs has increased as the state functions in a more managerial role, serving as clearinghouse to field the needs and responses created by global interdependence and to manage its own sovereign functions to meet the needs of its own people. "Socialization" occurs when states start to conform to certain behaviors over time by virtue of long-standing membership and ongoing interaction with other states in IOs.[67] The normative output of IOs comes in a variety of forms such as draft treaties, including provisional application of signed treaties before they formally enter into force, treaty-implementing standards, formal pronouncements, and informal consultations.[68] These are accepted by states as ways to respond quickly to emerging needs with relatively little start-up cost, since an institution is already in place to promulgate a regulation or standard and monitor its implementation.

Organs of institutions like the World Health Organization and the International Maritime Organization may be delegated authority by a standalone treaty to make determinations or to oversee updating the treaty's original provisions. The Convention on Psychotropic Substances (1971) allows the UN Commission on Narcotic Drugs to add or to remove substances from the Convention's schedules of controlled substances. The UN Commission in turn relies on World Health Organization expertise to determine whether a substance might be abused.[69]

Another example of international organizations' indirect standard and obligation setting is the *Codex Alimentarius* formulated by the joint *Codex Alimentarius* Commission of the Food and Agriculture Organization (FAO) and World Health Organization (WHO) to address food safety. Although its legal status is soft, since states can withdraw on notice, the *Codex* has taken on new importance because of reference to it in the WTO's Agreement on the Application of Sanitary and Phytosanitary Measures (SPS Agreement). This recognizes government health standards that are based on the *Codex Alimentarius*, even though the WTO prohibits any government actions to protect health that "arbitrarily and unjustifiably" discriminate against products from WTO member countries.

A similar generation of lateral obligation generation takes place when parties agree to an international convention that includes standards established by another convention or IO. The parties are thereby bound to those standards even if they are not members of the organization or parties to the referenced convention. We have an example of this in the UN Convention on the Law of the Sea, Annex VIII, Article 2, on Special Arbitration, which lists the International Maritime Organization (IMO) among specialized agencies that can provide experts in case of disputes regarding maritime safety or pollution control.[70] Should states accept IMO experts as arbitrators under this provision of the UN Law of the Sea Convention, they effectively accept IMO standards, even if they had not separately agreed to the relevant IMO treaties and standards.

In a review of codes and standards generated by the International Civil Aviation Organization (ICAO) and the International Atomic Energy Agency (IAEA), Frederic Kirgis concluded that they can have an effect "virtually, equal to, that of treaty obligations" because of their broad acceptance by those affected and their less controversial character.[71] In the case of ICAO standards and recommendations, members agree to "collaborate in securing the highest practical degree of uniformity" in complying with them and to notify ICAO if they find it impossible to do so. Given the stakes of safety and efficiency in commercial aviation and participation in formulating recommendations by all key players, including airline pilots and air traffic controllers, this soft form of obligation seems to have worked. IAEA recommendations work because they:

> enable a complex regulatory system to function smoothly without mandatory reliance on a cumbersome treaty-making or amending process while still allowing the option of (re)negotiating a treaty when consensus is available. Recommendations do not stand alone, independently of treaty obligations, and only rarely serve as precursors of binding obligations; instead, they follow treaty agreements generally and, because of this underpinning of "hard law", they are widely accepted and implemented.[72]

Both ICAO and IAEA exhibit high degrees of prescriptive legitimacy, since the interests of those actors being regulated converge substantially with those of the regulator.

Global administrative law is a term and concept coined by Benedict Kingsbury and his colleagues to bring together the myriad forms of law-making and law that now exist in the "global administrative space." As we have seen, "the administration of global governance is highly decentralized and not very systematic."[73] What ties together all the disparate elements of governance is the need for "transparency, consultation, participation, reasoned decisions and review mechanisms to promote accountability."[74] As Kingsbury points out, the demands for these qualities have a "common normative character, specifically an administrative law character."[75] Kingsbury draws the elements of global administrative law together "as an increasing commitment to publicness."[76] This is an important concept to bridge the gap when private actors like corporations or non-governmental organizations act in a public space, setting public standards or otherwise acting in some semi-official capacity. If a privately set standard meets the criteria of transparency and consultation, then it has acquired the character of global administrative law as it functions in the global arena. Its recognition therefore helps to move practice and compliance beyond the functional level to a legal one. As such, it may be easier for these administrative practices and standards to plug into legal infrastructure like courts and regulatory agencies at the national, transnational, and international levels.[77]

Global administrative law can therefore be understood as "the legal mechanisms, principles and practices, along with supporting social understandings, that promote or otherwise affect the accountability of global administrative bodies, in particular by ensuring that these bodies meet adequate standards of review of the rules and decisions these bodies make."[78] As such, the important insight that global administrative law provides is that forms that regulate global behavior can be put to a test to see if they might be considered part of the global governing environment. It also provides a statement of the values and preferences that we now seem to expect in legal and other obligations. The specific source, initiator, location of implementation, and form of the law become less important than the contextual, a framework within which to understand the normative underpinnings of the present global environment.

These proto-legal or non-legal mechanisms work because they meet desired normative and functional objectives. They meet these objectives through broad compliance and by providing acceptable means to settle differences or disputes. They may provide access to national, transnational, or international legal infrastructure like courts. They work because they provide opportunities for input by key players and are evaluated on a functional basis. This is particularly effective in areas where it is possible to measure whether a goal has been met. For example, does air traffic control provide for safer flying? Do these mechanisms allow for public commentary and review? Standards, codes, and global administrative law work because they can be readily known, tested, and changed. They are an important way to create governing capacity.

Summing up

We have seen in the preceding chapters how international relations in the twenty-first century now comprises an increased number of actors, institutions, and processes. The interactions and connections of these elements have created expanded political and juridical spaces at the international level. This includes expanded functions for existing institutions and procedures; new institutions and procedures; and old institutions and procedures adapted for new tasks. The range of institutional innovation and dynamism has been impressive at both the national and international levels. As part of the governing infrastructure and the outcome of these intensified interactions, law—both national and international—has also changed. In international law, we see the prominence of international institutions as law-makers. At the same time, we see a renewed reliance by international institutions on national courts and legislative processes to implement international obligations and standards. Yet, we also see how national practices and standards are now shaping international norms. Although this has created a rich international legal environment, the numbers and types of legal instruments and forums for resolution of disputes are creating concerns for the ongoing cohesion of international law as a legal system.

Johnston noted in 1997 that there were 82,000 publicized international agreements and possibly up to 100,000 official interstate agreements negotiated since the beginning of diplomatic history.[79] He further provided a list of "atypical" instruments that included: multilateral framework and other general declaratory instruments in treaty form; soft law in non-treaty form—codes of conduct, guidelines, statements of principles; memoranda of understanding and other informal implementation instruments; political accords; non-governmental organization implementation functions; UN General Assembly resolutions of law-making quality; UNSC resolutions; resolutions of other IOs with law-making capacity; and declarations of intergovernmental conferences.[80] To this list we might now add private standards and principles and practices agreed upon by states, IOs, non-governmental organizations, and other non-state actors.

All of these have become factors in global governance because they are part of the social structure that shapes the identity and interests of units within the international system today. Even if they lack the force of law or are not ripe for enforcement, recognition of their existence and attention to their requirements can create expectations and standards that move states towards incorporating these provisions in national law or general practice. They may also help to draw system-wide attention to problems or challenges for governance, even if there is no specific suggestion for a normative solution. And to the extent that no action is taken in the international sphere on the basis of these frameworks and standards, this may indicate the need for new capacities to carry out new responsibilities.

One way to determine international law's capacity to govern is to consider whether it has the basic tools to achieve its stated objectives. One way to do this is to organize international law's functions into two subsystems—an operating and a normative one. We are then better able to discern areas where international law is unable to meet its normative objectives. In such cases, international law continues to function in other areas, and the lack of effectiveness in enforcing a norm in no way detracts from the validity of the international norm *per se*. International law may not be able to give full effect to these norms without some system-wide change, but in the meantime, adaptations may be adopted to overcome the lack of such system-wide capacity. Apart from providing a means to overcome a specific incapacity, the adaptation itself may become so effective and widely recognized that it becomes part of international law's operating system when an opportunity for such formal change occurs.

One important way of coping with system-wide incapacity is to develop soft law or non-binding law. The term covers many forms of practices, regulation, and standards, which generally lack some attribute to make them formal international legal obligations. Although many soft law practices do become hard law obligations, social science studies have observed that soft law may be valuable in reshaping international politics. Using the language of the operating and normative systems, soft law may be able to reshape aspects of the operating system in a way to make it more responsive to the normative needs of international law. Soft law therefore relates to hard law as a precursor, supplement, or complement. It functions interactively with hard law and hard institutions at the international and national levels and fills in where there are normative or procedural gaps. As a body of practices that developed to fill hard law gaps, soft law practices are a valuable pool of experience on which to draw on if and when more permanent and formal changes are sought and from which to identify customary international law.

A more recent view of transnational practices is the emergence of a concept of global administrative law that emphasizes openness and participation in law-making and implementation and identifies "publicness" as a necessary factor in legitimate law-making today. The concept provides an example of new standards, expectations, and responsibility with regard to regulating behavior at the global level. In this view, it does not matter whether a legal obligation stems from the public or the private realm. If it aspires to have global effect, it should meet the new standards of global governance of which public accountability and responsibility are important.

The myriad forms of organizing behavior have made necessary an effort to understand norms "independent of the effects attributed to them."[81] In Legro's view, this can be achieved through better understanding of the organizational culture that affects the behavior of the unit in question. Legro, however, also rightly cautions that in seeking to identify organizational culture, we need to be careful not to exclude the domestic since it may be the domestic culture that is key to understanding a state's behavior with regard to particular norms. The research questions that he poses capture the issues that the global environment presents to the international legal system:

> How should we conceptualize the relative strength of different normative (and other) frameworks? When is it that unit-level ideologies and beliefs will supersede systemic ones? How do the two interact? Can synthetic cross-level ideational models be constructed?[82]

The answers to these questions could well signal a change in the understanding we bring to international law, where the domestic analogies of enforceable norms give way to concepts of coordination, facilitation, and standard-setting. Although this may sound like a softening of the normative value of international law, in fact, it can also provide a theoretical strengthening of the role that only international law can play—that of providing an authoritative pathway for various regulatory activities and practices to achieve system-wide acceptance and recognition.

6 Taking stock

Global governance in a post-Westphalian order

- Governance in a Westphalian order
- The twentieth-century international interlude
- Thickening forms of governance in the post-Westphalian order
- Prospects for research and global governance

Interactions and connections among the institutions and structures of global order, including law, have been the focus of this study. The thesis is that these interactions came about in response to specific needs and together have generated new capacities that in turn have changed the governance environment by producing new governing institutions, structures, partnerships, and relationships. They have empowered new actors and recognized new values that form the basis for governance today. They have also created new responsibilities and obligations. The cumulative effects of these interactions have generated some of the forces that produced globalization.

We can observe that governance today occurs in a much more open and participatory environment than was the case only a few decades ago in the mid-twentieth century. This move towards greater openness and participation is occurring at all levels of government, within international institutions and throughout the private sector in corporate and other non-state entities. There are three key developments: 1) the building of international institutions and structures that may constrain certain state behaviors in the short run, but are likely to contribute to a more stable and secure order in the long run; 2) the reliance on reporting and monitoring procedures as well as follow-up conferences in order to make states and other responsible parties review compliance with their obligations and gauge progress toward stated objectives; and 3) the culture of civil society, mass media, and early warning that is becoming more and more effective at putting the spotlight on emerging areas of potential international concern.

In matters of governance, three related elements are central: power, authority, and legitimacy. Order and control as features of governance can be achieved without all three elements present, but will be constrained if they are not. The questions that we face today with regard to governance relate to the presence and measure of these elements in practices we see in the globalized environment. The challenge is to assess and recognize the enduring elements of governance even if they may occur in different places with different actors under different circumstances at different times. This is the complex situation that requires a strong interdisciplinary framework to test and to understand the behaviors that we observe. Although describing organizational behavior, Andrew van de Ven and Marshall Scott Poole provide a succinct statement of the governance challenges of today: "The spacial dispersion of units and actors means that different influences may be acting simultaneously on different parts of the organization, each imparting its own particular momentum to the developmental process."[1] The policy and scholarly communities need to capture these individual developments and to understand what they may mean for the whole in global governance.

The move within international law and international relations to understand these interactions in a systematic, well-conceived, and theorized way has benefited from collaboration between the two fields. Groundwork for such collaboration was laid in the 1970s by those studying international cooperation—Robert Keohane, Joseph Nye, Leon Gordenker, Harold Jacobson, and Ernst Haas. International relations (IR) theorists like Hedley Bull made important contributions. Among legal scholars, members of the New Haven School, including Michael Reisman, Rosalyn Higgins, and Oscar Schachter, tried to understand the policy as well as the normative implications of various international undertakings. Edith Brown Weiss and Abram and Antonia Handler Chayes were among prominent legal scholars both promoting and pursuing interdisciplinary research to understand why states complied with international law.

Many of the scholars who were trained by those named above have been at the forefront of the increasingly rich collaboration now taking place between international relations and international legal scholars. Prominent international law (IL) and IR names associated with this phase are Michael Doyle, José Alvarez, Kenneth Abbott and Duncan Snidal, Anne-Marie Slaughter, MJ Peterson, Kathryn Sikkink and Margaret Keck, Martha Finnemore, Helen Milner, Michael Barnett, Alexander Wendt, Andrew Hurrell, Beth Simmons, Kal Raustiala, Ian Hurd, James Morrow, Laurence Helfer, Richard Steinberg, and Jonathan

Zasloff.[2] The founding of a *Journal of International Law and International Relations* based at the University of Toronto is another sign of the maturing of the collaboration between scholars of IL and IR. The Advisory Board for this journal includes many of those whose work has been referenced throughout this book.[3] The move towards scholars publishing in both IL and IR literature helps to direct readers to the relevant insights in both disciplines and is a promising development.[4]

Governance in a Westphalian order

This book has been about the changes that took place in governance as the international system moved through an international institutional interlude from a Westphalian to a post-Westphalian order. The interlude affected all levels of governance, whether international, national, subnational, public, or private. The demands and effects of globalization have put a spotlight on the institutions and processes of international governance. The book has proceeded from the assumption that understanding the present needs and capacities to govern requires understanding the issues and institutions—including law and regulation—that have helped to shape governance today. It further assumes that these sources and acts of governance continue to shape the new governing order that is now emerging. The book has focused on scholarly developments in IL and IR and particularly where the two fields of inquiry have converged to explain changes in governance and the shape of things to come.

The governance story told in this book starts with the formation of the state system that emerged from the Treaty of Westphalia in 1648. This was a political system of co-equals with no authority higher than that represented by the individual sovereign states. Its chief characteristic was expressed succinctly in the 1927 Permanent Court of International Justice Case of the *S.S. Lotus*: "states cannot be bound without their consent."[5] This voluntarist outcome of the Thirty Years' War was Europe's answer to the challenge Protestant monarchs and princes posed to the universal authority of the Catholic Church and its political agents. The Westphalian system emerged in a world where other systems were in existence and in operation. As the Christian rivals fought in Europe, China was on the eve of a shift in dynasties from the native Chinese Ming dynasty (1368–1644) to the non-Han Manchu Qing dynasty that would rule China for nearly 300 years from 1644 to 1912.[6]

China's tribute system was a stylized and formal system that revolved around recognition of the Emperor of China as the senior political figure in a regional world order where China was the dominant force.

The regular tribute missions that had the purpose of renewing the ties between China and the tribute states not only recognized China's privileged position in the region, but also provided recognition to those paying tribute as the legitimate authorities in those countries.[7] As we now know, the tribute system was more than political ritual. It was also a system of regional trade and exchange that facilitated contact among the diverse kingdoms, cultures, and political entities in the region reaching from Korea in the north to South Asia, touching on the Indian peninsula.

The Turkish Ottoman Empire was another major power with an empire that spanned three continents (southeastern Europe, western Asia, and north Africa) at its greatest extent. This empire with its system of provinces and vassal states lasted from 1299 to 1923.[8] In Africa, traditional tribal governance remains a factor in shaping the contemporary political order in countries like South Africa.

We focus on the Westphalian system because over time, the state system that Westphalia established became the accepted global standard for the conduct of international relations. It was a mutually re-enforcing system that rejected any alternative form of governance like the Chinese tribute system. To take this a step further, not only was any alternative order rejected, but any effort to assert one against the Westphalian standard provided grounds for military intervention and subjugation. The possession of superior technology made possible the successful wresting by the European powers of trade privileges, rights to mineral and resource exploration, and development, and eventually territorial control in the Americas, Asia, and Africa. Yet, the state form was not an easy fit for all—not even for central Europe that was the cradle of this system. The attempt to resolve the political, economic, and cultural issues raised by creating states has been the cause of many wars, mass brutality, and even genocide. Nevertheless, the state is the form of territorially-based political control that endures and it remains an important governance actor for the foreseeable future.

Still, we know that the independence and sovereignty that come with statehood are neither viewed nor exercised in the same way today as they were even a century ago. How a state will act is very much shaped by how it acquired sovereignty and independence. See, for example, Antony Anghie's observation that the exercise of sovereignty and independence of states emerging from the territories colonized by Europeans in the seventeenth, eighteenth, and nineteenth centuries is shaped by the colonial experience that judged them unable to carry out the sovereign responsibilities of statehood and therefore open to subjugation. Anghie's view is that these states have had a difficult, if not impossible, task to shake off that birthmark of conditional sovereignty as they now operate in the international system. The scars of the colonial legacy have produced some bloody consequences, as we have seen in Rwanda, Somalia, Sudan, and the Congo, to name a few protracted conflicts. From 1648 to 1918, much focus of international activity was on the development and strengthening of the state. Global governance in the Westphalian order was one of facilitating the relations among sovereigns and sovereign states. To the extent people benefited from any privileges like the freedom of religion, it was as a byproduct of state interest. The privilege won in the 1555 Peace of Augsburg, for example, provided for *cujus regio ejus religio*, which allowed religious freedom, but for the monarch or sovereign and not necessarily for their subjects. In fact, the Latin maxim provided that the people would follow the religion of their sovereign.[9] The sovereign would therefore dictate the religion of the realm without consideration as to the wishes or traditions of the people of that realm. Indeed, dissent from the established religion could result in persecution, including deprivation of property rights, lower status, and on occasion, pogroms or mass killings.

Early treaty-making reflects this focus on the state as the principal subject with a substantial portion of treaty activity devoted to such state interests as alliances, trade, and the waging of war.[10] These interests created the state values that became the values for global order: autonomy, mutual respect, and non-interference. The features of the Westphalian order were ones that focused on a balance of power among the most powerful states in order to maintain order and to preserve peace. When interests fell out of balance, conflict resulted. Individual quality of life and livelihood were determined by state authorities. To the extent that the treatment of people was an issue, it was one subject to the domestic values and policies of each individual country and its ruler.

As long as a state's actions did not spill over into another state, states were generally free to govern as they deemed appropriate. This changed in the late nineteenth and twentieth centuries as the requirements of industrialization forced states to act effectively across borders and as governments were increasingly expected to provide for their citizens. As Louis Henkin observe, the international system turned its attention away from state values to "human values" in its diplomatic activity and treaty-making. This was not done to the total exclusion of traditional state activities, but addressing areas of human concern became an increasingly large portion of what states did.

Technology steadily brought about more changes in the nature of state interactions. The first changes came through the recognition of the horrific and destructive nature of modern warfare. This can be seen in accounts of the early days of the US Civil War, when many in both the North and the South thought the war would end after one contest because one or the other side would be overwhelmed and lose heart.[11] In fact, those who thought this way underestimated the commitment individual soldiers had to their respective causes. Technological developments demonstrated in the Franco-Prussian War and the colonial wars to control territories in Africa and Asia in the late nineteenth century led to an arms race the Czar of Russia hoped to stem through the 1899 Hague Peace Conference. The Peace Conference also had on its agenda efforts to reduce the collateral damage of war on both individuals and their property.

While technology made modern warfare more deadly, at the same time, it made possible the reporting about war and soldiers' stories that put a face on war in ways that were not possible previously. The demands of industrialization also brought literacy to populations who had not only the education, but also the well-being and time to read reporting and become politically active in pacifist movements and humanitarian efforts like the founding of the Red Cross in 1863. While people, especially women, became more engaged in advocacy at an individual level, states were seeking ways to manage and to regulate new cross-border activities like telecommunications. As more and more people became politically active, new demands on states required them to develop new cross-border structures and capabilities.

The technological marvels of the nineteenth century were also reflected in important nation-building projects in countries like the United States and Canada. Municipal water works to provide safe drinking water and sanitation were introduced in New York City and Philadelphia, with large-scale engineering projects like the Croton Aqueduct in New York built to serve its growing population. Railroad building became a source of national pride and an important factor in nation-building itself. Typical of the time was British Columbia's insistence on a rail link to the east as a condition for joining the Confederation of Canada in 1871. The wagon road initially proposed became the national railroad that Canadian Prime Minister Sir John A. Macdonald saw as essential to a unified Canada. The project started in 1871 and was completed within 10 years.

In the United States, settlement and unification also drove the need for the national railway project completed in 1869 when the Union Pacific and Central Pacific Railroads met in Promontory Point, Utah. Such access to transportation lowered the cost of moving raw materials and manufactured goods and increased the mobility of populations within these countries. The next phase of infrastructure development driven by technology was the building of a transcontinental road system to accommodate the widespread automobile ownership made possible by Henry Ford's assembly line production methods and the availability of oil in the United States.

These developments created new demands that required government responses, which in turn created additional demands. The need for consistent and universal standards led people to rely on their governments to provide the means to meet their objectives. The US Interstate Commerce Commission (ICC), for example, was created in 1887 to regulate first railroads and then trucking, and to control rates. It provided recourse to communities along rail lines that felt unable to stand up alone to the power of the railroad companies and was eventually a major actor in desegregation when rail and bus passengers filed complaints of racial discrimination. Although the ICC was abolished in 1995, it was the first of many responses in the United States to situations where citizens sought the help of their government to equalize an imbalance.

During the Westphalian era, power, legitimacy, and authority all flowed from one source—the state. Having overthrown the hierarchy represented by the Pope and the Holy Roman Emperor, the international community in Europe opted for a governance system of states that operated freely within their realms and with little external regulation other than what they specifically agreed to. By the dawn of the twentieth century, the balance of power had become the operating mode, and states co-existed in an "anarchical society"—the title of Bull's classic text. The juxtaposition of the ideas of anarchy and of society is effective in making the point that even within a system of autonomous units, there are some agreed-on principles or rules that guide conduct. Wendt argues that the process and institutions of the "society" portion of the anarchical society actually mold and direct the "anarchy" by shaping the interests and identity of the members of the society.[12] Wendt sees this as occurring in three ways: the institution of sovereignty; the evolution of cooperation; and intentional efforts to transform egoistic identities into collective identities.[13]

Identity is important because it situates an entity in the broader political, social, cultural, and legal context. Where an entity finds itself will help to define that entity's interests. For example, newly independent countries sought membership in the United Nations (UN) to affirm and to safeguard their independence. In turn, these newly independent states pursued a strategy of conveying the same status or identity on all territories, with little regard to a territory's ability either to govern itself or to carry out the responsibilities of statehood.

Understanding identity and interests in this way also helps to reconcile the existence of power and the institutions that may seek to constrain the use of that power. This is possible by taking an expansive view of what institutions regulate or to use self-help.[14] Institutions that compete with each other to shape interests and identities may take on more or less significant roles depending on circumstances that are conditioned by politics, sociology, culture, and history. When considering these circumstances, the domestic should not be overlooked, since a state's identity is usually created by domestic forces and society prior to its entry into international society.[15] Social structures are created by repetitive actions, and changing these actions "will change the intersubjective knowledge that constitutes the system."[16] For mature political societies or "mature anarchies," Wendt recognizes that process serves this role of creating structures of identity and interest.[17]

Early twentieth-century scholars supported the view that reasons of state drove international relations, as international law and diplomacy reflected the interests of powerful states. This seemed especially true when military power and technology joined forces to overwhelm and colonize territories and place them in a dependent or semi-dependent status. For example, the concept of overcoming an unequal treaty has been part of China's modern nation-building project since the overthrow of the imperial dynasty in 1911. The classic international law view was that the validity of coerced treaties provided a way to end conflict, but such treaties did not ensure equal rights or even necessarily survival of a defeated state.[18]

In the early twentieth century, a group of US lawyers—including such prominent figures as US Secretaries of State Elihu Root and William Howard Taft, hoped that law and legal institutions might serve as an alternative to this system that settled interstate disputes through military conflict. They drew on the experience of domestic law, where "law and legal institutions served as neutral, apolitical institutions and principles that could resolve conflicts while giving groups and individuals complete liberty within their respective spheres of action."[19] They believed that conflict resulted from a "failure to provide proper institutional mechanisms. ... Law was a science, and thus could be divorced sharply from politics."[20] These "classicists" believed that a community existed that could ameliorate conflict. They further believed that law evolved, so that over time, it would attain the proper institutional structure to end conflict through such mechanisms as arbitration.[21] This faith in law was an important pillar of US foreign policy in the years between the First and Second World Wars. President Calvin Coolidge, for example, declared that: "We wish to discard the element of force and compulsion in international agreements and conduct and rely on reason and law."[22]

The faith of Americans that legal reasoning could solve even seemingly irresolvable conflicts was not shared in Europe, but was paralleled there by the hope of early theorists of international relations that the horrors of war demonstrated in the First World War from 1914 to 1918 would deter destruction and conflict. E.H. Carr's admonition in *The Twenty Years' Crisis* of the dangers of ignoring power is well remembered for its critique of the dangers inherent in this view. It was ultimately discredited by the rise of facism in the 1930's.

Hans Morgenthau, whose later importance in IR masked his origins as an international lawyer, introduced to the United States the realism that would diminish to the point of disappearance the study of IL within social science. Morgenthau did so in the pages of the *American Journal of International Law* in 1940, where he chastised the founders and early leaders of the American Society of International Law, including three Secretaries of State and prominent practitioners, for missing the behavioralist revolution.[23] According to Morgenthau, they ignored the reality of IR and the interactions of power, IL, and state behavior. Legal realists argued that law was not neutral, but rather reflected power and politics. In this view, it was not impossible for states to hold norms in common, but international law mainly reflected the interests of the powerful states.[24]

Structural realists added international institutions, including law, to their analyses and concluded that to the extent states behaved cooperatively, it was a coincidence or to meet some basic need and little more.[25] Within realism, a further variation was a realist–institutionalist hybrid that agreed that power shapes international law, but argued that international law could work in both a cooperative and a coercive mode. Wolfgang Friedmann's distinction between a law of cooperation and a law of co-existence exemplifies this outlook.[26]

The twentieth-century international interlude

As we saw in Chapter 2, international organizations (IOs) were created to enhance the ability of states to pursue their interests and to carry out their functions. Starting from structured, but non-institutionalized meetings, groups of states would gather to address problems of common concern. It seems commonplace today for an IO like the UN to call attention to an area of international concern, but the creation of such a voice independent of states in the early twentieth century was accepted with extreme caution and skepticism. Although the League of Nations may be principally remembered for its failure to live up to its promise to prevent war, it created an international platform that has endured. The concepts and structures started under the League provided the procedural and institutional templates that guided the planners and founders of the post-Second World War international institutions. More significantly, the political environment created by the presence of an IO was something on which other actors like non-governmental organizations capitalized. IOs provided them a readily accessible platform and connection to a worldwide audience through which to promote their agendas. International law-making and implementation became more generally accessible and participatory, not on a one person, one vote basis, but still more than at any other time in the development of political institutions. The creation of a place where all states are represented and where the public could gain more and more access to decision-makers fulfilled Woodrow Wilson's vision of "open covenants openly arrived at." This combination of universal representation and general participation also provides international institutions like the UN with a legitimacy and even authority that is unique.[27]

For such changes to have occurred, Wendt identifies two conditions. The first is "a need to think of oneself in novel terms," that is, for an existing structure or institution to realize it is unable to meet a new or emerging need. The second condition is to fashion a solution where the cost of giving up the "old way" of doing things does not exceed the rewards and benefits of the "new way."[28] The inability of the League of Nations system to control the use of force demonstrated that an adequate political and normative consensus did not exist to meet these conditions. The creation of a new multilateral framework and structure to handle disputes was not sufficient to overcome the failure of states to agree that the new way of doing business was necessary and that the benefits of acting within the new framework were greater than pursuing objectives in the old way. Given the continued existence of war even under the UN system, we can see an inadequate commitment to eliminate war as a means to settle disputes.

That reality, however, should not mask the fact that almost a century of efforts to control the use of force has had a moderating effect on state behavior. As noted in Chapter 4, states—even powerful states—now make considerable effort to have any use of military force legitimated by United Nations Security Council (UNSC) or General Assembly action.[29] UNSC resolution 1973 authorizing the imposition of a "no-fly zone" in Libya in 2011 is but yet another example of such legitimation. The UN's action was bolstered by participation in these operations by members of the Arab League.[30]

Wendt provides a three-phase outline of how system-wide or governance changes take place even within the "anarchy" of multiple autonomous actors:[31]

1   *Recognition: when a breakdown of consensus about identity occurs.* An example is the changing definition of a UN Charter Chapter VII threat to the peace and the evolution of the concept of a responsibility to protect when states are seen brutalizing their own people. Although international action was proscribed by the Westphalian principle of non-interference into the domestic affairs of a state, the hard shell of sovereignty is being eroded by the countervailing principle that the safety and well-being of its population are a state's responsibility. Failure to discharge this responsibility or a willful determination to do so can now invite international action. This occurred when UNSC resolution 1973 authorized action against Libya in 2011.[32] The change is from the "old way" of the state functioning in a community of autonomous units where restraints on state behavior, if any, were self-imposed. The "new way" is one where the community of autonomous units has determined that community-wide restraints are worth pursuing. In such a situation, the old value of non-interference gives way to a new value of community scrutiny and action. This, however, still remains a work in progress, and community scrutiny does not always lead to community action, as in the cases of Rwanda and Darfur. And when international action is taken, as in the 2011 case of Libya, it is not yet clear what the ultimate responsibility is of those states that have intervened.

2   *Evaluation: the breakdown of consensus leads to a "critical examination of old ideas about self and other and, by extension, of the structures of interaction by which the ideas have been sustained."*[33] This examination was the task put to the International Commission on Intervention and State Sovereignty that adopted the concept of a responsibility to protect as a means to overcome the barriers of sovereignty that prevented international action in cases of organized violence and mass brutality against a population. The responsibility to protect attempted to define both the obligations of states to their people internally—the basis for international scrutiny—and those of the international community to people being victimized anywhere— the basis for international action. Preventing brutality, however, may not provide a solution to the problem that precipitated the violence.

3   *Output: the rethinking paves the way for a third stage of new practice.* In the case of the responsibility to protect, the new practice has

been to increase awareness of the importance of preventing mass violence and to adapt the procedures and mechanisms in the UN Charter that were formulated for inter-state conflict to address the new needs of intra-state conflict. Since states still maintain control of the military and other resources required to respond effectively to these situations, mobilizing international action remains uncertain. And, as we can see in the case of Libya in 2011, the ultimate outcome of having used force beyond some level of protection can be unclear.

We have seen and can anticipate the continued, if not intensified, need for this progression of recognition, evaluation, and output in norms and governing processes as the forces of globalization continue to shape international relations. These forces include the compression of space and time; the intensification of interactions among units of governance both public and private; and individuals pursuing a host of endeavors in all aspects of life, for good and for ill. The tidy units of governance that regulated state activity and separately regulated public and private activity no longer exist. Today, units of governance govern multiple forms and entities that were not previously within their realms of responsibility. Conceptually and theoretically, it may be useful to recall the observation of Stephen Jay Gould that the act triggering system-wide changes may be sudden and abrupt, but that it takes much longer for the changes to move through the system.[34] Van de Ven and Poole's observation that each unit and actor within an organization imparts its own momentum to the development process is also part of the theoretical challenge we face in trying to recognize and to explain the emerging governance system.

Despite the powerful arguments advanced in academic circles by the realists, bolstered by the events that led up to the Second World War, there were those who took exception to the realist outlook. Indeed, we can now see that the inter-war period represented phase two in Wendt's three part progression of change, where a critical examination was undertaken by states of the old ideas and the structure of their inter-action. Scholars contributed to this effort by applying social science methods to understand where international law and international institutions did matter and could externally influence state behavior. The New Haven School that encompassed the work of Harold Lasswell and Myres McDougal took this approach. It "relied heavily upon intensive fact investigation: they wanted social problems to be 'mapped' through deep case studies, employing the best social science methods of the day, and appropriate legal rules and procedures were to be prescribed through specific 'principles of procedure' that would help realize those values [of security, wealth, respect, well-being, skills, enlightenment, rectitude, and affection]."[35]

International legal process is another approach that gained prominence in the 1970s, drawing inspiration from sociology, and set out to understand how international law shapes state behavior. The "managerial" view of international law put forward by Chayes and Chayes builds on this. A point of convergence with international relations can be found in rationalist institutionalism and its leading scholar, Keohane. In this view,

> [I]nternational organizations, creatures of international law, could provide venues for the repeated interaction that would yield a cooperative solution. More generally, international institutions could reduce the cost transaction and information solution. Such information sharing favors cooperation, reduces uncertainty about intentions, and facilitates international stability.[36]

This outlook reopened international law for political scientists who used "rationalism to identify means by which international law could facilitate cooperation that would otherwise not occur."[37]

The twentieth-century international interlude created institutions and practices that now serve legitimating functions in global affairs. According to one definition: "Legitimacy is a generalized perception or assumption that the actions of an entity are desirable, proper, or appropriate within some socially constructed system of norms, values, beliefs, and definitions."[38]

Legitimacy may be "possessed objectively," but is "created subjectively." It is socially constructed and therefore "reflects a congruence between the behaviors of the legitimated entity and the shared (or assumedly shared) beliefs of some social groups ... "[39] As a social phenomenon, legitimacy is subject to change. It therefore has to be managed and renewed because entities whose conduct is deemed to provide legitimacy must continuously earn their legitimating function, maintain it, and renew it, including "repairing it" where it may require change or adjustment.[40]

The post-Second World War international institutions, including the UN and its members, are presently in the throes of developing these maintenance and repair functions. It is not an easy task, as we can see from the difficulties encountered in trying to modify the permanent membership of the UNSC or the governing structure of institutions like the World Bank and in dealing with the democratic deficit in the decision-making processes of the European Union and other international institutions. The ability of existing international institutions to develop and to maintain these legitimacy maintenance and repair functions will be an important factor in determining their future effectiveness and survival.

These institutions are in a situation similar to that in which states found themselves in the late nineteenth and early twentieth centuries. At that time, the state's ongoing legitimacy and vitality depended on its finding ways to meet the increasing demands of its people and the cross-border needs of a modernizing and industrializing world. The solution was a system of cooperative, coordinating, and information-gathering structures or "functional unions" that worked to facilitate activity in specific areas like labor, telecommunications, postal services, public health, and the like. These developments mirrored changes within states themselves as governments began to take on more active roles in promoting the well-being of their citizens.

Many of these steps were taken by governments in order to stave off more radical solutions inspired by communist and fascist revolutions. In the wake of the 1930s Great Depression, there was little disagreement that governments had some responsibility to contribute to the health and well-being of their citizens. After the Second World War, the point of contention was no longer *whether* governments should be involved in providing for and safeguarding the well-being of their citizens but rather *how much* governments should do. The disagreement in the United States about whether government is responsible for creating jobs or for providing the conditions that will create jobs is a continuing example of this debate. Since the 2008 financial crisis, the question is also one of how much governments *can* do in a globalized world. In international institutions, the pressure is for consultation with and participation of those most affected by international actions, whether a World Bank loan or prosecution of international crime.

As a socially constructed phenomenon, legitimacy needs to be communicated and tested. This can be confusing in an environment where there are multiple sources of legitimacy, each functioning at a different level of start-up, management, or repair. These legitimacies may support each other or may compete with each other. An important example of legitimation is UN membership. Since the twentieth century interlude of international institution-building, states seek and use UN membership as evidence that they have achieved status, stature, and recognition by existing states in the international system. UN membership is now a collectivized version of the self-promotion that Hendrik Spruyt noted, when the state form once attained, became the standard to which all would be held.[41] International institutions now play a major role in conferring this status and recognition.

Despite their importance in organizational behavior, little is known about the conditions that "are distinctly congenial to particular types of legitimacy or distinctly conducive to particular legitimation strategies."[42] Mark Suchman provides two general types of legitimacy as part of a framework to understand these conditions. One is a *pragmatic legitimacy* where the interests and expectations of those principally affected closely match the actions to be legitimated. The other is a *cognitive legitimacy* that is further removed from any immediate pay-off or benefit, but stems from social norms "that furnish plausible explanations for the organization and its endeavors."[43] UN General Assembly resolutions and UN conference action plans are examples of how pronouncements acquire a measure of authority because of cognitive legitimacy.

Where there are strong technical components to issues, Suchman finds that legitimacy is likely to have a pragmatic basis. This was the case with the early international institutions that focused on specific issues like telecommunications and transportation. In these areas, the actions of social movements, non-governmental organizations, and non-state entities are given legitimacy because of the recognized technical competence of these actors. Where there is a strong institutional environment like the UN, there is greater need for what Suchman calls cognitive legitimacy.[44]

In these cases, the legitimacy of the institution has to be maintained as much as the legitimacy of its specific actions. An institution may therefore fail to maintain its legitimacy if it strays too far from the values of its constituents. However, as we saw in Chapter 4, structure and process can shape identities and interests so that over time constituents themselves change their values by virtue of their membership and participation in various institutions. The ability to differentiate between the forms, functions, and dynamics of legitimacy makes possible a better understanding of the conduct and behavior of actors on the global scene that either claim or seek to convey legitimacy.

It is also important to recognize that changes in legitimacy are less a wholesale rejection of an established order than an adjustment needed in light of changed conditions and needs. The ability to change in response to new circumstances is therefore key to long-term institutional viability. There is nothing novel in adaptability as a requirement for institutional survival. What is different is the accelerated pace of change that now demands accommodation. Each new development provides opportunities for institutions—including states, international organizations, and non-state actors, but it also places greater demands on these global actors.

Put in international law and international relations terms, we can see legitimacy as derived from "the substance of the rule or from the procedure or source by which it was constituted."[45] In Hurd's view, coercion, self-interest, and legitimacy are the three "modes of social control" or ways to induce behavior.[46] Although all three are present in functioning systems of order, Hurd finds that "few complex social orders are primarily based on coercion," largely because it is very costly and self-limiting to do so.[47] Even the area of self-interest is not as straightforward as it might seem because self-interest changes and can be shaped. It is neither uni-dimensional nor linear, so that self-interest in the long term allows for short-term trade-offs. We see this in cases where states participate in processes in order to shape them over the long run rather than to achieve specific aims in a particular case. US participation in the WTO dispute settlement system is an example of this. Nevertheless, self-interest, even broadly defined, as a mode of control is limited. Hurd notes that "a social system that relies primarily on self-interest will necessarily be thin and tenuously held together and subject to drastic change in response to shifts in the structure of payoffs."[48]

In contrast, legitimacy is deep-seated. According to Hurd, "[a] rule will become legitimate to a specific individual, and therefore become behaviorally significant, when the individual internalizes its content and reconceives his or her interests according to the rule."[49] This is no less true of states and other global actors. Coercion, self-interest, and legitimacy are related, interact, and together create the incentives and bases for social order and control. Key to governance, then, is how to determine legitimacy—how to understand the "motives for behavior rather than simply measuring the behavior itself."[50] We can look at what decision-makers say when they comply or fail to comply with a rule. We can observe how readily others within a community join a particular action or follow a particular behavior. We can see if patterns repeat and whether practices remain stable. And we can search for sources of authority or legitimized power.[51]

In Chapter 4, we observed the interactions between the international order and states, including their domestic political and legal institutions. These institutions, including law, remain important to give effect to international norms and standards. We have also seen that domestic incorporation and adaptation may not necessarily lead to cooperation, but they do change the nature of competition. Although studies like that of Andrew Cortell and James Davis highlight the importance of pathways for the international to play a role in the domestic, we find that the reverse also occurs.[52] The pathways that allow the international to enter the domestic sphere also become the channels for domestic social and political forces to reach the international sphere and thereby shape those institutions. This happens, for example, when the International Labor Organization adapts its agreements and recommendations to conform to existing domestic practices.[53]

As the international becomes a factor in domestic politics, it can affect the balance of power within domestic government. For example, the US Congress insisted that the President seek a UN mandate prior to acting against Iraq in response to its invasion of Kuwait in 1990. The UN Charter effectively gave Congress an additional lever to pull in its struggle to maintain Congressional prerogatives in the area of authorizing the use of the US military.[54] According to public opinion polls, the US public prefers US military action to have a UN mandate, if possible, and the failure of the United States to receive a UN mandate also makes building coalitions difficult. In the 2003 war against Iraq, President George W. Bush took pains to note that 35 countries had joined in the effort when he announced the start of combat operations in Iraq to the American people. Multinational support, if not a UN mandate, was regarded as necessary to legitimize the US-led invasion.[55] As the 2011 military actions against Libya demonstrate, however, a UN mandate does not guarantee executive-legislative harmony in the United States in matters regarding the use of force; policy differences still surface on the level of involvement and a mission's objectives.

The possibility that international obligations will change the balance among the institutions of government is a perennial topic and source of concern among politicians, academics, and commentators. From an IR perspective, this means that it is useful to focus "on domestic structure as an intervening variable."[56] And, the two aspects particularly to consider are "the domestic structural context and the domestic salience of the international rule or norm."[57] Cortell and Davis conclude that "international norms can shape state behavior by becoming entangled in the domestic political process [and] that regime strength and regime change are functions of such processes [regime dynamics]."[58] This dynamic, in turn, provides further support for the constructivist perspective in both international relations theory and international law—that frameworks can shape interests and goals.

The twentieth-century international interlude further facilitated and supported the development of an active and strong civil society of social movements and non-governmental organizations. The structure of international institutions and their modes of conducting business lent themselves to fostering participation by non-state actors. In 2010, the non-governmental organization branch of the UN Economic and Social Council listed more than 3,200 non-governmental organizations as accredited observers to the UN. They not only maintain a watchful public eye over the activities of international institutions, but also increasingly provide these institutions with a ready connection to domestic constituencies that can, in turn, put pressure on governments to act in certain ways. The most dramatic example of this may be the short 15 years between the conclusion of the Helsinki Final Act in 1975 and the collapse of the eastern European dictatorships and the Soviet Union and the end of the Cold War in 1989–91. With the passage of time, there is an increasing body of evidence that international norms and institutions shape state behavior and eventually change states' definition of their interests and pursuit of international politics.[59]

Nevertheless, the perspectives of the realists and the regime theorists remain relevant. Interests and power continue to drive action and policy choices, as do the internal politics of states and international institutions. The norms and structures of international activity shape both identity and interests. These, in turn, will shape the pursuit of interest and choice of strategy. The international interlude, therefore, added international institutions and social movements to the world scene as governing forces through their growing role as a constitutive touchstone for international activity. Transparency and public participation in conducting international affairs; ongoing review, scrutiny, and monitoring by public and private international institutions; and growing state acceptance—as a formal matter on the part of governments and as an informal matter as a factor in domestic politics—of findings of international concern are hallmarks of the twentieth-century international interlude.

What has not yet been fully developed is a consensus on the outcomes of forms of collective action. As the growing experience with UN peacekeeping and peacebuilding operations now demonstrates, even with the engagement of international attention and relevant national forces, long-term stability and peace ultimately remain in the hands of the people in conflict areas who must themselves set up new and sustainable forms of government. From both the policy and academic perspectives, modes of engagement between the international and the national—whether at the outset of an operation, during an operation, or after an operation—remain an area for development and theorizing. As shown by the multiplicity of states, IOs, and non-governmental organizations engaged in efforts to define and implement a responsibility to protect operation in Libya in early 2011, these activities will take place in the expanded political and juridical space where more issues are addressed in more forums with increased individual and group participation.

Thickening forms of governance in the post-Westphalian order

In the short period of a century, new institutions and processes of governance have burst onto the scene and are now finding their place in the global governance environment. The twentieth-century international interlude of institution building created the present system of state conduct based not only on the power of one or more states, but also on the power that comes from the authority and legitimacy that an institution or community possesses. Governance has thickened in the same ways that globalization has thickened. If thin globalization is represented by trade on the Silk Route in comparison to globalization today, then thin governance can be seen as the Westphalian state moving towards the functional units and conferences of the early twentieth century in comparison to the thicker governance, including international governance, in operation today. In the emerging system, multiple actors share responsibilities at many levels.

Figure 6.1 captures some of the major units active in governance today. As we know, these units did not become recognized as units of governance immediately, but have each been tested over time. Some of the elements are more mature as governing units than others, but all are developing through interactions and connections with each other.

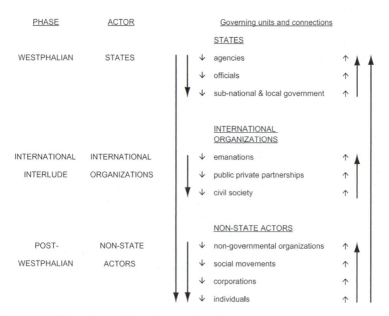

Figure 6.1 Governing units and connections

Figure 6.1 further identifies the sub-units functioning within each cluster of major actors. We can see that there is a complex relationship within each group of actors as well as between the groups. This does not mean, however, that the "old ways" of governing have been completely abandoned. States remain responsible for their internal affairs, and in fact, are now held to account not only by other states individually, but also by states collectively through a variety of institutions, if they fail to discharge their obligations. Still, IOs created by multilateral treaties remain constrained by the resources that member states provide to them for their operations, even while demanding that these organizations do more and more. And even if soft law can provide effective regulation, it does not provide the level of structural support that hard law might, for example, in access to courts and dispute resolution.

This takes us to Figure 6.2, which sets out the capacities of these units to govern, broken down into three conceptual elements: power, authority, and legitimacy. Not surprisingly, we see the densest clustering of capacities with the most mature governing unit, the state. Yet we see that IOs and non-state actors are starting to develop clusters of capacities and in doing so are redefining existing capacities.

In Figure 6.3, we see that a state's power to act begins with establishing its legitimacy internally, but because of the maturing of IOs

PHASE	ACTOR	Capacities to govern		Governing units and connections
				STATES
WESTPHALIAN	STATES	power ✓✓	↓	↓ agencies ↑
		authority ✓✓		↓ officials ↑
		legitimacy ✓✓	▼	↓ sub-national & local government ↑
				INTERNATIONAL ORGANIZATIONS
INTERNATIONAL	INTERNATIONAL	power ✓	↓	↓ emanations ↑
INTERLUDE	ORGANIZATIONS	authority ✓		↓ public private partnerships ↑
		legitimacy ✓✓	▼	↓ civil society ↑
				NON-STATE ACTORS
POST-	NON-STATE	power ✓	↓	↓ non-governmental organizations ↑
WESTPHALIAN	ACTORS	authority ✓		↓ social movements ↑
		legitimacy ✓		↓ corporations ↑
			▼ ▼	↓ individuals ↑

Figure 6.2 Governing capacities, units, and connections

Capacities	Actor		
	State	International organization	Non-state actor
Power	✓✓	✓	✓
Authority	✓✓	✓	✓
Legitimacy	✓✓	✓✓	✓

Figure 6.3 Governing capacity and global actors

in governance, state legitimacy alone is often no longer sufficient to support an action. In some areas like the use of force, the legitimacy provided by an IO may not always be available to a state (or coalition of states), but in less than a century, it has become highly desirable. Over time, the capacities of the institutions that comprise IOs and non-state actor clusters will increase to constrain further the autonomy of states to act. Putting this in Figure 6.3 terms, each part of the grid in the figure will eventually have two check marks indicating the denser and more complex governing environment. This is not to say that states will not be able to act autonomously, only that the transaction costs for such actions will be higher if state behavior does not meet international standards and expectations. Particularly in the area of military force, these transaction costs may be so high that a state may have physical capabilities that are, nevertheless, in the literal sense, use-less without international authorization.

The actual costs of operations undertaken under international mandates are increasing as missions become more complicated and as states rely on international institutions to do more and more. It is useful to remember that the maintenance of legitimacy domestically does not stand still, either, and that governments—even well-established governments— have to continue to earn their legitimacy and authority. Figures 6.1, 6.2, and 6.3 together provide a picture of what is happening, but do not explain how global governance may be developing. Van de Ven and Poole again provide a helpful framework for analysis. They identify two modes of change: prescribed and constructive.

A *prescribed* mode of change channels the development of entities in a prespecified direction, typically of maintaining and incrementally adapting their forms in a stable, predictable way. A *constructive* mode of change generates unprecedented, novel forms that, in retrospect, often are discontinuous and unpredictable departures from the past. A prescribed mode evokes a sequence of change events in accord with a preestablished program or action routine. A constructive mode, in contrast, produces new action routines that may (or may not) create an original (re)formulation of the entity.[60]

In global governance today, both modes of change are in operation and having an impact on international law and politics.

An example of this can be seen in what Vaughan Lowe has called an "interstitial norm," a kind of connective norm that draws together differing norms from hard and soft law as well as domestic and transnational law.[61] The 1997 International Court of Justice ruling in the *Gabcikovo Case* between Hungary and Slovakia shows how this happens when the two objectives of economic development and environmental protection collided. The outcome was a resort to the principle of sustainable development.[62] However, as Lowe rightly notes, there is not sufficient state practice to support the idea that sustainable development has acquired the status of a norm of customary international law. Instead, he finds this to be an interstitial principle that establishes "the relationship between the neighbouring primary norms when they threaten to overlap or conflict with each other."[63] Lowe explains how interstitial norms work:

> They have no independent normative charge of their own. They do not instruct persons subject to the legal system to do or abstain from anything, or confer powers, in the way that primary norms do. They direct the manner in which competing or conflicting norms that do have their own normativity should interact in practice.[64]

As a means to address the growing complexity of contemporary life—the impact of globalization, we can anticipate the increased appearance of such interstitial norms.

Another example of an interstitial norm is the principle of the responsibility to protect that attempts to balance the norm of non-intervention in the internal affairs of a state with that of the norm to protect the human rights of people. In that case, the report of the International Commission on Intervention and State Sovereignty outlined a process to operationalize such a connective or interstitial norm. It recognized the Security Council is recognized as the principal authority to mandate action when states brutalize their own populations. However, the report provides for autonomous state action even if the Security Council fails to act, although it does call on states to seek some form of multilateral authorization whenever possible.

Another characteristic of the new global environment is what Lowe calls "secularization," where "basic principles, structures, and processes of the normative system are transferred out of the system itself and into other areas of life."[65] This has become more significant as the daily lives of people are more intensely linked through the cross-border actions of corporations, private standard-setting organizations, and elements of civil society. Lowe concludes that "the conceptual framework of international law is likely to become diffused throughout the vast web of non-State international dealings."[66] The extent of this diffusion, the variety of modes and actors, and the length of time this has been happening now make possible rigorous examination and study to explain how institutions, including law, work to shape and to direct behavior. The explanations are not only of academic interest, but also important to sound policy development. Understanding how and what works in governance and how it will help all participants identify the formal and informal frameworks that can channel pressures for change and the normative and institutional efforts to address them. Understanding the functioning of today's political, economic, and social environment is crucial to its effective governance. This effort not only benefits from employing social science methods to explore legal phenomena, but also from developing cross-disciplinary theoretical perspectives to understand them.

As we see from Figures 6.1, 6.2, and 6.3 above, the complex phenomena within each set of governance actors is made more complicated by their increasing operation within a more complex global governing environment. From the standpoint of research and explanation, Van de Ven and Poole describe the natural constraints that occur when only part of a phenomenon is examined:

> ... it is not always clear from the outset what forces are influencing a complex developmental process. Indeed, if it is true that the interplay of multiple forces often drives development, then conducting research with a simple *a priori* theory in mind actually may impede adequate explanation. The researcher may look only for indicators of that particular theory, ignoring other possible explanations. In the best case, this myopia results in an incomplete account of development and change; in the worst case, the researcher may incorrectly reject his or her model because complexities introduced by other motors covered over evidence of its adequacy.[67]

A full understanding of global governance will therefore require strong interdisciplinary collaboration and interaction.

Prospects for research and global governance

This study has undertaken two things: 1) to acknowledge and to recognize the strides made in interdisciplinary studies between international law and international relations; and 2) to describe the complex global human and institutional interconnections that have emerged since the start of the twentieth century to shape and to govern our lives. We have seen how these connections created both new capacity and additional demands in the international arena and national systems of government. We have seen the leveraging of domestic, international, and non-state systems, each set of which generates its own further capacities, demands, and dynamics. In such a complex environment, the ability to draw on a variety of modes of explanation enhances our ability to understand the totality of the changes and conditions we are presently experiencing. Twenty years ago, the call was to engage in dialogue and collaboration between international relations and international law scholars. Through the effort of scores of scholars, teachers, academic associations, and practitioners, much has been done to increase the sophistication and depth of research undertaken as a collaboration between a new generation of scholars in both disciplines. Their work has provided important insights into the forms of governance that exist in a post-Westphalian world.

Global actions and activities often directly affect individuals, but the channels that facilitate direct participation by individuals in global governance exist only in segments that have not yet been fully connected. Nevertheless, we can see that the relationship between public authority and individuals is changing, with a much more active individual voice now present in national and international decision-making and implementation of programs and initiatives. Public power and authority are also becoming more diffuse as state functions and responsibilities have migrated to international organizations and non-state actors.

The twentieth century contributed the procedural and institutional modes through which to develop appropriate operating capacity and means. On the procedural side, we see the increasing reliance on openness and participation, access to information, regular reporting and review, and monitoring as part of international conduct. These procedural modes join the system-wide values of autonomy and responsibility that characterized the classical Westphalian system. If we take a closer look at the governing characteristics of the twentieth century, they remind us of the values that convey legitimacy and authority in a democratic society, where they take the form of debates, elections, participation, and service by individual citizens. Officials are elected or appointed to act on behalf of the general citizenry, not simply to accrue power or to exercise authority for its own sake.

At the international level, it seems that the pathways to values that convey legitimacy and authority will—for now—be principally through national channels. For the foreseeable future, even the engagement of civic groups will generally take place within traditional domestic political communities, although the effects of their advocacy or interests will reach across borders. As in domestic societies, international procedural values will change over time as a result of evolving connections and interactions, facilitated by rapidly changing global communications. No process or value stands still. Understanding how incremental steps fit into a broader scheme of both prescribed and constructive change will be critical to understanding and shaping a system of global governance.

Both scholars and practitioners of global governance today need a view that can provide an integrated understanding of the functions and capacities of each governing unit. As Spruyt traced the triumph of the state to the need for centralized resources in order to field armies, we are all now involved in the emergence of the next dominant governance form to meet the complex and diffuse needs of a global society. It is a form that will be open and malleable, but still authoritative and structured. The task of shaping it will require the drawing together of disparate modes of inquiry and theoretical bases from once discrete disciplines and the blending of several into something new. We have the opportunity to articulate new concepts and to develop a new understanding of the needs and modes of governance in a globalized world. And we have the opportunity to advance a central role for international law—broadly understood—as a significant enabling platform for the pursuit of global activities and development of a new definition of international relations.

In order to pursue rigorous and systematic study, we must maintain focus on the purpose of our scholarly projects and their scrutiny by the academic community. However, in a world of rapid changes, it is equally important that our findings are made accessible to a wider public and policy audience. Professional, academic organizations and think tanks can play a particularly valuable role in encouraging informed and appropriate use of scholarly findings by broader audiences, facilitating the wider distribution of information about current global governance practices and activities, and building communities of interest among practitioners and scholars from varied backgrounds and disciplines.

From an academic perspective, the present transitional environment provides much opportunity for research as we seek to understand the new requirements of global governance. This environment lends itself to cooperation not only between disciplines, but also between the academy and the policy world as decision-makers make policy choices and undertake long-term strategic planning. Responding to the governance tasks at hand requires that we, as scholars, recognize where we have been constrained by our disciplinary, intellectual, and professional borders. The changing governance environment requires of scholars that we reconsider our traditional outlook on engagement with the world of policy and practice.

In fostering collaboration between international law and international relations, we have made great progress. Now, like the academics who helped keep the Cold War cold by their contributions to deterrence theory in the 1950s and 1960s, we need to facilitate broader interactions between global governance scholars and practitioners today. This is not to encourage pre-judging the outcomes of an inquiry. It is only a reminder that good policy depends on a sound understanding of the issues and the likely implications of particular actions, based on rigorous scholarship.

This book has presented a number of examples—human rights, international criminal law, and protection against mass brutality, to name a few—where there has been a consensus on the existence of a problem and on the desired normative objectives. Yet this consensus did not prevent a considerable lag in developing the connections and relationships to achieve those objectives, if they were achieved at all. We live in a world in which global issues emerge from a number of different sources, but the frameworks and structures to deal with them have not kept pace, and remain largely conditioned and shaped by a smaller number of governing units. This means that the established units and systems of governance represent particular interests and values in which some actors are deeply invested, which in turn makes the units difficult to change. One manifestation of this that all proposals since the end of the Cold War to reform the structure of the UNSC have collided with this reality and failed.

It seems clear that we are on a path to a world in which countries and their citizens add a sense of global responsibility, authority, and identity to their existing, recognized national and international responsibilities. We lack a widely accepted means of recognizing when an initially *ad hoc* practice has acquired the legitimacy, power, and authority that make it part of the general governing environment. The global political decision-making environment remains fragmented, given the number of voices present in global politics and the wide range of actors' capacity and experience. This puts a premium on developing ways to understand rigorously and systematically actions undertaken to respond to global needs—a role ideally suited for interdisciplinary academic scholarship. As new conditions emerge, academics can make a great contribution to the policy world by categorizing a problem, examining the elements needed to address it, and developing the means to assess the immediate and longer-term effects of the individual and collective responses of states and other actors.

We can justifiably be proud of the collaborative efforts of IL and IR scholars in the late twentieth century that produced valuable scholarship in globalization and governance. Such collaborative scholarship and rigorous inquiry need to accelerate as the pace of events and technological developments that affect the daily lives of people around the world continues to accelerate. Like all scholarship, our future work will require rigorous testing and understanding within the academic community, but its results will then also be tested in the policy arena. To carry out new global governance tasks, local, national, and international actors, public and private, need the means to understand when and how a temporary adjustment to the system becomes permanent. Sound scholarship addressing its results to a broader audience will aid decision-makers in developing responses that can be employed in the short term as well as a range of future options.

It will not be easy to reach consensus on values and objectives in such a diverse and complex governance environment, but the only path to a constructive global political process will be a robust analytical and conceptual framework that supports engagement and debate among multiple actors. It seems only appropriate that, in a world where political, social, and juridical boundaries are shifting, intellectual and academic boundaries must shift as well. In a globalized world, we scholars need to cross our own conceptual borders.

Notes

Foreword by the series editors

1 Paul Diehl and Charlotte Ku, *The Dynamics of International Law* (Cambridge: Cambridge University Press, 2010); and Harold D. Jacobson and Charlotte Ku, eds., *Democratic Accountability and the Use of Force in International Law* (Cambridge: Cambridge University Press, 2002).

Introduction

1 Richard H. Steinberg and Jonathan Zasloff, "Power and International Law," *American Journal of International Law* 100, no. 1 (2006): 66.
2 Ibid.
3 Every US Secretary of State from 1889 to 1945 was a lawyer—three, Elihu Root, William Howard Taft, and Robert Lansing also served as president of the American Society of International Law.
4 Elihu Root, "The Need for Popular Understanding of International Law," *American Journal of International Law* 1, no. 1 (1907): 1–2.
5 See also Edward A. Kolodziej, Director, Center for Global Studies, University of Illinois (in an unpublished paper), "The World Society and Global Governance: Central Concerns of Global Studies Programs," 2009, 3, in which he states that we need: " ... not only recourse to the proven disciplinary and professional knowledge available to the academy, but also the synthesis of these partial perspectives to capture more credibly than we can now the complexity of the world society and to identify more precisely that confronting the world's populations."
6 See Robert Beck in a presentation entitled "Globalization Bytes: Exploring the 'Digital Divide' and the 'Global Technological Revolution,'" 2001 Global Studies Summit Institute, University of Wisconsin, Milwaukee.
7 UN Secretary-General Kofi A. Annan, *We the Peoples: The Role of the United Nations in the 21st Century* (New York: United Nations, 2000), 9.
8 See Alberto Alemanno, "The European Volcanic Ash Crisis: Between International and European Law," *ASIL Insights* 14, no. 21 (2010).
9 Simon Winchester ruminated on the effects of the Krakatoa eruption in 1883 that colored the atmosphere in such a way as to have inspired many works of art and helped discover the jet stream by making possible the tracking of the volcano's colored ash around the world. See Simon

Winchester, "A Tale of Two Volcanoes," *New York Times*, 16 April 2010, www.nytimes.com/2010/04/16/opinion/16winchester.html.

10 Alemanno, "The European Volcanic Ash Crisis."
11 David Held and Anthony McGrew, "Introduction," in *Governing Globalization: Power, Authority and Global Governance*, ed. David Held and Anthony McGrew (Cambridge, UK: Polity Press, 2002), 1–2.
12 UN Secretary-General Millennium Report, *We the Peoples*, 11.
13 Robert O. Keohane and Joseph S. Nye, "Introduction," in *Governance in a Globalizing World*, ed. Joseph S. Nye and Robert O. Keohane (Washington, DC: Brookings Institution Press, 2000), 11.
14 Ibid., 7.
15 Ibid., 11.
16 Ibid., 14.
17 James N. Rosenau, *Turbulence in World Politics: A Theory of Change and Continuity* (Princeton, N.J.: Princeton University Press, 1990), 60.
18 Ibid., 61.
19 Ibid., 63.
20 See, for example, Rosenau, *Turbulence*, 195.
21 Rosenau, *Turbulence*, 194.
22 See Scott Shane and Andrew W. Lehren, "Leaked Cables Offer Raw Look at US Diplomacy," *The New York Times*, 29 November 2010, www.nytimes.com/2010/11/29 and www.wikileaks.org.
23 Rosenau, *Turbulence*, 59.
24 See, for example, Charlotte Ku and Harold K. Jacobson, eds., *Democratic Accountability and the Use of Force in International Law* (Cambridge, UK: Cambridge University Press, 2002).
25 Rosenau, *Turbulence*, 111.
26 Ibid., 111–112.
27 Hendrik Spruyt, *The Sovereign State and Its Competitors* (Princeton, N.J.: Princeton University Press, 1994), 6.
28 Ibid.
29 The institutional innovations undertaken by the European Union are an important example of a multilayered system of governance, but may be too specific to the historic experience and financial resources of Europe to be readily duplicated more generally. Nevertheless, EU institution-building clearly has much to teach us in this area. See for example, Anne-Marie Burley (Slaughter) and Walter Mattli, "Europe Before the Court: A Political Theory of Legal Integration," *International Organization* 47 (1993): 41–76; and Karen Alter, *The European Court's Political Power: Selected Essays* (Oxford: Oxford University Press, 2009).
30 Paul Kennedy, Dirk Messner, and Franz Nuscheler, eds. *Global Trends & Global Governance* (London: Pluto Press, 2002), 59.
31 Robert O. Keohane, "Global Governance and Democratic Accountability," in *Taming Globalization: Frontiers of Governance*, ed. David Held and Mathias Koenig-Archiburgi (Cambridge: Polity Press, 2003), 131–132.
32 Keohane and Nye, "Introduction," 13.
33 Saskia Sassen, *Territory, Authority, Rights: From Medieval to Global Assemblages* (Princeton, N.J.: Princeton University Press, 2006), 419.
34 Spruyt, *The Sovereign State*, 184.

35 Instead of organization, for purposes of this study, one should substitute system.
36 Andrew H. van de Ven and Marshall Scott Poole, "Explaining Development and Change in Organizations," *Academy of Management Review* 20, no. 3 (July 1995): 526.
37 Ibid., 515.
38 Ibid., 519.
39 Ibid., 523.
40 Ibid., 520.
41 Ibid., 521–522.
42 Ibid., 522.
43 Rosenau, *Turbulence*, 60.
44 Van de Ven and Poole, "Explaining Development," 523.
45 Thanks to Alan James for pointing this out and to Peter Wilson, London School of Economics, for providing a sample course outline for Course 529: The Sociology of International Law.
46 Louis Henkin, *How Nations Behave* (New York: Columbia University Press, 1979), 47.
47 Conversation with Laurence Helfer, 25 March 2009, Washington, DC.
48 See, for example, John King Gamble, Jr., "Reservations to Multilateral Treaties: A Macroscopic View of State Practice," *American Journal of International Law* 74, no. 2 (April 1980): 372–394.
49 In the last systematic survey of this topic conducted by the American Society of International Law in 1990, project director John Gamble found 160 individuals teaching international law regularly in departments of political science in the United States and Canada. This conclusion was drawn from a survey sent to the 900 departments of political science in the United States and Canada identified in the Guide to Graduate Study in Political Science, 1989, and the Directory of Undergraduate Political Science Faculty. The number of international law courses taught regularly in departments of political science was therefore relatively small, with a faculty whose average age at the time of the survey was 53. It is difficult to know what the present situation is without undertaking an update of this survey. See John King Gamble, *Teaching International Law in the 1990s* (Washington, DC: The American Society of International Law, 1992), 39–65.
50 David Forsythe, *Human Rights in International Relations* (Cambridge: Cambridge University Press, 2000); Jack Donnelly, *International Human Rights* (Boulder, Colo.: Westview Press, 2006) and *Universal Human Rights in Theory and Practice* (Ithaca: Cornell University Press, 2003); and R.J. Vincent, *Human Rights and International Relations* (Cambridge: Cambridge University Press, 1986).
51 Representative work of these scholars follows: M.J. Peterson, "Whalers, Cetologists, and the International Management of Whaling," in *Knowledge, Power, and International Political Coordination*, Special Issue of *International Organization* 46 (1992): 147–186; Margaret E. Keck and Kathryn Sikkink, *Activists Beyond Borders* (Ithaca: Cornell University Press, 1998); Karen Alter, *The European Court's Political Power: Selected Essays* (Oxford: Oxford University Press, 2009); Paul Diehl and Gary Goertz, *War and Peace in International Rivalry* (Ann Arbor: University of Michigan Press, 2000); Margaret P. Karns and Karen A. Mingst, *International*

Organizations: The Politics and Processes of Global Governance (Boulder, Colo.: Lynne Rienner Publishers, 2009); and Beth A. Simmons, *Mobilizing for Human Rights* (New York: Cambridge University Press, 2009).

52 An indication of the growing interdisciplinary orientation of legal education can be gleaned from 2006 data showing that among the top 14 law schools in the United States, as ranked by *US News and World Report*, three schools had more than 40 percent of their faculty with PhDs in addition to the JD, five had between 30 and 40 percent, and five schools were at or below 20 percent. See Faculty Research & Achievement, www.law.northwestern.edu/faculty.

53 Conversation with José Alvarez, 28 January 2009, New York.

54 Lucy Reed, President, American Society of International Law, "Careers in International Law," University of Illinois College of Law, 22 February 2010, Champaign, IL.

1 Points of departure

1 Portions of this section have appeared in Charlotte Ku and Thomas G. Weiss, "Introduction: The Nature and Methodology of the Fields," in *Toward Understanding Global Governance: The International Law and International Relations Toolbox*, ed. Charlotte Ku and Thomas G. Weiss, ACUNS Reports and Papers No. 2 (1998), 1–9.

2 See, for example, Thomas Friedman, *The World is Flat* (New York: Farrar, Straus & Giroux, 2005); Anne-Marie Slaughter, *A New World Order* (Princeton, N.J.: Princeton University Press, 2004); and James N. Rosenau, *Turbulence in World Politics: A Theory of Change and Continuity* (Princeton, N.J.: Princeton University Press, 1990).

3 See Daniel C. Thomas, *The Helsinki Effect: International Norms, Human Rights, and the Demise of Communism* (Princeton, N.J.: Princeton University Press, 2001); and Thomas Buergenthal, "CSCE Human Dimension: The Birth of a System," in *Collected Course of the Academy of European Law* (1992).

4 As quoted in Thomas, *The Helsinki Effect*, 120.

5 This section included "human contacts" and provided for contacts and regular meetings on the basis of family ties, reunification of families, marriage between citizens of different states, travel for personal or professional reasons, improvement of conditions for tourism on an individual or collective basis, meetings among young people, sport, and expansion of contacts.

6 Henry A. Kissinger, *Years of Renewal: The Concluding Volume of His Memoirs* (New York: Simon & Schuster, 1999), 663. See also William Korey, *NGOs and the Universal Declaration of Human Rights: A Curious Grapevine* (New York: Palgrave, 1998), 247, about Kissinger's skepticism of the utility of Basket III.

7 See Audie Klotz, "Norms Reconstituting Interests: Global Racial Equality and U.S. Sanctions against South Africa," *International Organization* 49, no. 4 (1995): 451–478.

8 See Tables of Accession, American Convention on Human Rights at www.oas.org/juridico/english/sigs/b-32.html, and for the European Convention on Human Rights at http://conventions.coe.int/treaty.

9 See Edward C. Luck, *The UN Security Council: Practice and Promise* (Oxford: Routledge, 2006); James Raymond Vreeland, *The International Monetary Fund: Politics of Conditional Lending* (Oxford: Routledge,

2007); and Katherine Marshall, *The World Bank: From Reconstruction to Development to Equity* (Oxford: Routledge, 2008).

10 See "History of the World Treaty Index" http://depts.washington.edu/hrights/Treaty/history.html and Glenda Pearson, "Rohn's World Treaty Index: Its Past and Future," *International Journal of Legal Information* 29, no. 3 (2001): 543–559; and Michael J. Bowman and D.J. Harris, the University of Nottingham Treaty Centre, Multilateral Treaties—Index & Current Status (1984).

11 John King Gamble, Comprehensive Database of Multilateral Treaties (CDMT), The Behrend College, Pennsylvania State University (2000).

12 Beth A. Simmons and Richard H. Steinberg, eds., *International Law and International Relations* (Cambridge: Cambridge University Press, 2006), xxx.

13 Harold K. Jacobson, "Doing Collaborative Research on International Legal Topics: An Autobiographical Account," in "Exploring International Law: Opportunities and Challenges for Political Science Research: A Roundtable," ed. Charlotte Ku, *International Studies Review* 3 (2001): 15–21.

14 See John J. Mearsheimer, "The False Promise of International Institutions," *International Security* 19, no. 3 (1994/1995): 5–49.

15 Jonathan I. Charney, "Universal International Law," *American Journal of International Law* 87, no. 4 (1993): 529–551; Stephen Toope and Jutta Brunnée, *Legitimacy and Legality in International Law: An Interactional Account* (Cambridge: Cambridge University Press, 2010); Jack L. Goldsmith and Eric A. Posner, *The Limits of International Law* (New York: Oxford University Press, 2005); Kal Raustiala, "Form and Substance in International Agreements," *American Journal of International Law* 99, no. 3 (2005): 581–614; Andrew Guzman, *How International Law Works: A Rational Choice Theory* (New York: Oxford University Press, 2008); Laurence Helfer, "Exiting Treaties," *Virginia Law Review* 91, no. 7 (2005): 1579–1648; and Joel Trachtman, *The Economic Structure of International Law* (Cambridge, Mass.: Harvard University Press, 2008).

16 Statute of the International Court of Justice Article 38.

17 Robert O. Keohane, "International Relations and International Law: Two Optics," *Harvard Journal of International Law* 38 (1992): 492.

18 Martti Koskieniemmi, *The Gentle Civilizer of Nations: The Rise and Fall of International Law 1870–1960* (Cambridge: Cambridge University Press, 2001), 436–494.

19 Harold K. Jacobson, "Studying Global Governance: A Behavioral Approach," in ed. Charlotte Ku and Thomas G. Weiss, *Toward Understanding Global Governance*, ACUNS Papers and Reports, no. 2 (1998), 15.

20 Ibid.

21 Edward Hallett Carr, *The Twenty Years' Crisis, 1919–1939: An Introduction to the Study of International Relations* (London: Macmillan, 1949); Hans J. Morgenthau, *Politics among Nations: The Struggle for Power and Peace* (New York: Alfred A. Knopf, 1949); and Quincy Wright, *A Study of War* (Chicago: University of Chicago Press, 1942).

22 Jacobson, "Studying Global Governance," 16.

23 Ibid., 20.

24 Beth A. Simmons, "International Law: Stepchild in Political Science Research? A Rejoinder to Paul Diehl," in ed. Charlotte Ku, "Exploring International Law: Opportunities and Challenges for Political Science Research: A Roundtable," *International Studies Review* 3 (2001): 11–12.

25 Beth A. Simmons, *Mobilizing for Human Rights: International Law in Domestic Politics* (New York: Cambridge University Press, 2009), 10.
26 Helen Milner, *Interests, Institutions, and Information: Domestic Politics and International Relations* (Princeton, N.J.: Princeton University Press, 1997).
27 Simmons, *Mobilizing for Human Rights*, 10.
28 See Anne-Marie Slaughter, "The Real New World Order," *Foreign Affairs* 76 (1997): 183–198, and *A New World Order* (Princeton, N.J.: Princeton University Press, 2004).
29 See Anne-Marie Slaughter and William Burke-White, "The Future of International Law is Domestic (or, the European Way of Law)," *Harvard Journal of International Law* 47, no. 2 (2006): 327–352.
30 Andrew Linklater and Hidemi Suganami, *The English School of International Relations: A Contemporary Reassessment* (Cambridge: Cambridge University Press, 2006), 44.
31 Jutta Brunée and StephenToope, "International Law and Constructivism: Elements of an Interactional Theory of International Law," *Columbia Journal of Transnational Law* 39 (2000–2001): 48.
32 Brunée and Toope, "International Law and Constructivism," 65.
33 Quoting Gerald Postema, "Implicit Law," *Law & Philosophy* 13 (1994): 256–265, in Brunée and Toope, "International Law and Constructivism," 49.
34 Brunée and Toope, "International Law and Constructivism," 53.
35 Subtitle of the International Law Commission Report on *Fragmentation of International Law: Difficulties Arising from the Diversification and Expansion of International Law,* UN General Assembly Doc A/CN.4/ L.682 (13 April 2006).
36 *Fragmentation of International Law*, para. 481.
37 Christine Chinkin, "The Challenge of Soft Law: Development and Change in International Law," *International and Comparative Law Quarterly* 38 (1989): 866.
38 *Fragmentation of International Law*, para. 10, 12.
39 Ibid., para. 49, 31.
40 See José E. Alvarez, *International Organizations as Law-Makers* (Oxford: Oxford University Press, 2005).
41 See Paul F. Diehl and Charlotte Ku, *The Dynamics of International Law* (Cambridge: Cambridge University Press, 2010).
42 *Fragmentation of International Law*, para. 8, 11.
43 See for example Matthew Partridge, "It's short-sighted to give North Korea aid without strings," 17 July 2010, www.guardian.co.uk/commentisfree/ 2010/jul17/north-korea-aid.
44 *Fragmentation of International Law*, para. 492.
45 Sally Engle Merry, "Legal Pluralism," *Law & Society Review* 22, no. 5 (1988): 870.
46 Brunée and Toope, "International Law and Constructivism," 65.
47 Ibid., 68.
48 Ibid., 70.

2 International concerns and the international community of states

1 Hendrik Spruyt, *The Sovereign State and Its Competitors* (Princeton, NJ: Princeton University Press, 1994), 6.

2 Ibid., 178.
3 Ibid., 178–179.
4 Montevideo Convention on the Rights and Duties of States, 26 December 1933, 165 *League of Nations Treaty Series* 19.
5 See International Court of Justice, Western Sahara Advisory Opinion, 16 October 1975, www.icj-cij/docket.
6 See, for example, *Clipperton Island Case* in *American Journal of International Law* 27 (1933), reporting on the decision of Italy's King Victor Emmanuel III in 1931 to award the island to France in a dispute between France and Mexico. France was the older claimant but it had not occupied the island.
7 See James Crawford, *The International Law Commission's Articles on State Responsibility: Introduction, Text and Commentaries* (Cambridge: Cambridge University Press, 2002), 1.
8 Ibid., 2.
9 As quoted in ibid., 17.
10 US Joint Forces Command, The JOE 2010: Joint Operating Environment, 65: www.peakoil.net/files/JOE2010.pdf.
11 Abram Chayes and Antonia Handler Chayes, *The New Sovereignty: Compliance with International Regulatory Agreements* (Cambridge, Mass.: Harvard University Press, 1995) 5.
12 Ibid.
13 Ambassador Richard Benedict as quoted in Chayes and Chayes, *The New Sovereignty*, 5.
14 Inis L. Claude, Jr., *Swords into Plowshares* (New York: Random House, 1984), 21.
15 Alexander Cooley and Hendrik Spruyt, *Contracting States: Sovereign Transfers in International Relations* (Princeton, N.J.: Princeton University Press, 2009).
16 Ibid., 19.
17 See Sino-British Joint Declaration at www.gov.cn/english/2007–06/14/content_649468.htm; see also "End of an Experiment: The introduction of a minimum wage marks the further erosion of Hong Kong's free-market ways," *The Economist*, 15 July 2010.
18 Jed Rubenfeld, "The Two World Orders," *Wilson Quarterly* 27, no. 4 (2003): 34.
19 Thomas M. Franck, "Can the United States Delegate Aspects of Sovereignty to International Regimes?" in *Delegating State Powers: The Effect of Treaty Regimes on Democracy and Sovereignty*, ed. Thomas M. Franck (New York: Transnational Publishers, 2000), 2.
20 The Tenth Amendment states that: "The powers not delegated to the United States by the Constitution, nor prohibited by it to the states, are reserved to the states respectively, or to the people."
21 Rubenfeld, "The Two World Orders," 27.
22 Ibid.
23 UN Charter Article 50 includes non-member states in the obligation to carry out decisions made under Charter Chapter VII.
24 See Summary of Contributors of Military and Police Personnel: www.un.org/en/peacekeeping/contributors.
25 Claude, *Swords*, 24.
26 Ibid.

27 See G-20 Information Centre, www.g20.utoronto.ca.

28 See, for example, 1960 United Nations General Assembly Resolution 1514, the Declaration on the Granting of Independence to Colonial Countries and Peoples.

29 See M.J. Peterson, *The UN General Assembly* (Oxford: Routledge: 2005).

30 See http://socialinvesting.about.com.

31 See Edward C. Luck, *The UN Security Council: Practice and Promise* (London: Routledge, 2006).

32 Claude, *Swords*, 34.

33 For information about the International Labour Organization, www.ilo.org, see also Steve Hughes, *The International Labour Organization: Coming in from the Cold* (London: Routledge, 2011).

34 Laurence R. Helfer, "Monitoring Compliance with Unratified Treaties: The ILO Experience," *Law and Contemporary Problems* 71, no. 1 (2008): 200.

35 Ibid., 201.

36 Ibid., 202–203.

37 See International Civil Aviation Organization, www.icao.int.

38 See David P. Forsythe, *The International Committee of the Red Cross: A Neutral Humanitarian Actor* (London: Routledge, 2007).

39 See International Committee for the Red Cross (www.icrc.org) and Hague Conference on Private International Law (www.hcch.net).

40 See Craig N. Murphy and JoAnne Yates, *The International Organization for Standardization: Setting Standards* (London: Routledge, 2009); and Kenneth W. Abbott and Duncan Snidal, "The Governance Triangle: Regulatory Standards Institutions and the Shadow of the State," in *The Politics of Global Regulation*, ed. Walter Mattli and Ngaire Woods (Princeton, N.J.: Princeton University Press, 2009), 51.

41 See the UN Administrative Tribunal, www.untreaty.un.org.unat.

42 Cheryl Shanks, Harold K. Jacobson, and Jeffrey H. Kaplan, "Inertia and Change in the Constellation of International Governmental Organizations, 1981–92," *International Organization* 50 (1996): 599.

43 See Global Environmental Facility, www.thegef.org.

44 See Clive Archer, *The European Union* (London: Routledge, 2008).

45 Shanks, Jacobson, and Kaplan, "Inertia and Change," 600.

46 See Jonathan I. Charney, "Universal International Law," *American Journal of International Law* 87, no. 4 (1993): 529–551.

47 Ibid., 551.

48 Quoting Article 22 of the League of Nations Covenant, Balakrishnan Rajagopal, *International Law from Below: Development, Social Movements and Third World Resistance* (Cambridge: Cambridge University Press, 2003), 56.

49 Quincy Wright, "Status of the Inhabitants of Mandated Territory," *American Journal of International Law* 18 (1924): 306.

50 Rajagopal, *International Law from Below*, 57.

51 Ibid., 67–68.

52 See Wunsz King, *Woodrow Wilson, Wellington Koo, and the China Question at the Paris Peace Conference* (Leyden, Netherlands: A.W. Sythoff, 1959).

53 See Tse-tsung Chow, *The May Fourth Movement* (Stanford: Stanford University Press, 1960); and Jonathan D. Spence, *In Search of Modern China* (New York: Norton, 1999), 309–310.

54 As quoted in Julius Stone, "Procedure under the Minorities Treaties," *American Journal of International Law* 26 (1932): 502.
55 Ibid.
56 Ibid., 509.
57 Ibid.
58 See Leon Gordenker, *The UN Secretary-General and Secretariat* (London: Routledge, 2005).
59 Permanent Court of International Justice, Series A/B, No. 64, 6 April 1935. The dispute was between Albania and Greece over the closing of private schools that provided education to the Greek minority. Albania defended its action as one that applied to both majority and minority populations in Albania. The PCIJ concurred and did not find Albania in violation of its obligations to protect the Greek minority within its borders.
60 Permanent Court of International Justice, Series A/B, No. 6, 10 September 1923. At issue was whether German leases granted prior to the First World War would be recognized in Poland. The PCIJ found that Poland did have to recognize these leases as part of its minorities obligation.
61 Permanent Court of International Justice, Series A/B, No. 65, 4 December 1935. The question here was whether amendments to the Danzig penal code and code of penal procedure violated the Constitution of the Free City of Danzig's protection of individuals against the State. In this case, the Court found that the amendments did indeed violate the Free City's Constitution.
62 F.D. Roosevelt, Four Freedoms Speech, 6 January 1941, wiretap.area.com/gopher/gov/US-history, 4.
63 See William Korey, *NGOs and the Universal Declaration of Human Rights* (New York: Palgrave, 2001).
64 See Korey, *NGOs and the Universal Declaration*, 29–42.
65 Also Professor of the History of International Relations at Columbia University from 1937 and later President of the Carnegie Endowment for International Peace (1949–50).
66 Korey, *NGOs and the Universal Declaration*, 39.
67 Emphasis added. Buergenthal, "The Evolving International Human Rights System," 787.
68 Ibid.
69 See UN Economic and Social Council Resolution 1503 (XLVIII), 27 May 1970.
70 Buergenthal, "The Evolving International Human Rights System," 783.
71 See Human Rights Committee General Comments, www2.ohchr.org/english/bodies/hrc/comments.htm.
72 Buergenthal, "The Evolving International Human Rights System," 789.
73 UN General Assembly Resolution 377, 1950.
74 International Commission on Intervention and State Sovereignty (ICISS), *The Responsibility to Protect: Report of the International Commission on Intervention and State Sovereignty* (2001), 1–2.
75 See Lee Feinstein and Anne-Marie Slaughter, "A Duty to Prevent," *Foreign Affairs* 82, no. 1 (2004): 136–150; and Charlotte Ku, "Legitimacy as an Assessment of Existing Legal Standards: The Case of the 2003 Iraq War," in *The Iraq Crisis and World Order, Volume 1: Structural, Institutional and Normative Challenges*, ed. Ramesh Thakur and W.P.S. Sidhu (United Nations University Press, 2006).

76 ICISS, *Responsibility to Protect*, 2.
77 Human Security Report, 2003, 6, www.humansecurity-chs.org.
78 See International Commission on Intervention and State Sovereignty, *Responsibility to Protect Core Principles: A Synopsis*, (2001), xiii.
79 "A More Secure World: Our Shared Responsibility," Report of the Secretary-General's High-level Panel on Threats, Challenges and Change, UN General Assembly doc. A/GA/565, 2 December 2004, 1.
80 Ibid., vii.
81 See William Burke-White and Anne-Marie Slaughter, "The Future of International Law is Domestic (or, The European Way of Law)," *Harvard Journal of International Law* 47, no. 2 (2006): 327–352.

3 The expanded international political and juridical arenas

1 See Hendrik Spruyt, *The Sovereign State and Its Competitors* (Princeton, N.J.: Princeton University Press, 1994), 189.
2 Ronald A. Brand, "Sovereignty: The State, the Individual, and the International Legal System in the Twenty-First Century," *Hastings International & Comparative Law Review* 25 (2002): 290.
3 Louis Henkin, *International Law: Politics and Values* (Dordrecht, Netherlands: Martinus Nijhoff Publishers, 1995), 284.
4 John King Gamble, Comprehensive Database of Multilateral Treaties (CDMT), The Behrend College, Pennsylvania State University (2000).
5 For a list of important human rights treaties, see *United Nations Millennium Summit Multilateral Treaty Framework*, 6–8 September 2000, at http://treaties.un.org.pages/TreatyEvents; and Charlotte Ku, *Global Governance and the Changing Face of International Law*, Academic Council on the United Nations System Reports and Papers No. 2 (2001), 2–5.
6 See Beth A. Simmons, *Mobilizing for Human Rights: International Law in Domestic Politics* (New York: Cambridge University Press, 2009), xxx.
7 Thomas Buergenthal, "The Evolving International Human Rights System," *American Journal of International Law* 100 (2006): 804.
8 See "About the IMF," www.imf.org/external.about.htm. See also James Raymond Vreeland, *The International Monetary Fund* (London: Routledge, 2007).
9 See World Bank Group, web.worldbank/org. See also Katherine Marshall, *The World Bank* (London: Routledge, 2008).
10 See Bernard M. Hoekman and Petros C. Mavroidis, *The World Trade Organization* (London: Routledge, 2007).
11 See Anne-Marie Burley (Slaughter), "Regulating the World: Multilateralism, International Law, and the Projection of the New Deal," in *Multilateralism Matters: The Theory and Praxis of an Institutional Form*, ed. John Gerard Ruggie (New York: Columbia University Press, 1993), 144, 146.
12 The ICSID was established by the Convention on the Settlement of Investment Disputes between States and Nationals of Other States. It was negotiated by the Executive Directors of the World Bank and entered into force in 1966. Some 146 countries are party to this convention.
13 Ronald A. Brand, "Sovereignty," 293.
14 See Geoffrey Jones, "Restoring a Global Economy, 1950–80," *Harvard Business School Working Knowledge*, http://hbswk.hbs.edu/cgi-bin/print?id=4961.

15 See UNCTAD *World Investment Report 2010*, www.unctad.org.
16 Spruyt, *The Sovereign State*, 189.
17 Anne-Marie Burley (Slaughter) and Walter Mattli, "Europe before the Court: A Political Theory of Legal Integration," *International Organization* 47 (Winter 1993): 42.
18 UN Secretary-General Kofi A. Annan, *We the Peoples: The Role of the United Nations in the 21st Century* (New York: United Nations, 2000), 7.
19 M.J. Peterson, "Transnational Activity, International Society, and World Politics," *Millennium* 21, no. 3 (1992): 371–388.
20 Margaret E. Keck and Kathryn Sikkink, *Activists beyond Borders: Advocacy Networks in International Politics* (Ithaca, N.Y.: Cornell University Press, 1998), 39.
21 See Balakrishnan Rajagopal, *International Law from Below: Development, Social Movements and Third World Resistance* (Cambridge: Cambridge University Press, 2003), 281.
22 Keck and Sikkink, *Activists beyond Borders*, 111.
23 See ibid., 60–66.
24 Ibid., 200.
25 Ibid., 202.
26 Ibid., 214 (emphasis added).
27 Rajagopal, *International Law from Below*, 270.
28 Sidney Tarrow, *The New Transnational Activism* (Cambridge: Cambridge University Press, 2005), 12.
29 See Rajagopal, *International Law from Below*, 120–127.
30 Keck and Sikkink, *Activists beyond Borders*, 200–201.
31 See Xinyuan Dai, *International Institutions and National Policies* (Cambridge: Cambridge University Press, 2007).
32 See Cynthia A. Williams and John M. Conley, "An Emerging Third Way? The Erosion of the Anglo-American Shareholder Value Construct," *Cornell International Law Journal* 38 (2005): 493.
33 See *UN Principles for Responsible Investment*, www.unpri.org/principles.
34 See ibid.
35 The UN Global Compact was an initiative undertaken by UN Secretary-General Kofi Annan in 1999 in an address at the World Economic Forum in Davos, Switzerland, suggesting that the business community join with the UN in a "global compact" of shared values and principles "to give a human face to the global market." See George Kell, United Nations, "Towards Universal Business Principles," Remarks to the Dilemmas in Competitiveness, Community and Citizenship, Business and Human Rights Seminar, London School of Economics, 21 May 2001, www.unglobalcompact.org/newsandevents/speeches_and_statements/london_school_of_economics.General information on the UN Global Compact, including its 10 Principles in the areas of human rights, labor, the environment, and anti-corruption, is available at www.unglobal compact.org.
36 See Paul F. Diehl and Charlotte Ku, *The Dynamics of International Law* (Cambridge, UK: Cambridge University Press, 2010), 103–128.
37 See Choike: A Portal on Southern Civil Society, www.choike.org.
38 John Rawls, *The Law of Peoples* (Cambridge, Mass.: Harvard University Press, 1999), 36.

39 For a complete list of Special Rapporteurs, Special Representatives, and Independent Experts working either on country or thematic mandates, see *Special Procedures of the Human Rights Council*, www2.ohchr.org/English/bodies/chr/special.

40 Steven Erlanger, "Thinker led president to war," *International Herald Tribune* (2–3 April 2011): 2.

41 Massimo Calabresi, "Advocate of Intervention: U.N. Ambassador Susan Rice made the case for humanitarian action in Libya," *Time*, 4 April 2011, 43.

42 J.W. Salacuse and H.P. Sullivan, "Do BITs Really Work? An Evaluation of Bilateral Investment Treaties and Their Grand Bargain," *Harvard Journal of International Law* 46, no. 1 (2005): 67–130.

43 See Diehl and Ku, *The Dynamics of International Law*, 135.

44 The London Court of Arbitration, www.lcia.org.

45 Catherine A. Rogers, "The Vocation of the International Arbitrator," *American University International Law Review* 20, no. 5 (2005): 1004.

46 See Cheryl Shanks, Harold K. Jacobson, and Jeffrey H. Kaplan, "Inertia and change in the constellation of international governmental organizations, 1981–92," *International Organization* 50 (Autumn 1996).

47 Buergenthal, "Evolving International Human Rights System," 791.

48 Ibid., 793.

49 See Council of Europe, Convention for the Protection of Human Rights and Fundamental Freedoms, http://conventions.coe.int/treaty.

50 Buergenthal, "Evolving International Human Rights System," 794.

51 See European Court of Human Rights, "50 Years of Activity: The European Court of Human Rights, Some Facts and Figures," http://echr.coe.int.

52 See Inter-American Commission on Human Rights, www.cidh.oas.org.

53 Buergenthal, "Evolving International Human Rights System," 795.

54 See Inter-American Commission on Human Rights, Chapters II and III *Annual Report* (2009), http://cidh.oas.org.

55 African (Banjul) Charter on Human and Peoples' Rights, Article 31,www.africa-union.org/official-documents.

56 See Organs of the African Union, www.african-union.org; and Malcolm Evans and Rachel Murray, eds., *The African Charter on Human and Peoples' Rights* (Cambridge: Cambridge University Press, 2002).

57 See *Freedom in the World Methodology*, www.freedomhouse.org.

58 Simmons, *Mobilizing for Human Rights*, 360.

59 Data from European Court of Human Rights, "50 Years of Activity: The European Court of Human Rights Facts and Figures," www.echr.coe.int. Note that Russia has only been party to the European Convention since 1990 while Turkey and Italy have been parties since the start of the European Court.

60 See International Criminal Court for the Former Yugoslavia, www.icty.org and International Criminal Court for Rwanda, www.ictr.org.

61 See ICTY Global Legacy, www.icty.org and Kelly Askin, "Reflections on Some of the Most Significant Achievements of the ICTY," *New England Law Review* 37 (2002–3).

62 See "ICC Prosecutor presents case against Sudanese President Hassan Ahmad Al Bashir, for genocide, crimes against humanity and war crimes in Darfur," ICC Press Release, 2008, www.icc-cpi.int.

63 See Article 17 of the Rome Statute of the International Criminal Court, www.icc-cpi.int.

64 See International Criminal Court, www.icc-cpi.int.

65 Cesare P.R. Romano, "The Proliferation of International Judicial Bodies: The Pieces of the Puzzle," *New York University Journal of International Law and Politics* 31 (1999): 709–710.

66 See International Court of Justice, "Reparations for Injuries Suffered in the Service of the United Nations," Advisory Opinion, 11 April 1949, www.icj-cij.org/docket.

67 Romano, "Proliferation of International Judicial Bodies," 740–741.

68 Ibid., 747.

69 Ibid., 748.

70 Zachary Douglas, "The Hybrid Foundations of Investment Treaty Arbitration," *British Yearbook of International Law* 74 (2003): 151.

71 International Court of Justice, Application of the Convention on the Prevention and Punishment of the Crime of Genocide (Bosnia and Herzegovina v. Serbia and Montenegro), 2007, www.icj-cij.org/docket.

72 Jonathan I. Charney, "The Impact on the International Legal System of the Growth of International Courts and Tribunals," *New York University Journal of International Law and Politics* 31 (1999): 699.

73 Campbell McLachlan, *Lis Pendens in International Litigation* (Leiden: Martinus Nijhoff Publishers, 2009), 13–14.

74 See McLachlan, *Lis Pendens*, 14–15.

75 Charney, "The Impact on the International Legal System of the Growth of International Courts and Tribunals," 699.

76 See Georges Abi-Saab, "Fragmentation or Unification," *New York University Journal of International Law and Politics* 31 (1999): 919–933.

77 See the Project on International Courts and Tribunals, "The International Judiciary in Context," www.pict-pcti.org/publications/synoptic_chart/synop_c4.pdf.

78 Charney, "The Impact on the International Legal System of the Growth of International Courts and Tribunals," 700.

79 McLachlan, *Lis Pendens*, 465.

80 See Michael G. Schechter, *United Nations Global Conferences* (Oxford, UK: Routledge: 2005).

81 See International Criminal Court, www.icc-cpi.int.

82 See About the Court, at www.icc-cpi.int.

83 Burley (Slaughter) and Mattli, "Europe Before the Court."

84 Karen J. Alter and Laurence Helfer, "Nature or Nurture? Judicial Lawmaking in the European Court of Justice and the Andean Tribunal of Justice," *International Organization* 64 (2010): 563–592.

85 The Human Rights Committee (HRC) is a body of experts created by the International Covenant on Civil and Political Rights (ICCPR) to review the periodic reports submitted by ICCPR members as well as to review any inter-state complaints among ICCPR members. The First Optional Protocol to the ICCPR further allows individual complaints to the HRC from nationals of states that accept this Protocol. See Human Rights Committee General Comments, www2.ohchr.org/english/bodies/hrc/

86 See Human Rights Committee General Comments, www2.ohchr.org/english/bodies/hrc/comments.htm.

87 See Malcolm Shaw, *International Law* (Cambridge: Cambridge University Press, 2008), 356.
88 See *Handyman v. UK*, Series A, vol. 24, 58 ILR (1981), 150. See also *Brannigan and Mahoney v. UK*, Series A, No. 258-B (1994), para. 43.
89 See José E. Alvarez, *International Organizations as Law-Makers* (Oxford: Oxford University Press, 2005).
90 Harold K. Jacobson, William M. Reisinger, and Todd Mathers, "National Entanglements in International Governmental Organizations," *American Political Science Review* 80 (March 1986): 148.
91 Ibid.
92 See Jack L. Goldsmith and Eric A. Posner, *The Limits of International Law* (Oxford, UK: Oxford University Press, 2005).
93 The New Deal is the name given to the economic programs passed by Congress to respond to the Great Depression during Franklin Roosevelt's first term (1933–37). The term was used both in Roosevelt's 1932 campaign and inaugural address.
94 Burley (Slaughter), "Regulating the World," 146.
95 Paul Berman, "A Pluralist Approach to International Law," *Yale Journal of International Law* 10, no. 2 (2007): 320.
96 Sally Engle Merry, "Legal Pluralism," *Law and Society Review* 20 (1988): 870.
97 Ibid., 871.
98 Ibid., 783.
99 David Kennedy, "My Talk at ASIL," *ASIL Proceedings* (2000), 104.
100 Ibid.
101 Ibid., 121.
102 See Christine Chinkin and Hilary Charlesworth, *The Boundaries of International Law: A Feminist Analysis* (Manchester, UK: Manchester University Press, 2000).
103 See Antony Anghie, *Imperialism, Sovereignty and the Making of International Law* (Cambridge, UK: Cambridge University Press, 2007). For a representative sample of critical legal studies scholarship in international law, see David Kennedy's compilation, "New Approaches to International Law: A Bibliography," *Harvard Journal of International Law*, 35 (1994): 417–460.
104 David Kennedy and Chris Tennant, "New Approaches to International Law: A Bibliography," *Harvard Journal of International Law* 35 (1994): 418.
105 See David Held, *Democracy and the Global Order: From the Modern State to Cosmopolitan Governance* (Palo Alto: Stanford University Press, 1995).
106 Keck and Sikkink, *Activists beyond Borders*, 213.
107 Ibid., 26. See, for example, the International Campaign to Ban Landmines www.icbl.org, and Richard Price, "Reversing the Gun Sights: Transnational Civil Society Targets Land Mines," *International Organization* 52 (1998): 613–644.
108 Simmons, *Mobilizing for Human Rights*, 3.

4 International relations in a global context

1 Anne-Marie Slaughter, *A New World Order* (Princeton, N.J.: Princeton University Press, 2004), 5.
2 Rome Statute of the International Criminal Court, 17 July 1998, UNTS 90.

3 High Level Conference on the Future of the European Court of Human Rights Interlaken Declaration, 19 February 2010, www.eda.admin.ch.

4 Ibid.

5 UK Parliament, Joint Committee on Human Rights, "Enhancing Parliament's role in relation to human rights judgments," HL Paper 85, HC455, 26 March 2010.

6 Ibid., 11.

7 See Chapter 3 for a full discussion of the European Court of Human Rights.

8 Slaughter, *A New World Order*, 7.

9 Anne-Marie Slaughter and William Burke-White, "The Future of International Law is Domestic (or, The European Way of Law)," *Harvard International Law Journal* 47 (2006): 339.

10 Ibid., 344 (emphasis added); quote from original text of UN Security Council Resolution 1373, 28 September 2001, para. 2c–d.

11 Slaughter and Burke-White, "The Future of International Law," 345.

12 In addition to the mandates of former German colonies, disputes over the status of territories like the Saar and Danzig were temporarily settled through special arrangements made in the peace treaties that ended the First World War and placed under the supervision of the League of Nations.

13 Slaughter and Burke-White, "The Future of International Law," 333.

14 Ibid., 350.

15 Ibid., 346.

16 Harold Hongjuh Koh, "Why Do Nations Obey International Law?" *The Yale Law Journal* 106 (June 1997): 1,657.

17 See Government of Canada, International Treaties: Canadian Practice, http://asp-psd.pwgc.gc.ca.

18 International Court of Justice, Avena and Other Mexican Nationals, *Mexico vs. the United States of America*, No. 128, 31 March 2004.

19 ICJ, Avena: 66, para. 143.

20 ICJ, Avena: 72, para. 152 subparagraph 9.

21 Oklahoma Court of Criminal Appeals: *Osbaldo Torres v. State of Oklahoma* (No. PCD-04-442), 13 May 2004. See also Damrosch, Brief of International Law Experts and Former Diplomats as *Amici Curiae* in Support of Petitioner, appeal from the District Court of Oklahoma, State of Oklahoma Case No. CF-1993-4302, 30 April 2004.

22 See J.L. Brierly, *The Law of Nations* (Oxford, UK: Oxford University Press, 1963), 86–93.

23 Anne-Marie Slaughter and David Bosco, "Plaintiff's Diplomacy," *Foreign Affairs* 79 (2000): 102–106.

24 Thomas R. Phillips, "State Supreme Courts: Local Courts in a Global World," *Texas International Law Journal* 38 (Special 2003): 564–565.

25 Ibid., 558.

26 Ibid.

27 Michael Barnett and Raymond Duvall, "Power in global governance," in *Power in Global Governance*, ed. Michael Barnett and Raymond Duvall (New York: Cambridge University Press, 2005), 5.

28 Inis L. Claude, Jr. "Collective Legitimization as a Political Function of the United Nations," *International Organization* 20 (Summer 1966): 367.

29 Andrew Hurrell, "Power, institutions, and the production of inequality," in *Power in Global Governance*, ed. Michael Barnett and Raymond Duvall (New York: Cambridge University Press, 2005), 55.

30 Mark Leffey and Jutta Weldes, "Policing and Global Governance," in *Power in Global Governance*, ed. Michael Barnett and Raymond Duvall (New York: Cambridge University Press, 2005), 72.

31 Michael Barnett and Martha Finnemore, "The power of liberal international organizations," in *Power in Global Governance*, ed. Michael Barnett and Raymond Duvall (New York: Cambridge University Press, 2005), 166.

32 Ibid., 173.

33 Dag Hammarskjöld, "International Cooperation within the United Nations," in *Dag Hammarskjöld: Servant of Peace*, ed. Wilder Foote (New York: Harper and Row, 1962), 93.

34 Barnett and Finnemore, "The power of liberal international organizations," 174.

35 Harold K. Jacobson, William M. Reisinger, and Todd Mathers, "National Entanglements in International Governmental Organizations," *American Political Science Review* 80 (March 1986): 142.

36 Ibid.

37 Hammarskjöld, "International Cooperation," 94.

38 Barnett and Finnemore, "The power of liberal international organizations," 183.

39 Ibid., 184.

40 See Larry Elliott, "Greece's financial crisis puts the future of the euro in question," *The Observer*, 7 February 2010, www.guardian.co.uk/business/2010/feb/07.

41 Barnett and Finnemore, "The power of liberal international organizations," 182.

42 See Public Law 101–246, www.state.gov.

43 Robert C.R. Siekmann, "The legal responsibility of military personnel," in *Democratic Accountability and the Use of Force in International Law*, ed. Charlotte Ku and Harold K. Jacobson (Cambridge, UK: Cambridge University Press, 2002), 109.

44 "Observance by United Nations Forces of International Humanitarian Law," Secretary-General's Bulletin (UN Doc. ST/SGB/1999/13), 6 August 1999.

45 "Comprehensive review of the whole question of peacekeeping operations in all their aspects," UN General Assembly Doc A/59/710, 24 March 2005, 4.

46 Ibid., 7.

47 "Observance by UN Forces," ST/SGB/2003/13.

48 UN, "Comprehensive review," 11.

49 See also United Nations Department of Peacekeeping Operations, *United Nations Peacekeeping Operations: Principles and Guidelines* (2008), www.un.org.

50 Dag Hammarskjöld, "Introduction to the Annual Report, 1959–60," in *Dag Hammarskjöld: Servant of Peace*, ed. Wilder Foote (New York: Harper and Row, 1962), 312.

51 See Terence C. Halliday and Bruce G. Carruthers, *Bankrupt: Global Lawmaking and Systemic Financial Crisis* (Stanford: Stanford University Press, 2009).

52 Terence C. Halliday and Bruce G. Carruthers, "The Recursivity of Law: Global Norm Making and National Lawmaking in the Globalization of Corporate Insolvency Regimes," *American Journal of Sociology*, 112, no. 4 (January 2007): 1,187.
53 Ibid., 1,188.
54 Ibid.
55 Kal Raustiala, "Domestic Institutions and International Regulatory Cooperation: Comparative Responses to the Convention on Biological Diversity," *World Politics* 49 (Summer 1997): 482–483.
56 Daniel W. Drezner, *All Politics is Global: Explaining International Regulatory Regimes* (Princeton, N.J.: Princeton University Press, 2007), 4.
57 Harold K. Jacobson and Edith Brown Weiss, "A Framework for Analysis," in *Engaging Countries: Strengthening Compliance with International Environmental Accords*, ed. Edith Brown Weiss and Harold K. Jacobson (Cambridge, Mass.: MIT Press, 1998), 2.
58 Ibid., 11.
59 Harold K. Jacobson and Edith Brown Weiss, "Assessing the Record and Designing Strategies to Engage Countries," in *Engaging Countries*, ed. Brown Weiss and Jacobson, 554.
60 See Chicago Council of Global Affairs, *Worldviews 2002*, www.thechicagocouncil.org.
61 Nigel White, *Democracy Goes to War* (Oxford: Oxford University Press, 2009), 288.
62 See Charlotte Ku and Harold K. Jacobson, eds. *Democratic Accountability and the Use of Force in International Law* (Cambridge: Cambridge University Press, 2002).
63 Rapport Commissie van Onderzoek Besluitvorming Irak, January 2010, paragraph 20, 531.
64 Ibid.
65 International Court of Justice, reports, 1949, 179.
66 International Law Association, Final Report, Committee on the Accountability of International Organizations, 2004, 26, www.ila-hq.org.
67 ILA Final Accountability Report, 27.
68 Ian Hurd, "Legitimacy, Power, and the Symbolic Life of the UN Security Council," *Global Governance* 8 (2002): 36.
69 See Ku, "When Can Nations Go to War? Politics and Change in the UN Security System," *Michigan Journal of International Law* 24, no. 4 (Summer 2003): 1,077–1,120.
70 See Harold K. Jacobson, *Networks of Interdependence* (New York: Alfred Knopf, 1984), 10.
71 See Steve Charnovitz, "Nongovernmental Organizations and International Law," *American Journal of International Law* 100 (2006): 361.
72 Ibid., 351.
73 Elihu Root, "The Function of Private Codification in International Law," *American Journal of International Law* 5 (1911): 577, 583.
74 Charnovitz, "Nongovernmental Organizations," 349.
75 As quoted in ibid., 361, footnote 95.
76 See, for example, Germany's objections to NGO participation at international conferences in Roger Chickering, *Imperial Germany and a World Without War* (Princeton, N.J.: Princeton University Press, 1976).

77 Charnovitz, "Nongovernmental Organizations," 348.
78 See Kal Raustiala, "The 'Participatory Revolution' in International Environmental Law," *Harvard Environmental Law Review* 21 (1997): 537–586.
79 See Lesley Wexler, "The International Deployment of Shame, Second-Best Responses and Norm Entrepreneurship: The Campaign to Ban Landmines and the Landmine Ban Treaty," *Arizona Journal of International and Comparative Law* 20 (2003): 561–606.
80 "The Institute of International Law is a purely scientific and private association, without official character, whose objective is to promote the progress of international law by: formulating general principles; cooperating in codification; seeking official acceptance of principles in harmony with the needs of modern society; contributing to the maintenance of peace or to the observance of the laws of war; proffering needed judicial advice in controversial or doubtful cases; and contributing, through publications, education of the public, and any other means, to the success of the principles of justice and humanity which should govern international relations." See www.nobelprize.org.
81 Charnovitz, "Nongovernmental Organizations," 350.
82 Ibid., 351.
83 See *Integrated Civil Society Organization System*, http://esango.un.org/civilsociety. General estimates on the number of NGOs in operation today exceed 30,000.
84 See International Union for Conservation of Nature, www.iucn.org.
85 See Parliamentarians for Global Action, www.pgaction.org.
86 See United Cities and Local Governments, www.cities-localgovernments.org.
87 In the case of the International Labor Organization, trade unions and businesses are represented in national delegations and participate in ILO deliberations with representatives of states. In the case of the World Tourism Organization, the private sector is represented through affiliate membership. There are presently 409 Affiliate Members of the World Tourism Organization representing airlines, hotels, travel agents, trade unions, business schools, universities, and environmental organizations (see www.unwto.org).
88 Measured on a per capita basis, Africa and Asia still lag behind Europe and North America in the number of NGOs. See http://esango.un.org/civilsociety.
89 See Manley O. Hudson, "The First Conference for the Codification of International Law," *American Journal of International Law* 24 (1930): 451, noting that organizations of women sent representatives to the conference at the Hague and that a conference committee devoted a session to hearing statements from the organizations on the subject of the nationality of women.
90 Franz von Benda-Beckmann, Keebet von Benda-Beckmann, and Julia Eckert, "Rules of Law and Law of Ruling: Law and Governance between Past and Future," in *Rules of Law and Law of Ruling: Law and Governance between Past and Future,* ed. Franz von Benda-Beckmann, Keebet von Benda-Beckmann, and Julia Eckert (Surrey: Ashgate Publishing, 2009), 3.
91 Ann Marie Clark, Elisabeth J. Friedman, and Kathryn Hochstetler, "The Sovereign Limits of Global Civil Society," *World Politics* 51 (October 1998): 9.

92 See Dinah Shelton, "The Participation of Nongovernmental Organizations in International Judicial Proceedings," *American Journal of International Law* 88 (1994): 641–642.

93 Raustiala, "The 'Participatory Revolution,'" 559.

94 Ibid., 560.

95 Ibid.

96 See, for example, discussion of delegation-NGO consultations during the Rome Conference in Zoe Pearson, "Non-Governmental Organizations and the International Criminal Court: Changing Landscapes of International Law," *Cornell International Law Journal* 39 (2006): 243–284.

97 See Charnovitz, "Nongovernmental Organizations," 354.

98 Christine Chinkin, "Human Rights and the Politics of Representation: Is There a Role for International Law?" in *The Role of Law in International Politics*, ed. Michael Byers (Oxford: Oxford University Press, 2000), 139–140.

99 See International Court of Justice, Legality of the Threat or Use of Nuclear Weapons, Advisory Opinion, 1996 ICJ Reports, Separate Opinion of Judge Guillaume, 288, www.icj-cij.org.

100 Peter M. Haas, "Introduction: Epistemic Communities and International Policy Coordination," *International Organization* 46, no. 1 (Winter 1992): 1–35.

101 UN Secretary-General, *Preface to the Statute of the International Criminal Court*, UN Doc A/CONF/183/9, 1999.

102 See Pearson, "Non-governmental Organizations."

103 William Korey, *NGOs and the Universal Declaration of Human Rights* (New York: Palgrave, 2001), 171.

104 See Alan Boyle and Christine Chinkin, *The Making of International Law* (Oxford: Oxford University Press, 2007), 67–68.

105 Charlotte Ku and John King Gamble, "International Law—New Actors and New Technologies: Center Stage for NGOs?" *Law and Policy in International Business* 31, no. 2, (2000): 221–262.

106 Chinkin, "Human Rights," 137.

107 UN Commission on Human Rights, "On the Question of Integrating the Human Rights of Women Throughout the United Nations System," E/CN.4/1998/49, 23 March 1998.

108 See Pearson, "Non-governmental Organizations," 266.

109 See Coalition for the International Criminal Court, www.iccnow.org.

110 Ibid.

111 See UN Report of the Independent Panel on Safety and Security of UN Personnel in Iraq, 20 October 2003, www.un.org/News/dh/iraq/safety-security-un-personnel-iraq.pdf.

112 See Abram Chayes and Antonia Handler Chayes, *The New Sovereignty: Compliance with International Regulatory Agreements* (Cambridge, Mass.: Harvard University Press, 1995), 253–254.

113 Amnesty International *Annual Report 2011: The State of the World*, at www.amnesty.org

114 Charnovitz, "Nongovernmental Organizations," 370.

115 See "League to Enforce Peace is Launched," *New York Times*, 18 June 1915.

116 See David Caron, "War and International Adjudication: Reflections on the 1899 Peace Conference," *American Journal of International Law* 94 (2000): 8.

117 Ibid., 10.
118 Ibid., 16.
119 Ibid., 8.
120 See Cynthia Price Cohen, "The Role of Nongovernmental Organizations in the Drafting of the Convention on the Rights of the Child," *Human Rights Quarterly* 12 (1990): 137–145, and Charnovitz, "Nongovernmental Organizations."
121 See Office of the United Nations High Commissioner for Human Rights, Convention on the Rights of the Child, www2.ohchr.org/English/law/crc/htm.
122 See Global Environmental Facility, www.thegef.org, and Charnovitz, "Nongovernmental Organizations," 368.
123 The International Committee of the Red Cross describes itself as "an independent, neutral organization ensuring humanitarian protection and assistance for victims of war and armed violence": www.icrc.org/eng.
124 Peter Willets, "From 'Consultative Arrangements' to 'Partnership': The Changing Status of NGOs in Diplomacy at the UN," *Global Governance* 6 (2000): 193.
125 See Raustiala, "The 'Participatory Revolution.'" Although it is common-place to see provisions for IO consultations with NGOs in areas of their competence, NGO participation is not a foregone conclusion. The 1974 Convention for the Prevention of Marine Pollution from Land-Based Sources and the 1979 Convention on Long-Range Transboundary Air Pollution, for example, do not mention NGOs.
126 Anna Spain, "Who's Going to Copenhagen? The Rise of Civil Society in International Treaty-Making," *ASIL Insights* 13 (December 11, 2009) available at http://www.asil.org.
127 Jessica T. Mathews, "Power Shift," *Foreign Affairs* (1997): 50.
128 Charlotte Ku, "Strengthening international law's capacity to govern through multilayered strategic partnerships," *South African Yearbook of International Law* 32 (2007): 107–23.
129 See Richard Price, "Reversing the Gun Sights: Transnational Civil Society Targets Land Mines," *International Organization* 52 (1998): 613–644.
130 M.J. Peterson, "Whales, Cetologists, Environmentalists, and the International Management of Whaling," *International Organization* 46 (1992): 147–186.
131 Gian Luca Burci, "Institutional Adaptation without Reform: WHO and the Challenges of Globalization," *International Organizations Law Review* 2 (2005): 442.
132 Charnovitz, "Nongovernmental Organizations," 348–372; Pearson, "Non-governmental Organizations," 243–284; Chinkin, "Human Rights," 131–148; Raustiala, "The 'Participatory Revolution,'" 537–586; and Dianne Otto, "Nongovernmental Organizations in the United Nations System: The Emerging Role of International Civil Society," *Human Rights Quarterly* 18 (1996): 107–141.
133 Martin Shapiro quoted in Raustiala, "The 'Participatory Revolution,'" 576.
134 Raustiala, "The 'Participatory Revolution,'" 576.
135 See Environmental Protection Agency, www.epa.gov.
136 See Pearson, "Non-governmental Organizations," 2006.
137 Kathryn Sikkink, "Human rights, principled issue-networks, and sover-eignty in Latin America," *International Organization* 47, no. 3 (Summer 1993): 412.

5 International law in the global environment

1 Portions of this chapter are adapted from Paul F. Diehl and Charlotte Ku, "Extra-systemic adaptations to system imbalance," in *The Dynamics of International Law* (Cambridge: Cambridge University Press, 2010).

2 UN Secretary-General Kofi A. Annan, *We the Peoples: The Role of the United Nations in the 21st Century* (New York: United Nations, 2000), 11.

3 See Harold Nicolson, *Diplomacy*, 3rd edition (Washington, DC: Georgetown University Institute for the Study of Diplomacy, 1988).

4 Douglas M. Johnston, *Consent and Commitment in the World Community* (Irvington-on-Hudson, N.Y.: Transnational Publishers, Inc., 1997), 15.

5 See Cindy Skrzycki, "The Federal Register Turns 70," *Washington Post*, 7 March 2006.

6 See the International Network for Environmental Compliance and Enforcement at www.inece.org.

7 Saskia Sassen, *Territory, Authority, Rights* (Princeton, N.J.: Princeton University Press, 2006), 8.

8 Ibid.

9 See Diehl and Ku, *The Dynamics of International Law*, 28–46.

10 See José E. Alvarez, *International Organizations as Law-Makers* (Oxford: Oxford University Press, 2005).

11 Jonathan I. Charney, "Universal International Law," *American Journal of International Law* 87 (1993): 547.

12 The Human Rights Committee is a body of independent experts charged with monitoring the implementation of the International Covenant on Civil and Political Rights by state parties. All state parties are obligated to provide regular reports to the Committee on how rights are being implemented. See www2.ohchr.org.

13 See Thomas Buergenthal, "The Evolving International Human Rights System," *American Journal of International Law* 100 (2006): 804–806.

14 Johnston, *Consent and Commitment*, 38.

15 José E. Alvarez, "The New Treaty-Makers," *Boston College of International and Comparative Law Review* (2002): 217.

16 Ibid., 223–232.

17 See *Review of the Statute of the Administrative Tribunal of the United Nations* (UN General Assembly Doc A/C.6/55/L.18), 20 November 1989; and Christiane E. Philipp, "The International Criminal Court – A Brief Introduction," in *Max Planck Yearbook of United Nations Law*, vol. 7, ed. A. von Bogdandy and R. Wolfrum (The Netherlands: Koninklijke Brill NV, 2003): 331–339.

18 See Alvarez, "The New Treaty-Makers," 220, and Arthur Eyffinger, *The 1899 Hague Peace Conference: The Parliament of Man, the Federation of the World* (The Hague: Kluwer Law International, 1999).

19 Even with existing infrastructure, negotiating multilateral treaties is a major undertaking. "A normal negotiation may require four or five intergovernmental negotiating sessions of one to two weeks each during a period of eighteen months to two years. The Climate Convention negotiations required six sessions of two weeks each in less than sixteen months, in addition to regular meetings of the Intergovernmental Panel on Climate Change and various other informal meetings involving subsets of

countries. Despite this very full and expensive schedule of negotiations, the Climate Convention negotiations were only one of more than a half dozen global or regional environmental agreement negotiations occurring more or less at the same time. During this period there were also important international negotiations for the conclusion of nonbinding legal instruments, such as the Arctic Protection Strategy, the Rio Declaration on Environment and Development, Forest Principles, and Agenda 21." Edith Brown Weiss, "International Environmental Law: Contemporary Issues and the Emergence of a New World Order," *Georgetown Law Journal* 81 (1992–93): 698.

20 Ibid.

21 Charney, "Universal International Law," 529.

22 Paul Diehl and I take a different view and argue that international law's system of rule recognition is embedded in it as the operating system. See Hart, *The Concept of Law*, 209, on international law and its lack of secondary rules of recognition and adjudication.

23 Charney, "Universal International Law," 547.

24 Dinah Shelton, "Introduction: Law, Non-Law and the Problem of Soft Law," in *Commitment and Compliance: The Role of Non-Binding Norms in the International Legal System,* ed. Dinah Shelton (Oxford: Oxford University Press, 2000), 8.

25 Ibid., 10.

26 Christine Chinkin, "Normative Development in the International Legal System," in *Commitment and Compliance: The Role of Non-Binding Norms in the International Legal System*, ed. Dinah Shelton (Oxford: Oxford University Press, 2000), 25–29.

27 Edwina S. Campbell, *Consultation and Consensus in NATO: Implementing the Canadian Article* (Lanham: University Press of America, 1985).

28 Michael Schechter's study on UN-sponsored World Conferences concluded that the greatest normative and political contributions were made by follow-up meetings to such conferences and not the conferences themselves. The conferences provided the impetus to come together to address an issue, but actual changes might come years after the conference itself concluded. See Michael G. Schechter, "Conclusions," in *United Nations-sponsored World Conferences: Focus on Impact and Follow Up*, ed. Michael G. Schechter (Tokyo: United Nations University Press, 2001), 218–222.

29 Chinkin, "Normative Development," 29.

30 Xinyuan Dai, *International Institutions and National Policies* (Cambridge, UK: Cambridge University Press, 2007); Dinah Shelton, ed., *Commitment and Compliance: The Role of Non-Binding Norms in the International Legal System* (Oxford: Oxford University Press, 2000); Edith Brown Weiss and Harold K. Jacobson, *Engaging Countries: Strengthening Compliance with International Environmental Accords* (Cambridge, Mass.: MIT Press, 1998); and Abram Chayes and Antonia Handler Chayes, *The New Sovereignty: Compliance with International Regulatory Agreements* (Cambridge, Mass.: Harvard University Press, 1995).

31 Jeffrey W. Legro, "Which Norms Matter: Revisiting the 'Failure' of Internationalism," *International Organization* 51(Winter 1997): 35.

32 Ibid., 44.

33 Christine Chinkin, "The Challenge of Soft Law: Development and Change in International Law," *International and Comparative Law Quarterly* (1989): 850–866.

34 See Westfield, 2001–2; Isabella D. Bunn, "Global Advocacy for Corporate Accountability: Transatlantic Perspectives from the NGO Community," *American University International Law Review* 19, no. 6 (2004): 1265–1306.

35 Kenneth Abbott and Duncan Snidal, "Hard and Soft Law in International Governance," *International Organization* 54 (2000): 421–456.

36 Ibid., 423.

37 See Forest Stewardship Council United States, www.fscus.org.

38 Andrew Guzman, *How International Law Works* (Oxford: Oxford University Press, 2005).

39 Ibid.

40 See Richard L. Williamson, Jr., "International Regulation of Land Mines," in *Commitment and Compliance*, ed. Dinah Shelton (Oxford: Oxford University Press, 2000), 505–521.

41 Chinkin, "Normative Development," 42.

42 Dai, *International Institutions*, 151.

43 Shelton, "Introduction," 18.

44 Laurence Boisson de Chazournes, "Policy Guidance and Compliance: The World Bank Operational Standards," in *Commitment and Compliance*, ed. Shelton, 289.

45 See Francis Maupin, "International Labor Organization Recommendations and Similar Instruments," in *Commitment and Compliance*, ed. Shelton, 373–374.

46 Ibid., 386.

47 Ibid., 384.

48 *Compilation and Analysis of Legal Norms* (UN Economic and Social Council Document E/CN.4/21996/52/Add.2) May 12, 1995, ap.ohchr.org/documents.

49 Walter Kälin, "Origin, Content and Legal Character of the Guiding Principles on Internal Displacement," in *The Guiding Principles on Internal Displacement and the Law of the South Caucasus: Georgia, Armenia, Azerbaijan*, ed. Roberta Cohen, Walter Kälin, and Erin Mooney (Washington, DC: American Society of International Law, 2003), xiv.

50 Ibid., xiv.

51 Ibid.

52 Ibid., xviii.

53 Ibid., xxv.

54 See International Commission on Intervention and State Sovereignty, *Responsibility to Protect Core Principles: A Synopsis* (2001), xi, para 2.29.

55 *A More Secure World: Our Shared Responsibility*, Report of the Secretary-General's High-level Panel on Threats, Challenges and Change (UN General Assembly document A/59/565), 2 December 2004, 1.

56 Emphasis added. *A More Secure World: Our Shared Responsibility*, 9.

57 See the Constitutive Act, www.africa-union.org/root/au/AboutAu/Constitutive_Act_en.htm.

58 See 2005 World Summit Outcome Document, www.un.org/summit2005.

59 *Implementing the Responsibility to Protect*, Report of the Secretary-General, (United Nations General Assembly Doc/63/677), 12 January 2009, 2.
60 See UN Doc SG/A/1120, 21 February 2008.
61 Alex J. Bellamy, "The Responsibility to Protect—Five Years On," *Ethics & International Affairs* 24, no. 2 (Summer 2010): 144.
62 Abbott and Snidal, "Hard and Soft Law," 456.
63 Shelton, "Introduction," 15.
64 Lesley Wexler, "The International Deployment of Shame, Second-Best Responses, and Norm Entrepreneurship: The Campaign to Ban Landmines and the Landmine Ban Treaty," *Arizona Journal of International and Comparative Law* 20 (2003): 599.
65 José E. Alvarez, *International Organizations as Law-Makers* (Oxford: Oxford University Press, 2005), 217.
66 Frederic L. Kirgis, "Specialized Law-Making Processes," in *The United Nations and International Law*, ed. Christopher C. Joyner (Cambridge: Cambridge University Press, 1997), 65.
67 See Legro, "Which Norms Matter"; and Derek Jinks and Ryan Goodman, "How to Influence States: Socialization and International Human Rights Law," *Duke Law Journal* (2005): 621–704.
68 Kirgis, "Specialized Law-Making Processes," 90.
69 See Article 2, Convention on Psychotropic Substances, 1971, www.incb.org.
70 See 1982 UN Law of the Sea Convention, Annex VIII: Special Arbitration, Article 2, www.un.org/Depts/los/convention_agreements/texts/unclos/unclos_e.pdf.
71 Kirgis, "Specialized Law-Making Processes," 87–88.
72 Barry Kellman, "Protection of Nuclear Materials," in *Commitment and Compliance*, ed. Shelton, 487.
73 Benedict Kingsbury, "The Concept of 'Law' in Global Administrative Law," *European Journal of International Law* 20 (February 2009): 25.
74 Ibid.
75 Ibid.
76 Ibid., 57.
77 Ibid.
78 Ibid., 25.
79 Johnston, *Consent and Commitment*, 8–9.
80 Ibid., 25.
81 Legro, "Which Norms Matter," 57.
82 Ibid., 58–59.

6 Taking stock: global governance in a post-Westphalian order

1 Andrew H. van de Ven and Marshall Scott Poole, "Explaining Development and Change in Organizations," *Academy of Management Review* 20 (1995): 526.
2 With thanks to Michael Doyle for making this point. Conversation on 22 January 2009, New York.
3 See *Journal of International Law and International Relations*, www.jilir.org.
4 Examples of these paired publications are: Kenneth Abbott and Duncan Snidal, "International Regulation without International Governance: Imposing International Organization Performance through Orchestration,"

Review of International Organizations (2010): 315–344; and Kenneth W. Abbott and Duncan Snidal, "Strengthening International Regulation through Transnational New Governance," *Vanderbilt Journal of International Law* 42 (2009): 501–579; Karen Alter and Laurence Helfer, "Nature or Nurture: Judicial Lawmaking in the European Court of Justice and the Andean Tribunal of Justice," *International Organization* 64 (2010): 563–592; Laurence Helfer and Karen Alter, "The Andean Tribunal of Justice and its Interlocutors: Understanding Preliminary Reference Patterns in the Andean Community," *New York University Journal of International Law and Politics* 41 (2009): 871–930; and Beth A. Simmons, "International Law and State Behavior: Commitment and Compliance in International Monetary Affairs," *American Political Science Review* 94 (2000): 819–835, and "Money and the Law: Why Comply with the Public International Law of Money," *Yale Journal of International Law* 25 (2000): 323–362.

5 Permanent Court of International Justice, *Case of the S.S. Lotus* (France v. Turkey), Judgement, 7 September 1927, www.worldcourts.com.

6 According to a 2000 census, Han Chinese make up 91.5% of China's population with the balance made up of Manchu, Hui, Tibetan, Zhuang and other nationalities. *CIA Factbook*, China, www.cia.gov.

7 The last recorded tribute mission was from Nepal in 1908. See John K. Fairbank and Teng Ssu-yu, "On the Ch'ing Tributary System," *Harvard Journal of Asiatic Studies* 6 (1941): 193.

8 See Norman Itzkowitz, *Ottoman Empire and Islamic Tradition* (Chicago: University of Chicago Press, 1972).

9 Measures of religious freedom did exist, but to the extent that religious tolerance was practiced, it was as a matter of state policy or action that could be changed. See, for example, the revocation of the 1589 Edict of Nantes that for nearly a century had provided some tolerance for the Protestant Huguenots in France. Many of these Huguenots fled to The Netherlands and to Prussia following this act. See Leo Gross, "The Peace of Westphalia, 1648–1948," *American Journal of International Law* 42 (1948): 22.

10 See Comprehensive Database of Multilateral Treaties as cited in Charlotte Ku, "Global Governance and the Changing Face of International Law," 2001 John W. Holmes Memorial Lecture, ACUNS Reports & Papers no. 2 (2001), 4.

11 See James M. McPherson, *This Mighty Scourge: Perspectives on the Civil War* (New York: Oxford University Press, 2007), 155–166.

12 Alexander Wendt, "Anarchy is What States Make of it: The Social Construction of Power Politics," *International Organization* 46 (1992): 391–425.

13 Ibid., 395.

14 Ibid., 399.

15 Ibid., 402.

16 Ibid., 406–407.

17 Ibid., 409.

18 Emmerich de Vattel, *The Law of Nations*, ed. Joseph Chitty (Philadelphia: T. & J.W. Johnson, 1854; reprinted by The Lawbook Exchange, 2004), 200–204.

19 Richard H. Steinberg and Jonathan M. Zasloff, "Power and International Law," *American Journal of International Law* 100 (2006): 66.

20 Ibid.

21 Ibid.
22 Ibid., 69.
23 See Hans J. Morgenthau, "Positivism, Functionalism, and International Law," *American Journal of International Law* 34 (1940): 260–284.
24 See Stanley Hoffman, "International Law and the Control of Force," in *The Relevance of International Law*, ed. Karl Deutsch and Stanley Hoffman (New York: Schenkman Publishing, 1968).
25 See, for example, the work of Jack L. Goldsmith and Eric Posner in *The Limits of International Law* (2005), and Clyde Eagleton's comment that the "UN Charter does very little to strengthen the law of nations," in "International Law and the Charter of the United Nations," *American Journal of International Law* 39 (1945): 751.
26 Wolfgang Friedmann, *The Changing Structure of International Law* (New York: Columbia University Press, 1964).
27 See Jonathan I. Charney, "Universal International Law," *American Journal of International Law* 87 (1993): 529–551.
28 See Wendt, "Anarchy," 419.
29 See ibid. and Charlotte Ku and Harold K. Jacobson, eds., *Democratic Accountability and the Use of Force in International Law* (Cambridge: Cambridge University Press, 2002).
30 UN Department of Public Information (UN Security Council document SC/10200), "Security Council approves 'No-Fly Zone' over Libya, authorizing 'all necessary measures' to protect civilians, by vote of 10 in favour with 5 abstentions," 17 March 2011.
31 Wendt, "Anarchy," 420–421.
32 See "The Situation in Libya," UN Security Council document S/RES/ 1973, 17 March 2011.
33 Wendt, "Anarchy," 421.
34 Van de Ven and Poole citing Gould at Van de Ven and Poole, "Explaining Development," 423.
35 Steinberg and Zasloff, "Power," 77.
36 Robert Keohane and Joseph Nye, "Introduction," in *Governance in a Globalizing World*, ed. J. Nye and J.D. Donahue (Washington, DC: Brookings Institution Press), 18.
37 Steinberg and Zasloff, "Power," 79.
38 Mark C. Suchman, "Managing Legitimacy: Strategic and Institutional Approaches," *Academy of Management Review* 20 (1995): 574.
39 Ibid.
40 Ibid., 601–602.
41 Hendrik Spruyt, *The Sovereign State and Its Competitors* (Princeton, N.J.: Princeton University Press, 1994), 178–179.
42 Suchman, 604.
43 Suchman, 582.
44 Suchman.
45 Ian Hurd, "Legitimacy and Authority in International Politics," *International Organization* 53 (1999): 381.
46 Ibid., 383.
47 Ibid., 385.
48 Ibid., 387.
49 Ibid., 388.

50 Ibid., 390.
51 See Helen V. Milner, *Interests, Institutions, and Information: Domestic Politics and International Relations* (Princeton, N.J.: Princeton University Press, 1997).
52 Andrew Cortell and James Davis, "How Do International Institutions Matter? The Domestic Impact of International Rules and Norms," *International Studies Quarterly* 40 (1996): 451–478.
53 See Francis Maupin, "International Labor Organization Recommendations and Similar Instruments," in *Commitment and Compliance*, ed. Dinah Shelton (Oxford, UK: Oxford University Press, 2000).
54 See Cortell and Davis, "How Do International Institutions Matter?" 465.
55 See "Presidential Speech Launching Iraq Invasion," http://uspolitics. about.com/od/wariniraq/a/bush_2003march.htm.
56 Cortell and Davis, "How Do International Institutions Matter?" 471.
57 Ibid., 451.
58 Ibid., 472.
59 See, for example, cases included in Beth A. Simmons, *Mobilizing for Human Rights* (New York: Cambridge University Press, 2009).
60 Van de Ven and Poole, "Explaining Development," 522.
61 See Vaughan Lowe, "The Politics of Law-Making," in *The Role of Law in International Politics*, ed. Michael Byers (Oxford: Oxford University Press, 2000), 212–221.
62 See International Court of Justice, Judgment of 25 September 1997, *Gabcikovo-Nagymaros Project* (Hungary/Slovakia),www.icj-cij.org/docket.
63 Lowe, "The Politics of Law-Making," 216.
64 Ibid.
65 Ibid., 224.
66 Ibid., 225.
67 Van de Ven and Poole, "Explaining Development," 533.

Select bibliography

"Centennial Essays," *American Journal of International Law* 100, nos. 1–4 (2006): Thomas Buergenthal, "The Evolving Human Rights System"; Steve Charnovitz, "Nongovernmental Organizations and International Law"; and Richard Steinberg and Jonathan M. Zasloff, "Power and International Law." These essays were commissioned to mark the centennial of the founding of the American Society of International Law. They provide an overview of developments in international law throughout the twentieth century.

José E. Alvarez, *International Organizations as Law-makers* (New York: Oxford University Press, 2005) is an information-packed, comprehensive, and conceptually rich review of the evolving relationship between international law and international organizations.

Antony Anghie, *Imperialism, Sovereignty, and the Making of International Law* (Cambridge, UK: Cambridge University Press, 2007) is a path-breaking study that examines how a state's sovereignty is shaped if acquired following a period of colonialism.

Michael Barnett and Raymond Duvall, eds. *Power in Global Governance* (Cambridge, UK: Cambridge University Press, 2005) is an insightful and important collection of reflections on how and why to factor power into understanding the structures and frameworks of global governance.

Jutta Brunnée and Stephen Toope, *Legitimacy and Legality in International Law: An Interactional Account* (Cambridge, UK: Cambridge University Press, 2010) is an important application of the constructivist approach to understanding international law in a globalized environment.

Edward Hallett Carr, *The Twenty Years' Crisis: 1919–1939* (New York: Harper & Row, Publishers, 1945) is the classic treatment of power, international relations, and international law.

Jonathan I. Charney, "Universal International Law," *American Journal of International Law* 87 (1993) is an important early work considering the potential law-making role of international organizations.

Christine Chinkin and Hilary Charlesworth, *The Boundaries of International Law* (Manchester: University of Manchester Press, 2000) is a path-breaking study on the gendered nature of international law and its consequences.

Paul F. Diehl and Charlotte Ku, *The Dynamics of International Law* (Cambridge, UK: Cambridge University Press, 2010) presents a new operating system and normative system framework for understanding international law, its capacities, and its evolving role in global governance.

Daniel W. Drezner, *All Politics is Global: Explaining International Regulatory Regimes* (Princeton, N.J.: Princeton University Press, 2007) is an insightful study that examines the differing roles played by and influences wielded by— the powerful and less powerful public and private global actors.

Sally Merry Engle, "Legal Pluralism," *Law and Society Review* 20 (1998) is an important foundational overview of the concept of legal pluralism.

David Held, *Democracy and the Global Order: From the Modern State to Cosmopolitan Governance* (Stanford, Cal.: Stanford University Press, 1995) is a classic statement of the changing world order and its implications for governance.

Douglas Johnston, *Consent and Commitment in the World Community* (Irvington-on-Hudson, N.Y.: Transnational Publishers, Inc., 1997) is an innovative study of the broad array of international commitments beyond treaties.

Margaret E. Keck and Kathryn Sikkink, *Activists beyond Borders: Advocacy Networks in International Politics* (Ithaca, N.Y.: Cornell University Press, 1998) is a classic treatment of how organized private movements can influence politics and developments within countries.

Vaughan Lowe, *International Law* (New York: Oxford University Press, 2007) is a modern general account of international law in the spirit of J.L. Brierly's classic *Law of Nations*.

Walter Mattli and Ngaire Woods, eds., *The Politics of Global Regulation* (Princeton, N.J.: Princeton University Press, 2009) is a collection of case studies selected to illustrate the characteristics and capacities that equip actors to engage in global regulation.

Helen V. Milner, *Interests, Institutions, and Information: Domestic Politics and International Relations* (Princeton, N.J.: Princeton University Press, 1997) is an innovative study of how and why information from outside a country can shape and influence politics and developments within.

Balakrishnan Rajagopal, *International Law from Below: Development, Social Movements and Third World Resistance* (Cambridge, UK: Cambridge University Press, 2003) is an innovative study on how social movements have empowered local populations as they face powerful external institutions and forces.

James N. Rosenau, *Turbulence in World Politics* (Princeton, N.J.: Princeton University Press, 1990) is a thoughtful early reflection about the changes underway in international politics.

Saskia Sassen, *Territory, Authority, Rights: From Medieval to Global Assemblages* (Princeton, N.J.: Princeton University Press, 2006) is a rich and informative study of how governance has changed from the early modern to the present global period. It introduces the idea of "switching", where old capacities and habits take on new functions or significance.

Dinah Shelton, ed., *Commitment and Compliance: The Role of Non-Binding Norms in the International Legal System* (New York: Oxford University Press, 2000) is as innovative effort to understand the phenomenon of soft law through a collection of case studies.

Beth A. Simmons, *Mobilizing for Human Rights: International Law in Domestic Politics* (New York: Cambridge University Press, 2009) is an important and rigorous study of the influence of international human rights in domestic politics. This is a classic study and a model for empirical work in international law and politics.

Anne-Marie Slaughter, *The New World Order* (Princeton, N.J.: Princeton University Press, 2004) is a creative and important effort to understand the diffusion of power, government, and governance functions in the early twenty-first century.

Hendrik Spruyt, *The Sovereign State and Its Competitors* (Princeton, N.J.: Princeton University Press, 1994) is a fine analysis of the political and economic conditions that led to the eventual dominance of the state over other governing forms in the sixteenth and seventeenth centuries.

Alexander Wendt, "Anarchy is What States Make of It: The Social Construction of Power Politics," *International Organization* 46, no. 2 (1992): 391–425, is an important study of how interests and politics create the general environment within which they operate, and how the environment in turn shapes interests and politics.

Index